John Ashton

Hyde Park from Domesday-book to Date

John Ashton

Hyde Park from Domesday-book to Date

ISBN/EAN: 9783337826093

Printed in Europe, USA, Canada, Australia, Japan

Cover: Foto ©Andreas Hilbeck / pixelio.de

More available books at **www.hansebooks.com**

FROM

DOMESDAY - BOOK TO DATE

BY

JOHN ASHTON

AUTHOR OF "SOCIAL LIFE IN THE REIGN OF QUEEN ANNE," ETC., ETC.

ONE MAP AND TWENTY-ONE ILLUSTRATIONS

London
DOWNEY & CO.
YORK STREET, COVENT GARDEN, LONDON
1896

PREFACE.

The only History of Hyde Park, at all worthy of the name, is Vol. I. of "The Story of the London Parks," by Jacob Larwood. But, its author says, definitely, "What happened in Hyde Park subsequently to 1825, approaches too near to contemporary history to be told in these pages." This (for Hyde Park has a history since then), added to the inaccuracies and imperfections of the book, has induced me to write a History of Hyde Park from Domesday Book to Date.

JOHN ASHTON.

CONTENTS.

CHAPTER I.

The forests round London—The Manor of Eia in Domesday Book—Its subdivision—The Manor of Hyde—The Manor of Ebury—The Manor of Neate—The Neat houses—Henry VIII. and Hyde Park—Queen Elizabeth and Hyde Park—James I.—The deer in the Park—Last shooting therein—Foxes—The badger . . . 1

CHAPTER II.

Hyde Park in the early Commonwealth—Its sale—Toll on horses and carriages—A hurling match—Cromwell's accident—Attempts to shoot him in the Park—Notices against trespassers—The Park at the Restoration . . 14

CHAPTER III.

The camp in Hyde Park during the Plague of 1665—Boscobel Oaks in the Park—When first opened to the public—What it was then like—The Cheesecake House—Its homely refections—Orange girls 24

CHAPTER IV.

Foot and horse racing in the Park—Prize fighting—Duelling—The duel between Lord Mohun and the Duke of Hamilton 32

CHAPTER V.

Duelling in Hyde Park 39

CHAPTER VI.

Skating on the ponds and Serpentine—The Ring—Many notices thereof—Fireworks in the Park—Bad roads therein, and accidents caused thereby—Regulations in the time of Queen Anne—Making the drive—Riding in the Park 49

CHAPTER VII.

Rotten Row, the King's Old Road—The New King's Road made and lighted—The Allied Sovereigns in the Park—The Park after the Peninsular War—The Duke of Wellington in the Park—The Queen and Royal Family in the Park 61

CHAPTER VIII.

The springs in Hyde Park—Used as water supply for Westminster—Horses in the Park—The Westbourne—Making the Serpentine—The "Naumachia" thereon—Satires about it—The Jubilee Fair 65

CHAPTER IX.

Coronation of George IV.—Boat-racing on the Serpentine—Illumination of the Park—Fireworks—Coronation of Queen Victoria—Fair in the Park—Fireworks in Hyde Park, at "Peace rejoicing," May, 1856 75

CHAPTER X.

The Great Exhibition of 1851 94

CHAPTER XI.

Royal Humane Society's Receiving House—Boats and bathing—The Dell—Chelsea Water Works reservoir—Walnut-trees—Flower-walk—Military executions—The Magazine, Whip, Four-in-hand and Coaching Clubs—Their dress—Satire on Coaching—The Park as a military centre—The first review—Fort at Hyde Park Corner—Guard-house—Camp in Hyde Park—Insubordinate troops 120

CHAPTER XII.

Grand Reviews in 1660-1661-1668, 1682-1695-1699—Camps in 1715-1716-1722—Poem on the latter—Reviews in 1755-1759-1760 132

CHAPTER XIII.

Reviews in 1763-1764—Shooting-butts in 1778—Camp in 1780—Severe sentence of a Court-martial—Volunteer Reviews, 1799-1800—The rain at the latter . . . 142

CHAPTER XIV.

Volunteer Reviews of 1803—Review in honour of the Allied Sovereigns, 1814—Popularity of Blücher—Review by the Queen in 1838—Volunteer Review, 1860 . . 152

Contents.

CHAPTER XV.

Volunteer Reviews, 1864, 1876—Mobs in the Park—Funeral of Queen Caroline 163

CHAPTER XVI.

Commencement of the reign of King Mob—Sunday Trading Bill, 1855—Riots—Withdrawal of the Bill—Meetings about high price of food, 1855—Rough play and window smashing 177

CHAPTER XVII.

Sympathy with Italy, 1859—Garibaldi riots, 1862—Reform League Meeting, 23rd July, 1866—Police proclamation against it—Attempt to hold it—Hyde Park railings destroyed 187

CHAPTER XVIII.

Reform League Meeting of 25th July, 1866—Burning a tree —Stone-throwing—Temporizing policy of the Government—Special constables sworn in—Meeting abandoned —Return of police injured—Meeting of "Working Men's Rights Association," 1867—Reform League Meeting of 6th May, 1867—Police warning—Legal opinions —Meeting held—Meeting on 5th August, 1867 . . 200

CHAPTER XIX.

Demonstrations against the Irish Church, 1868—In favour of Fenians, 1869—Regulations made by Commissioners of Works—Fenian Demonstration, 1872—A speaker sentenced—Meeting about the Eastern Question, 1878— Fight—Preaching in the Park—Modern instances—May-Day and May 6, 1894—Against the House of Lords, Aug. 26, 1894 212

CHAPTER XX.

The Children's Fête in Hyde Park, 1887 . . . 224

CHAPTER XXI.

List of Rangers—A horse jumping the wall—Highwaymen —Horace Walpole robbed—Other robberies—Assaults, offences, etc., in the present reign—A very recent case . 235

CHAPTER XXII.

The Gates—That into Kensington Gardens—Improvements in the Park—Encroachments—The case of Ann Hicks and the other fruit-sellers—Seats in the Park—New house in ditto 253

CHAPTER XXIII.

Works of art in the Park—Drinking fountain—Marble Arch—Hyde Park Corner—Achilles statue—Walk round the Park—Cemetery of St. George's, Hanover Square—Sterne's tomb and burial—Tyburn tree—The Tybourne—People executed—Henrietta Maria's penance—Locality of the gallows—Princess Charlotte—Gloucester House—Dorchester House—Londonderry House—Apsley House—Allen's apple stall—The Wellington Arch—Statues of the Duke—St. George's Hospital, Knightsbridge—A fight on the bridge—Albert Gate and George Hudson—Knightsbridge Barracks 265

LIST OF ILLUSTRATIONS.

	PAGE
Exhibition of 1851: Osler's Glass Fountain and the Transept	Frontispiece
Boscobel Oaks, 1804	27
Cheesecake House, 1826	30
Duel between Lord Mohun and the Duke of Hamilton	37
Duel between George Garrick and Mr. Baddeley, 1770	42
Winter Amusement, 1787	50
The Row, 1793	62
„ „ 1814. The Allied Sovereigns .	62
„ „ 1834	62
The Duke of Wellington . . .	64
A Spring in the Park, 1794	65
Houses in the Park, 1794	66
A Man of War, 1814	73
"Albert, spare those trees!"	103
Tailpiece: Col. Sibthorpe and Exhibition of 1851 .	119
Map of Hyde Park from "Roque's Survey," 1741—1745 .	120
Volunteer Review by George III., 1799	143
The Soldiers' Toilet, 1780	145
Returning from the Review, 1800	150
Popularity of Blücher, 1814	157
The Broken Windows at Apsley House, 1831 . . .	280

HYDE PARK.

CHAPTER I.

The forests round London—The manor of Eia in Domesday Book—Its subdivision—The Manor of Hyde—The Manor of Ebury—The Manor of Neate—The Neat houses—Henry VIII. and Hyde Park—Queen Elizabeth and Hyde Park—James I.—The deer in the park—Last shooting therein—Foxes—The badger.

In old times London was surrounded by forests, of which the only traces now remaining are at Bishop's Wood, between Hampstead and Highgate, and the Chase at Enfield. FitzStephen, who lived in the reign of Henry II., tells us, in his Description of London, that beyond the fields to the north of London was an immense forest, beautified with woods and groves—or in other words, park land—full of the lairs and coverts of beasts and game, stags, bucks, boars and wild bulls. Contrary to what one might expect, these forests were not reserved for the sole hunting of the King and his favourites; but, as we are informed by the same writer, many of the citizens took great delight in fowling, with merlins, hawks, etc. (which showed how wealthy they were at that time), and they had the right and privilege of hunting in Middlesex, Hertfordshire, in all the Chiltern country, and in

Kent, as far as the River Cray. And this forest of Middlesex was only disforested in 1218 (2 Henry III.).

If, however, Hyde Park was, primævally, a forest, it must have been cleared and brought into cultivation in the Saxon times, for there is no mention of a forest, or even woodland, in the Domesday Book account of the Manor of Eia—in which Hyde Park was situate : on the contrary, it seems as if it was highly cultivated, as is evidenced by the following translation of that portion of the book relating to this manor :—

"Ossulton Hundred. The land of Geoffrey Mannevile.[1] Geoffrey de Mannevile holds the Manor of Eia. It was assessed for 10 hides [2] /. The land is 8 carucates / [3]. In demesne 5 hides, and there are 2 ploughs / [4]. The villans [5] have 5 ploughs, and a 6th might be made. There is 1 villan with half a hide / and 4 villans each with 1 virgate,[6] and other 14 each with half a virgate / and 4 bordars [7] with one virgate, and 1 cottager. Meadow for 8 ploughs' teams, and of hay / 60s. of pasture 7s. In all the profits it is worth £8 / when received £6. In the time of King Edward £12 /. Harold, son

[1] Ancestor of the family of Mandeville, Earls of Essex.
[2] A hide was 100 or 120 acres—as much land as one plough could cultivate in a year.
[3] A Carucate was as much arable land as could be cultivated by one plough in a year, with sufficient meadow and pasture for the team.
[4] A plough is the same as a Carucate.
[5] These were not slaves, but persons used and employed in the most servile work, and belonging, both they and their children, and their effects, to the lord of the soil, like the rest of the cattle or stock upon it.
[6] A Virgate was from 8 to 16 acres of land.
[7] Bordars were peasants holding a little house, bigger than a cottage, together with some land of husbandry.

of Earl Radulf, held this manor, whom Queen / Editha had the custody of with this manor, on the day that King Edward was alive and dead. / Afterwards, William, the Chamberlain, held it of the Queen in fee for £3, / yearly to farm. And after the death of the Queen, he now holds it / of the King, in the same manner. It is now 4 years since William lost the manor, and nothing has been received from the King's farm, that is £12."

This Manor of Eia was bounded on the north by the *Via Trinobantina*, a road which crossed England from the coast of Suffolk to that of Hampshire, and we now call that portion by Hyde Park the Uxbridge Road: and on the east ran the *Watling Street*, a road from Chester to Dover (of which the Edgware Road is a portion), which crossed the *Via Trinobantina*, and continued down Park Lane to the Thames—which was the southern boundary of the manor.

About the compilation of Domesday Book the Manor of Eia (we know not why) was divided into three manors, named severally Hyde, Ebury (or Eubery), and Neate (or Neyt), and was given by Geoffrey de Manneville to the Monastery of St. Peter in Westminster, where his wife Athelais was interred, and it was in the possession of this monastery till 1536. The Manor of Neate was nearest the river, about Chelsea, and there it was that the abbots of Westminster had a pleasure house. We read [1] how Nicholas Littlington, who was prior of the Monastery, was made Abbot on the elevation of Abbot Simon Langham to the See

[1] An History of the Church of St. Peter, Westminster, by R. Widmore, 1751.

of Ely in 1362, and how "he improved the estate of the convent at Hyde"—and also how he died, November 29th, 1386, "at the Manor house of Neyte near Westminster, at that time thought a good building; for the Duke of Lancaster,[1] styling himself King of Castile, desired leave of the Abbot to reside there during a sitting of parliament at Westminster." And here also was born John, the fifth son of Richard, Duke of York, on November 7th, 1448. Here died (May 12th, 1532) John Islip, who was elected Abbot of Westminster October 27th, 1500, and was buried in a chapel in the Abbey, which he built and which is still called by his name. In his abbacy (1502-3) the building of Henry VII.'s Chapel was begun, and in 1532 he negotiated an exchange between the Abbey and the King; the latter had from the Abbey about one hundred acres of land, part of which was made into St. James's Park, and the former received in exchange the priory of Poughley, in Berks, of which Cardinal Wolsey had procured the dissolution, to help him endow the colleges he designed at Oxford and Ipswich.

Islip's successor was William Boston, and, in 1536, an Act of Parliament was passed (28 Henry VIII., c. 49) and confirmed by a conveyance dated July 1, 1537, granting the King the lands belonging to the Abbey of "Nete, within the towne and paryshes of Westmynster and Seynt Martyn's in the Felde," as also the manors of Neyte, Ebery, and Todington, of the advowson of Chelsea rectory, of some lands at Greenwich, and of several meadows and closes

---

[1] John of Gaunt, brother of Edward III., and titular King of Castile.

near the Horseferry: in return for which the Abbey was to receive the site of the newly dissolved Priory of Hurley, in Berkshire; which, somewhat singularly, formerly belonged to the same Geoffrey de Manneville who gave the Abbey the Manor of Eia.

The Manor of Ebury lay between the other two manors, and comprised the district now known as Belgravia and Pimlico. It never was historically famous, but it helped to swell the coffers of the Grosvenors, especially that of the present Duke of Westminster and his father, for the manor (of 430 acres) then called Eabury or Ebury Farm came into the possession, in 1656, of Sir Thomas Grosvenor, who married the daughter and sole heiress of Alexander Davies, Esq., of Ebury Farm, who never could have contemplated the princely fortune he was leaving to her descendants.

Once only do we hear anything particular of the Manor of Ebury, and that is in connection with Queen Elizabeth.[1] "That *Ebery Farm*, containing 430 Acres, Meadow and Pasture, which was holden of her Majesty by lease, was granted to one *Whashe*, who paid £21 *per Ann*. And the same was let to divers Persons, who, for their private Commodity, did enclose the same, and had made Pastures of Errable Land; thereby not only annoying her Majesty in her Walks and Passages, but to the hindrance to her Game, and great Injury to the Common, which, at *Lammas*, was wont to be laid open, for the most Part; as by ancient Precedents thereof made, do particularly appear, both in the Time of *Henry the Eighth, Edward the Sixth,* and *Queen Mary.* And by the Grant made from her

[1] Strype's edit. of Stow's Survey, ed. 1720. Book VI. p. 80.

Majesty to the new tenants, it appeareth, that they are to enjoy the same lands in such sort as their predecessors did, which was then always *Lammas* ground, and now enclosed about 20 years past."

At least this was the plea of those who broke down the fences, etc., in 1592. " The Parishioners, having, as they supposed, that Lord's[1] Countenance, sent divers Persons on the 1 of *August,* being *Lammas day*, who, with Pickaxes, and such like Instruments, pulled down the Fences, and brake the Gates, having with them the Bailiffs and Constables, to keep the Peace."

The Manor of Neate lay alongside the river Thames, and although we have seen that the old moated mansion was of some importance, still, at the time of the above dispute (in which it shared with the neighbouring manor), it was only termed *a farm*, the house and all the ground around it having been granted by Edward VI. to Sir Anthony Brown; still the name of the manor was perpetuated in the " Neat Houses "—which were places of rural entertainment, and which Strype (Book vi. p. 67) describes : " The *Neat Houses* are a Parcel of Houses, most seated on the Banks of the River *Thames*, and inhabited by Gardiners ; for which it is of Note, for the supplying *London* and *Westminster* Markets with *Asparagus*, *Artichoaks*, *Cauliflowers*, *Musmelons*, and the like useful Things that the Earth produceth ; which, by reason of their keeping the Ground so rich by dunging it (and through the nearness to *London*, they have the Soil cheap), doth make their crops very forward, to their great Profit in coming to such good Markets."

[1] Lord Burghley, High Steward of Westminster.

There are no traces of these "Neat Houses" now; they disappeared entirely before the destructive builder, but they were in existence during this century, and stood where now is St. George's Row, Warwick Street, Pimlico. Yet it is evident that before it sunk wholly into market gardens, the "Neat Houses" was a place of amusement where people of good standing in society might attend without prejudice. In those days people's tastes were much simpler than in our time, and drinking syllabubs, and playing at an imaginary Arcadian life with imaginary Chloes and Strephons was fashionable.

It would be hard, indeed, if Pepys had nothing to say about this suburban place of entertainment, where he takes his wife and Mistress Knipp, an actress, of whom his wife was jealous. "Aug. 1, 1667. After the Play, we went into the House, and spoke with *Knipp*, who went abroad with us, by coach, to the *Neat Houses*, in the way to *Chelsy*; and there, in a Box in a Tree, we sat and sang, and talked and eat; my wife out of humour, as she always is, when this women is by." And again, "May 28, 1668. Met *Mercer*[1] and *Gayet*, and took them by water, first to one of the *Neat Houses*, where walked in the Gardens, but nothing but a Bottle of Wine to be had, though pleased with seeing the garden; and so to Fox Hall, where with great pleasure we walked, and then to the upper end of the retired walk, and there sat and sang, and brought a great many gallants and fine people about us; and, upon the bench, we did by and by eat and drink what we had, and very merry."

[1] Who had formerly been a kind of companion to his wife.

It seems a pity after such a merry scene to chronicle a death, but it was not a common one. *Domestic Intelligencer, August 5th*, 1679. "We hear that Madam Ellen Gwyn's mother, sitting lately by the water-side at her house by the *Neate Houses*, near *Chelsea*, fell accidentally into the water, and was drowned."

There seems no reason to doubt but that Henry VIII. wanted these manors for the purpose of hunting, as they lay so contiguous to the 100 acres which, in 1532, he had added to St. James's Park; and that this was his intention is shown by a proclamation made in 1536, wherein the King, who was passionately fond of all field sports, and excelled in them, as in every other manly exercise, says, that being desirous of having hares, patridges, pheasants and herons preserved round about his Palace of Westminster, for his own disport and pastime, forbids anyone, under pain of imprisonment, and further punishment according to his will and pleasure, either to hunt or hawk "from the Palace of Westminster to St. Giles' in the Fields, and from thence to Islington, to Our Lady of the Oak, to Highgate, to Hornsey Park, and to Hampstead Heath."

Hyde Park was then of much greater extent than it is at present, and comprised 620 acres; but what with the portion taken to add to Kensington Gardens, and land taken away at Hyde Park Corner, it now does not measure 400 acres. There is very little doubt but that when this manor of Hyde came into the possession of Henry VIII. he fenced it round, because its northern, southern, and eastern boundaries were all public roads, and, although in all probability men would not dare to poach on this Royal manor, yet the *feræ naturæ* must necessarily have been kept within bounds if there was to be hunting or any other kind of sport. And it must have been a high fence, for deer were plentiful, and they certainly were hunted and shot. In a letter from the Lords of the Council to Sir John Masone,[1] ambassador from England at the French Court, dated June 2nd, 1550, and giving an account of the reception and amusement of the embassy of Messrs. de Chastillon, Mortier and Bouchetel, who were sent by Henry II. to receive Edward's ratification of the treaty by which Boulogne had been ceded to France for the sum of 400,000 crowns, we find that, " Upon Tuesday, the King's Majesty had them on hunting in Hyde Park, and that night they supt with his Highness in the Privy Chamber."

Queen Elizabeth also hunted in Hyde Park—and, like her brother, offered sport therein to noble visitors. For instance, she so entertained Count John Casimir, son of Frederick III., Elector Palatine, and a general in the Dutch service, as we learn from the Talbot Papers,[2] in a letter from Gilbert Talbot and his wife to the Earl and Countess of Shrewsbury, dated February 13th, 1578. " My L. of Lecester also hath geven him dyvers other thynges, as geldynges, hawks and houndes, woddknyves, falchyones, hornes, crossebowes, and sondry peces of brode clothe fytte for huntynge garmentes, bothe

---

[1] England under the reigns of Edward VI. and Mary, by P. F. Tytler. Lond. 1839, vol i. p. 288.
[2] Illustrations of British History, etc., by E. Lodge. Lond. 1791, vol. ii. p. 205.

for wynter and sumer, for he delyghtethe greatly in huntynge, and can chouse his wynter deere very well. He kylled a barren doe wth his pece this other daye in Hyde P'ke from emongst CCC other deere." And to show that the Queen herself, if she did not actually join in the sport, looked on, there is an entry in the accounts (1582) of the Board of Works, of a payment " for making of two new standings in Marybone and Hyde Park, for the Queen's Majesty and the Noblemen of France [1] to see the hunting." This is also mentioned by John Norden in his *Notes on London and Westminster* (1592). " Hyde Park substancially impayled with a fayre lodge and princelye standes therein. It is a stately parke and full of fayre game."

In the 1575 edition of Geo. Turberville's " *Noble Art of Venerie or hunting* " (p. 95) we have a fine picture of Queen Elizabeth on one of these stands, whilst, kneeling on the ground, and bareheaded, the royal huntsman presents the "fewmets," or droppings of the deer, on some leaves, in a plate, for the Queen's inspection ; and the following is " The report of a Huntesman upon the sight of an Hart, in pride of greace.

> " ' Before the Queen, I come report to make,
> Then husht and peace, for noble *Tristrame's* sake.
> From out my horne, my fewments first I drawe,
> And then present, on leaves, by hunter's lawe ;
> And thus I say ; my Liege, behold and see
> An Hart of tenne, I hope he harbored bee.
> For if you mark his fewmets every poynt,
> You shall them find long, round and well anoynt,
> Knottie and great, without prickes or cares,
> The moystness shewes what venison he beares.' "

Another engraving shows the Queen about to

[1] The Duke of Anjou and his Court.

take assay of the deer, the kneeling huntsman handing her a knife for the purpose. And this is "the English manner, in breaking up of the Deare.

"First, where hee appointeth the Deares foote to be cut off, and to be presented to the Queen or chiefe, our order is that the Queen or chiefe (if so please them) do alight and take assaye of the Deare with a sharpe knife, the which is done in this maner. The deare being layd upon his backe, ye Queen, chiefe, or such as they shall appoint, comes to it. And ye chiefe huntsman (kneeling, if it be to the Queen) doth hold the Deare by the fore foote, whiles the Queen or chiefe, cut a slit drawne alongst the brysket of the deare, somewhat lower than the brysket towards the belly. This is done to see the goodnesse of the fleshe, and howe thicke it is."

In the 1611 edition, James I. takes the place of Queen Elizabeth.

James I. no doubt, as he was so fond of hunting, hunted the deer here, although he had Theobalds and Windsor, with many another hunting ground. And the deer were kept up in Charles I.'s reign, when Hyde Park was still an enclosed and private Royal park: and the deer were still preserved, for, when the Park was sold according to a special Resolution of the House of Commons of the 1st Dec., 1652, what were left of the deer, during those troublous times, were sold for the benefit of the Navy, and they were valued in the specifications at £765 6s. 2d. I can find no record of their sale—but they were sold. And soon after the Restoration, when James Hamilton, Esq. (one of the Grooms of the Bedchamber), was Ranger—he advised the

Park being surrounded by a brick wall, and restocked with deer, which was done. But the deer no longer roamed the Park at will; they were confined in an enclosure, called Buckdean Hill, the Deer Harbour, or the Paddock, close by the Keepers' Lodge, admission to which seems to have been obtainable by payment of a shilling—at least, in 1751, as we see by the following extract from a poem by W. H. Draper, entitled, "The Morning Walk, or the City Encompass'd."

> "Behold the ranger [1] there! with gun aslant,
> As just now issuing from his cottage [2] fold,
> With crew *Cerberian*, prowling o'er the plain
> To guard the harmless deer, and range them in
> Due order set, to their intended use.
> Key he can furnish, but must first receive
> One splendid shilling, e'er I can indulge
> The pleasing walk, and range the verdant field."

As far as I can learn, the last Royal shooting of the deer in Hyde Park was on the 9th Sept., 1768, and it is the more interesting, considering how intimately we are now allied with the House of Saxe Cobourg Gotha. In *The Public Advertiser* of Sept. 12, 1768, we read: "Same day, their Serene Highnesses the two Princes of Saxe Gotha, and many other Foreigners of Distinction, together with a great Number of our own Nobility, and Gentry, attended the Diversion of Deer Shooting in Hyde Park, which continued all the Evening till Dark, when one was at last killed, after being shot at ten Times. What rendered it so difficult to kill him, was the Hardship of getting him from among the Deer, and no other was allowed to be shot at

---

[1] Keeper, whose duty was to shoot trespassing dogs, and foxes.
[2] His lodge.

but this one: Several Wagers were won and lost upon this Occasion."

The deer still remained, until early in this century, in this enclosure, which was in the northwest corner of the Park, bounded on the north by the Park wall, on the west by Kensington Gardens, on the south by the Serpentine, and on the east by a fence. Dogs were allowed in the other parts of the Parks, as our poet says,—

> "But lo! a faithful spaniel, there stretch'd out,
> Not food for powder meet, relentless gun!"

But the "relentless gun" was evidently necessary against the foxes, for there is a Minute of the Board of Green Cloth in 1798, by which Sarah Gray is granted a pension of £18 per annum, to compensate her somewhat for the loss of her husband, who was accidentally killed by a shot from the gun of a keeper, who was hunting for foxes in Kensington Gardens. It would be a thankless task to look for them there at the present time; but it is not very many years since there was a badger, who took up his abode in a drain in the Gardens, and could not be dislodged. Strange and weird legends were told concerning this badger, one of which was that he had devoured a policeman, clothing and all, with the exception of his boots and helmet. The badger was ultimately caught, and purchased, I believe, by the Baroness Burdett-Coutts, who sent it into the country, and there gave it its liberty.

CHAPTER II.

Hyde Park in the early Commonwealth—Its sale—Toll on horses and carriages—A hurling match—Cromwell's accident—Attempts to shoot him in the Park—Notices against trespassers—The Park at the Restoration.

IT was not until after the martyrdom of the King, and a little before Cromwell found himself strong enough to become Lord Protector of the three Kingdoms, that the Parks, etc., were sold. But on Dec. 31, 1652, was passed " An Act for the Exposing to Sale divers Castles, Houses, Parks, Lands and Hereditaments, Belonging to the late King, Queen, or Prince, Exempted from sale by a former Act:" and among them was "All that Park commonly called *Hide Park*, in the county of *Middlesex*, with all Houses, Woods and Perquisits thereunto belonging."

At the beginning of the troubles between the King and Parliament, the exclusiveness of the Park grew somewhat lax, and it became a place of fashionable resort; but the sour, puritanical spirit of the times prevailed, and, in 1645, it was ordered " that Hyde Park and Spring Gardens should be kept shut, and no person be allowed to go into any of those places on the Lord's day, fast and thanksgiving days, and hereof those that have the keeping of the said places are to take notice and see this order obeyed, as they will answer the contrary at their uttermost peril." And, presumably, this order was acted on until 1649, when it was resolved that the London Parks—Whitehall, Hampton Court, the New Park at Richmond, Westminster Palace, Windsor Castle and Park, and Greenwich House and Park—should be the property of the Commonwealth, and thrown open to the public.

But in 1652, it was thought fit to sell Hyde Park, Greenwich House and Park, Windsor Park and Meadows, Cornbury Park, Oxon, Somerset House, and Vauxhall House and Grounds, for the benefit of the Navy, and duly sold they were. Three lots were made of Hyde Park—called the Gravel Pit division, or that part abutting on the Bayswater Road, which was very well wooded; the Kensington division, which lay on the south, which was principally pasture land; whilst the third comprised what were termed the Middle, which comprised the Ring, the Banqueting division—in which was the Cake House—near the present site of the Receiving House of the Royal Humane Society; and the Old Lodge division, which said Old Lodge was near Hyde Park Corner; and this third lot was very well wooded.

The first lot was bought by Richard Wilcox for the sum of £4144 11s.; the second was secured by John Tracy for £3906 7s. 6d.; and the third fetched £9020 8s. 2d., and became the property of Anthony Dean, a ship-builder, who let the right of pasture of his portion; and the lessees immediately began to recoup themselves by exacting a toll on the carriages and horses entering the Park. Says Evelyn, in his diary, under date of April 11, 1653, "I went to take the aire in Hide

Park, where every coach was made to pay a shilling, and horse sixpence, by these sordid fellows who purchas'd it of the State as they were cal'd."

This toll seems afterwards to have been raised, or it might only have been for the occasion, which was the first of May, when it was fashionable to be seen in the Park; for, in a letter dated May 2, 1654,[1] J. B. informs Mr. Scudamore that "Yesterday, each coach (and, I believe, there were fifteen hundred) paid half-a-crown, and each horse one shilling. The benefit accrues to a brace of citizens, who have taken the herbage of the Park from Mr. Dean, to which they add this excise of beauty. There was a hurling in the *paddock course* by Cornish gentlemen, for the great solemnity of the day, which, *indeed* (to use my Lord Protector's word), was great. When my Lord Protector's coach came into the Park with Colonel Ingleby and my Lord's daughters only (three of them, all in green-a) the coaches and horses flocked about them like some miracle. But they galloped (after the mode court pace now, and which they all use wherever they go, round and round the Park,) and all that great multitude hunted them, and caught them still at the turn, like a hare, and then made a lane with all reverent haste for them, and so after them again, that I never saw the like in my life."

Cromwell himself was present at this hurling match, according to the *Moderate Intelligencer* of April 26—May 4, 1654. "This day there was a hurling match of a great ball by fifty Cornish gentlemen on the one side, and fifty on the other;

[1] Correspondence of Lord Scudamore, Ambassador at Paris in 1635, etc., privately printed.

one party played in red caps, and the other in white. There was present his Highness the Lord Protector, many of the Privy Council, and divers eminent gentlemen, to whose view was presented great agility of body, and most neat and exquisite wrestling at every meeting of one with the other, which was ordered with such dexterity, that it was to show more the strength, vigour and nimbleness of their bodies, than to endanger their persons. The ball they played withal was silver, and designed for that party which did win the goal."

But, if Cromwell could drive the coach of State, he could not always manage to drive his own, and there is one memorable instance of his coming to grief in Hyde Park, in 1654, in endeavouring so to do, the story of which is thus told by General Ludlow (who was no friend to the Protector) in his Memoirs.[1]

"In the mean time, *Cromwel* having assumed the whole Power of the Nation to himself, and sent Ambassadors and Agents to Foreign States, was courted again by them, and presented with the Rarities of several Countries; amongst the rest the Duke of *Holstein* made him a Present of a Set of gray *Frizeland* Coach-Horses, with which taking the Air in the Park, attended only with his Secretary *Thurlow*, and Guard of Janizaries, he would needs take the place of the Coachman, not doubting but the three pair of Horses he was about to drive would prove as tame as the three Nations which were ridden by him: and, therefore, not contented with their ordinary pace, he lashed them very furiously. But they, unaccustomed to such

[1] Vol. ii. p. 508.

a rough Driver, ran away in a Rage, and stop'd not till they had thrown him out of the box, with which Fall, his Pistol fired in his Pocket, tho without any hurt to himself; by which he might have been instructed how dangerous it was to intermeddle with those things wherein he had no Experience."

In Thurloe's *State Papers* (vol. ii. p. 652) there is another account of this accident, in a letter, dated October 16, 1654 (N.S.), from "The *Dutch* embassadors in *England*, to the States General.

My LORDS,—After the sending away of our letters of last friday, we were acquainted the next morning, which we heard nothing of the night before, that about that time a mischance happened to the lord protector, which might have been, in all likelihood, very fatal unto him, if God had not wonderfully preserved him; as we are informed the manner of it to be thus. His highness, only accompanied with Secretary Thurloe and some few of his gentlemen and servants, went to take the air in Hyde Park, where he caused some dishes of meat to be brought; where he made his dinner, and, afterwards, had a desire to drive the coach himself, having put only the secretary into it, being those six horses, which the earl of Oldenburgh had presented unto his highness, who drove pretty handsomely for some time; but, at last, provoking those horses too much with the whip, they grew unruly, and run so fast that the postillion could not hold them in; whereby his highness was flung out of the coach box upon the pole, upon which he lay with his body, and, afterwards, fell upon the ground. His foot getting hold in the tackling, he was carried away a good while in that posture, during which a pistol went off in his pocket; but, at last, he got his foot clear, and so came to escape, the coach passing away without hurting him. He was presently brought home, and let blood; and, after some rest taken, he is now pretty well again. The secretary, being hurt on his ancle with leaping out of the coach, hath been forced to keep his chamber hitherto, and been unfit for any business; so that we have not been able to further or expedite any business this week."

Larwood, in his *Story of the London Parks*, gives quotations from two poetical lampoons, which I have not been able to verify, and, therefore, give them on his authority. And, he says, there was a poem called *The Jolt*, by Sir John Birkenhead, treating of this accident. The first quotation he gives he does not say whence it is taken, and is as follows :

"Every day and hour has shown us his power,
And now he has shown us his art.
His first reproach was a fall from a coach—
And his next will be from a cart."

A pleasant allusion to his probable fate, for a criminal who was to be hanged, was taken to the gallows on a cart, and, the halter being round his neck, the horse was whipped, and the cart being drawn from under him, the unfortunate man was left swinging.

The other quotation, he says, occurs in a ballad called, "Old England is now a brave Barbary."

"But Noll, a rank rider, gets first in the saddle,
And make her show tricks, curvate and rebound;
She quickly perceived he rode widdle-waddle,
And, like his coach-horses, threw his Highness to the ground."

Hyde Park seems to have been fraught with danger to the Protector, for in 1657 there was a plot to have assassinated him. The chief conspirators were a man named Sindercombe, or Fish, a cashiered quarter-master in Monk's army, and another named Cecil, who turned approver; who in his evidence [1] said,

"That the first time they rode forth to kill him, was the latter end of *September* last, (*viz.*) the Saturday after he had left going to *Hampton Court*.

"That the second time was when he rode to *Kensington*, and thence, the back way to *London*.

"The third time, when he went to *Hide-Park* in his coach.

"The fourth time, when he went to *Turnham Green*, and so by *Acton* home, at which time they rode forth to kill him, and resolved to break through all difficulties to effect it.

"The fifth time, when he rode into *Hide-Park*, where his Highness alighting, asked him, the said *Cecil*, whose horse that was he rode on, *Sundercomb* being then on the outside of the Park; and then *Cecill* was ready to have done it, but doubted, his horse having at that time got a cold."

That they meant to kill the Protector there can be little doubt, and looked after their means of escape afterwards, for we read in the papers of the day [2] how—" Once, they thought to have done their work as his Highness was taking the aire in *Hide-Park;* and, to make way for their Escape, they had, in one place, Filed off the Hinges of the Gates,

---

[1] *Mercurius Politicus.* January 29—February 5, 1657.
[2] *Mercurius Politicus.* January 15—22, 1657, and *The Publick Intelligencer,* January 19—26, 1657.

and rode about with the train attending his Highness, with intent to have given him a fatall Charge, if he had chanced to have galloped out at any distance from the company." They also had pulled down some of the fencing, so as to leave them another place of egress.

Sindercombe was tried, found guilty, and sentenced to be hanged, drawn and quartered; but, on the night previous to his execution, he found means to poison himself, and so cheated the gallows. The coroner's jury found a verdict of *felo de se*,[1] and "On the same day, *February* 17, *Miles Sindercom* aforesaid, being found to have murthered himself, his Body was, according to Law, drawn to the open place upon *Tower Hill*, at a Horses Taile, with his head foreward, and there, under the Scaffold of Common execution, a Hole being digg'd, he was turned in stark naked, and a stake, spiked with Iron, was driven through him into the earth; That part of the stake which remaines above ground, being all plated with Iron, which may stand as an example of terror to all Traytors for the time to come."

Previous to this, it had been found necessary to protect the Park, by authority, as we see by two entries in the *Journals of the House of Commons*. "7 Oct., 1643. *Ordered*, That the Officers and Soldiers at the Courts of Guard be required not to permit any to cut down Trees or Woods in *Hyde Park*, or *Maribone Park*, but such as are authorized thereto by Ordinance of Parliament; and not to suffer any such persons to go out of the Works to cut the Woods in these two

[1] *Mercurius Politicus*. February 12—19, 1657.

Parks, or to bring any from thence, but by Warrant from the Committees appointed for that Ordinance: and the Officers and Soldiers at the Courts of Guard are required, from time to time, to be aiding and assisting to *Sir John Hippesley*, a Member of this House, on all Occasions, to prevent the cutting down or destroying of the said Parks, unless it be by Authority of the Ordinance aforesaid."

And there is another entry on Oct. 14, 1644. "Whereas Information hath been given, That several unruly and disorderly Persons have, in a tumultuous and riotous Manner, broken into *Hide Park*, pulled down the Pales to destroy his Majesty's Deer and Wood there, notwithstanding strict Command hath been given to the Contrary: It is *Ordered and Ordained*, by the Lords and Commons in Parliament, That the said Park and Deer, and the Woods and Pales, belonging to the said Park, are hereby protected from the Violence of any Person or Persons whatever: and that no Soldier, or other, shall presume to pull down, or take away, any of the Pales belonging to the same, nor kill, or destroy, any Deer therein; or cut, fell, or carry away, any Wood growing in or about the said Park, or Mounds thereof. And it is further *Ordered* for the better Prevention of the Mischiefs aforesaid, That all Captains and Commanders of Guards and Forts near the said Park, shall give Notice of this Ordinance to the Soldiers under their several Commands: And that they themselves likewise do their Uttermost Endeavours, that this Ordinance shall be obeyed in all Points: And, lastly, that if any Others, not being Soldiers, shall offend contrary to this Ordinance, that the Keepers of the said Park, or some of them may charge any of his Majesty's Officers with the said offenders: Who are to be brought before the Parliament, to be proceeded with according to their Demerits."

When the King "came to his own again," the gentlemen who had purchased Hyde Park, had to restore it to the Crown, on the grounds that the sale had never been ratified by Parliament: and an early Act of His Majesty's was to build a wall around the Park, and re-stock a portion of it with deer.

CHAPTER III.

The camp in Hyde Park during the Plague of 1665—Boscobel Oaks in the Park—When first opened to the public—What it was then like—The Cheesecake House—Its homely refections—Orange girls.

IN 1665, at the time of the great Plague, Hyde Park was put to a sad use, as is well described in a contemporary poem entitled " Hide Park Camp Limned out to the Life, etc."

" In *July*, Sixteen hundred sixty and five,
(O happy is the Man that's now alive)
When God's destroying Angel sore did smite us,
'Cause he from sin could by no means invite us:
When Lovely *London* was in Mourning Clad,
And not a countenance appear'd but sad;
When the Contagion all about was spread;
And People in the Streets did fall down dead.
When Money'd fugitives away did flee,
And took their Heels, in hopes to scape scot-free.
Just then we March't away, the more's the pitty,
And took our farewell of the Doleful City.
With heavy Hearts unto *Hide Park* we came,
To chuse a place whereas we might remain:
Our Ground we view'd, then streight to work we fall,
And build up Houses without any Wall.
We pitched our Tents on Ridges, and in Furrows,
And there encamp't, fearing th' *Almighty's Arrows*.
But O alass! What did all this avail:
Our men (ere long) began to droop and quail.
Our Lodgings cold, and some not us'd thereto,
Fell sick, and dy'd, and made us more adoe.
At length the Plague amongst us 'gan to spread,
When ev'ry morning some were found stark dead.
Down to another Field the sick were t'ane;
But few went down, that e'er came up again.
For want of comfort, many, I observ'd,
Perish'd and dy'd, which might have been preserv'd.
But that which most of all did grieve my Soul,

The Camp in 1665.

To see poor Christians drag'd into a Hole :
Tye Match about them, as they had been Logs,
And draw them into Holes, far worse than Dogs.
When each Man did expect his turn was next,
O then our Hearts with sorrow was perplext.
Our Officers amazed stood, for dread,
To see their men no sooner sick but dead.
But that which most of all did grieve them, Why?
To help the same there was no remedy.
A Pest-house was prepar'd, and means was us'd,
That none should be excluded, or refus'd :
Yet all would not avail, they dy'd apace,
As one dy'd out, another took his place.
A sad and dismal time, as ere was known,
When Corps, in the wide fields about was strown.

"But stay, my Muse; I think 'tis but a folly
To plunge ourselves too deep in Melancholly;
Let us revive a little, though in jest,
Of a bad Market we must make the best.
Is nothing left to chear us? not one Sup?
We'le try conclusions, ere the Game be up.
Methinks I hear some say, Friend, Prithee hark,
Where got you drink and Victuals in the *Park*?
I, there's the Query ; We shall soon decide it,
Why, We had Men, cal'd Sutlers, provided ;
Subtle they were, before they drove this Trade,
But by this means, they all were sutler made.
No wind, or weather, ere could make them flinch,
Yet they would have the Souldiers at a pinch.
For my part, I know little of their way,
But what I hear my fellow Souldiers say ;
One said, Their Meat and Pottage was too fat ;
Yes, quoth another, we got none of that :
Besides, quoth he, they have a cunning sleight,
In selling out their Meat by pinching weight ;
To make us pay sixpence a pound for Beefe,
To a poor Souldier, is no little grief.
Their Bread is small, their Cheese is mark't by th' Inch,
And, to speak truth, they're all upon the pinch.
As for their Liquor, drink it but at leisure,
And you shall ne're be drunk with over measure.
Thus would they often talk to one another ;
And, for my part, I speak it as a Brother,
They for the Sutlers put up many a Prayer,
When, for themselves they took not so much care.
This was, it seems, most of the Sutlers' dealings,
But yet, I say, there's none but have their failings.
They might do this (poor men), yet think no evil.
Therefore they'l go to God, or to the D——.

"But leave them now, because Tat-too has beat,
And fairly to our Tents let us retreat,
Where we keep such a coyl, and such a quarter,
And all to make the tedious nights seem shorter.
Then down we lie, until our bones do ake,
First one side, then the other weary make.
When frost did pinch us, then we shake and shiver,
And full as bad we were in stormy weather;
A boistrous blast, when men with sleep were dead,
Would bring their Houses down upon their head.
Thus in extremity, we often lay,
Longing to see the dawning of the day
Which brought us little comfort, for the Air
Was very sharp, and very hard our fare.
Our sufferings were almost beyond belief,
And yet we found small hopes to have relief.

"Our brave Commanders, Valiant, Stout and Bold,
Was neither pinch't with hunger, nor with cold,
They quaft the Bowls about, one to another,
With good Canary they kept out the weather;
And oft to one another would say thus,
(When we are gone, then gone is all with us)
And thus, in mirth, they chear'd their Spirits up,
By taking t'other Pipe, and t'other Cup:
Much good may it do their hearts; we should have done
The same ourselves, had we been in their room.
We were as glad when we got to a Cup
Of nappy Ale, to take a pretty sup;
But durst not go to Town, on any cause,
For fear the Martial catch us in his Claws.
About the *Park* to walk for recreation,
We might be free, we knew our Bounds and Station.
But not a Coach was stirring any where,
Unless t'were such as brought us in our Beer.
Alass, *Hide Park*, these are with thee sad dayes,
The Coaches all are turn'd to Brewers' Drayes;
Instead of Girls with Oranges and Lemons,
The Bakers' boys, they brought in loaves by dozens;
And by that means, they kept us pretty sober,
Until the latter end of wet *October*.
They promis'd we should march, and then we leapt,
But all their promises were broke (or kept).
They made us all, for want of Winter Quarters,
Ready to hang ourselves in our own Garters.

"At last, the Dove came with the Olive Branch,
And told, for certain, that we should advance
Out of the Field; O then we leapt for joy,
And cry'd with one accord, *Vive le Roy*.
What did the Sutlers then? nay, what do ye think?

BOSCOBEL OAKS, 1804.

For very grief, they gave away their drink:
But it's no matter, let them laugh that wins,
They were no loosers (God forgive their sins).

"Upon *Gunpowder Treason* day, (at Night)
We burnt our Bed-Straw, to make Bone fire light;
And went to Bed, that night, so merry hearted
For joy we and our Lodgings should be parted;
Next morning we were up by break of day,
To be in readinesse to march away.
We bid adue to *Hide Park's* fruitful Soil,
And left the Country to divide the Spoyl.
With flying Colours we the City enter,
And, then, into our Quarters boldly venture.
Our Land-Ladyes sayd *Welcome* (as was meet),
But, for our Landlords, some lookt sowr, some sweet.
So soon as we were got into warm Bed,
We look't as men new metamorphosed.
But now I think 'tis best to let them sleep,
Whilst I out of the Chamber softly creep,
To let you know, that now my task is done,
Would I had known as much when I begun.
A sadder time, I freely dare engage
Was never known before, in any Age.
God bless King Charles *and send him long to reign,
And grant we never may know the like again.*"

In connection with Hyde Park and the Restoration, I may mention the following, copied from *The Times*, December 18, 1862. "A RELIC OF THE PAST IN HYDE PARK. Perhaps few of the many who visit this Park are aware that on the right hand side of the Carriage drive, between the Receiving house and the Bridge, there still remains an interesting relic of the Stuart period. It is a tree, one of two planted by Charles II. from acorns taken from the Boscobel Oak, in Somersetshire, in *which his father successfully sought refuge*, and were planted here to commemorate the event. They have both been dead some years, and one, much decayed, was removed in 1854; the other, beautifully clothed with ivy, which gives it the appearance of life, still remains. In common with all the other old trees in the Park, it is protected by a fence of iron hurdles; but, surely, a relic like this deserves a handsome and appropriate railing, with a descriptive brass plate affixed, to point out to strangers this historical antiquity, now known only to local historians."

If the traditional lore of the writer of the above is on a par with his historical knowledge (*vide italics*) this statement has not much value. Indeed, a correspondent in *Notes and Queries* (3s. iii. 96), referring to this paragraph, and speaking of the trees, says "the tradition really and truly connected with them is the fatal duel fought by the fifth Lord Mohun and the Duke of Hamilton, in November, 1712."

Hyde Park seems to have been first opened to the public about 1637, for in the dedication of James Shirley's play of *Hide Parke* (published in that year) to the Right Hon. Henry, Earl of Holland, he says, " This Comedy in the title, is a part of your Lordship's Command, which heretofore grac'd, and made happy by your smile, when it was presented, after a long silence, *upon first opening of the Parke*." And it is from this contemporary play that we are able to learn somewhat of the Park itself. Nightingales and cuckoos abounded, and both are several times mentioned.

 Mistress Caroll. Harke, Sir, the Nightingale, there's better lucke
  Comming towards us.
 Fairfield. When you are out breath
  You will give over, and for better lucke,
  I do beleeve the bird, for I can leave thee,
  And not be in love with my owne torment.
 M. Ca. How, sir?

FA. I ha said, stay you and practise with the bird,
  'Twas Philomel they say; and thou wert one,
  I should new ravish thee.
  . . . . . .
MISTRESS BONAVENT. I heard it yesterday warble so prettily.
LACY. They say 'tis luckie, when it is the first
  Bird that salutes our eare.
BO. Doe you believe it?
TRYER. I am of his minde, and love a happy Augury.
LA. Observe the first note alwayes
  Cuckoo!
  Is this the Nightingale?

And then also there were refreshments to be taken at the Keeper's Lodge (sometimes called Price's Lodge, from Gervase Price, a keeper), as we read in *Hide Parke*.

RIDER. I wish your sillabub were nectar, Lady.
MISTRESS BONAVENT. We thank you, sir, and here it comes already.
  Enter MILKEMAIDE.
MISTRESS JULIETTA. So, so, is it good milke?
BON. Of a Red Cow.
MISTRESS CAROLL. You talke as you inclin'd to a consumption. Is the wine good?

Pepys mentions this Lodge and its refreshments more than once. "*June* 3, 1668. To the Park, where much fine company and many fine ladies, and in so handsome a hackney I was, that I believe, Sir W. Coventry and others who looked on me, did take me to be in one of my own, which I was a little troubled for: so to the Lodge and drank a cup of new milk, and so home."—"*April* 25, 1669. Abroad with my wife in the afternoon to the Park, where very much company, and the weather very pleasant. I carried my wife to the Lodge, the first time this year, and there, in our coach, eat a cheese cake and drank a tankard of milk."

Not to know the Lodge was to show oneself of small account, as we see in a comedy called "The

English Monsieur," by the Hon. James Howard, son of the Earl of Berkshire, acted with much applause at the Theatre Royal, in 1674.

"COMELY. Nay, 'tis no London female; she's a thing that never saw Cheesecake, Tart, or Syllabub at the Lodge in Hyde Park."

According to Thomas Brown, of Shifnall, the ladies also partook of refreshment in their coaches, for he says,—" See, says my *Indian*, what a Bevy of Gallant Ladies are in yonder Coaches; some are Singing, others Laughing, others Tickling one another, and all of them Toying and devouring Cheese Cakes, March-Pane, and *China* Oranges."[1] And this in the sober days of William and Mary!

About this time the name of "the Lodge" was generally dropped, and it was called the Cake House or Mince Pie House, until it was pulled down early middle of the century. It was situated nearly on the site of the present Receiving House of the Royal Humane Society, as is shown in a "Plan of Hyde Park, as it was in 1725. From a Plan of the Parish of St. George, Hanover Square, in the Vestry Room of that Parish."[2] It was made of timber and plaster, and must have had a very picturesque look when the accompanying illustration was taken in 1826. The other view of it, in 1804, shows its surroundings in the Park. "The Cake House" furnished the title of one of Charles Dibdin's table entertainments, first performed in 1800.

Then too there were the Orange girls, whose vocation was not entirely confined to the theatres,

[1] "Amusements Serious and Comical, Calculated for the Meridian of London." Lond. 1700, p. 55.
[2] "Environs of London." D. Lysons, 2nd ed. vol. ii. part i. p. 117.

CHEESECAKE HOUSE, 1826.

and who were chaffed by, and gave saucy answers to, the beaux. In a play by Thomas Southern (the author of *Isabella* and *Oroonoko*), published in 1693, called *The Maid's last Prayer, Or* Any, *rather than Fail*, we find (p. 37) Lord and Lady Malapert discussing the propriety of visiting their country seat.

L. MAL. Well, well, there are a thousand innocent diversions.
LA. MAL. What! Angling for Gudgeons, Bowls, and Nine-pins?
L. MAL. More wholesome and diverting than always the dusty Mile Horse driving in Hide-Park.
LA. MAL. O law! don't profane Hide-Park: Is there anything so pleasant as to go there alone, and find fault with the Company? Why, there can't a Horse or a Livery 'scape a Man, that has a mind to be witty. And then I sell bargains to the Orange Women.

CHAPTER IV.

Foot and horse racing in the Park—Prize fighting—Duelling—
The duel between Lord Mohun and the Duke of Hamilton.

THEN, also, there were races run in the Park, both horse, coach and foot. In Shirley's *Hide Parke* we read,—

L. BONAVENT. Be there any races here?
MR. LACY. Yes, Sir, horse and foot.

. . . .

MISTRESS BON. Prethee, sweetheart, who runnes?
LA. An Irish and an English footeman!
M. BON. Will they runne this way?
LA. Just before you, I must have a bet!   [*Exit.*
M. BON. Nay, nay, you shall not leave me.
MISTRESS CARROLL. Do it discreetely, I must speak to him,
 To ease my heart. I shall burst else.
 Weele expect 'em here, Cousen, do they runne naked?
M. BON. That were a most immodest sight.
M. CA. Here have bin such fellowes, Cousen.
M. BON. It would fright the women!
M. CA. Some are of opinion it brings us hither.
 Harke what a confusion of tongues there is.
 Let you and I venture a paire of Gloves
 Upon their feete; I'le take the Irish.
M. BON. 'Tis done, but you shall pay if you lose.
M. CA. Here's my hand, you shall have the Gloves if you
 winne.
M. BON. I thinke they are started.
   The Runners, after them the Gentlemen.
OMNES. A Teag, A Teag, make way for shame.
LA. I hold any man forty peeces yet.
VENTURE. A hundred pound to ten! a hundred peeces to ten!
 Will no man take me?
M. BON. I hold you, Sir.
VEN. Well, you shall see. A Teag! a Teag! hey!
TRYER. Ha! Well run, Irish!
BON. He may be in a Bogge anon.   [*Exeunt.*

The horse race is thus described.
Enter Jockey and Gentleman.
I. What dost thinke, *Jockey?*
II. The crack o' th' field against you.
Jo. Let them crack nuts.
I. What weightc?
II. I think he has the heeles.
III. Get but the start.
Jo. However, if I get within his quarters, let me alone.
[*Exeunt.*
Confused noise of betting within, after that, a shoute.
M. Ca. They are started.
Enter Bonvile, Rider, Bonavent, Tryer, and Fairefield.
Ri. Twenty pounds to fifteene.
L. Bon. 'Tis done we'e.
Fa. Forty pounds to thirty.
L. Bon. Done, done, Ile take all oddes.
Tr. My Lord, I hold as much.
L. Bon. Not so.
Tr. Forty pounds to twenty.
L. Bon. Done, done.
M. Bon. You ha' lost all, my Lord, and it were a Million.
L. Bon. In your imagination, who can helpe it?
La. *Venture* had the start, and keepes it.
L. Bon. Gentlemen, you have a fine time to triumph,
'Tis not your oddes that makes you win.
Within—Venture! Venture! [*Exeunt Men.*
Julietta. Shall we venture nothing o' th' horses?
What oddes against my Lord?
M. Ca. Silke stockings.
Ju. To a paire of perfum'd gloves, I take it.
M. Ca. Done!
M. Bon. And I as much.
Ju. Done with you both!
M. Ca. Ile have em Spanish sent.
Ju. The stockings shall be scarlet, if you choose
Your sent, Ile choose my sent.
M. Ca. 'Tis done, if *Venture*
Knew but my lay, it would halfe breake his necke now,
And crying *A Jockey! hay!* [*A shoute within.*
Ju. Is the wind in that coast, harke the noyse.
Is *Jockey* now?
M. Ca. 'Tis but a paire of gloves.
Ju. Still it holds. [*Enter My Lord.*
How ha' you sped, my Lord?
L. Bon. Won, Won, I knew by instinct
The mare would put some tricke upon him.
M. Bon. Then we ha' lost; but, good my Lord, the circumstance.

L. Bon. Great *John* at all adventure and grave *Jockey*
  Mounted their severall Mares, I sha'not tell
  The story out for laughing, ha, ha, ha,
  But this in briefe ; *Jockey* was left behind,
  The pitty and the scorne of all the oddes,
  Plaid 'bout my eares like Cannon, but lesse dangerous,
  I looke all still : the acclamations was
  For *Venture*, whose disdainful Mare threw durt
  In my old *Jockey's* face, all hopes forsaking us,
  Two hundred peeces desperate, and two thousand
  Oathes sent after them : upon the suddaine,
  When we expected no such tricke, we saw
  My rider, that was domineering ripe,
  Vault ore his Mare into a tender slough,
  Where he was much beholding to one shoulder
  For saving of his necke ; his beast recovered,
  And he, by this time, somewhat mortified,
  Besides mortified, hath left the triumph
  To his Olympick Adversary, who shall
  Ride hither in full pompe on his *Bucephalus*,
  With his victorious bagpipe.

These pedestrian races between " Running footmen" seem to have been common in Hyde Park, as Pepys notes under date August 10, 1660. " With Mr. Moore and Creed to Hyde Park by Coach, and saw a fine foot race three times round the Park, between an Irishman and Crow, that was once my Lord Claypole's footman." And for another instance of horse-racing in the Park we can find one in the comedy of *The Mulberry Garden*, by Sir Charles Sedley (1668), where, in Act I. Scene 2, Ned Estridge, speaking of Sir John Everyoung, says, " 'Tis a pleasant old fellow. He has given me a hundred pounds for my *Graybeard*, and is to ride himself, this day month, twice round the Park, against a bay stone horse of *Wildishe's*, for two hundred more." Whilst for a different kind of race we have the testimony of Evelyn, who says : " May 20th, 1658. I went to see a coach race in Hide Park, and collationed in Spring

Garden." In *The Merry Life and mad Exploits of Captain* James Hind, *The great Robber of England*, a noted highwayman *temp.* Charles II., is a story of " How *Hind* robbed a Gentleman in *Hide Park* of a Bag of Money. *Hind* being well mounted, went one Evening into *Hide Park*, to see some Sport, and riding by a Gentleman's Coach, espied a Bag of Money, upon which *Hind* used some Discourse about the Race that was going to be run; but the Race beginning, the Gentleman caused his Coach to stand still, that he might the easier judge which of the Horses run best. Hind's head not being idle, rode close to the Coach side, took the Bag of Money in his hands, and rode away with it. The Gentleman presently missing his Bag of Money, cries out, *Stay him, Stay him, I am robbed.* Many rode after him, especially the Captain whom he robbed at *Chalk Hill*, who pursued him very hard. *Hind* riding by *St. James's*, said to the Soldiers, *I have won the Wager;* but holding of the Bag fast, his Cloak fell off, which he left for them that came next. But when he came to his companions, he said, *I never earned a hundred pounds so dear in all my life.*"

Larwood says that foot-racing was carried on till early in the present century, and gives instances down to 1807; the only one I am at all able to verify was one run by two boys on 5th March, 1807—when one dropped down dead—*but that race was run in St. James's Park.*

In the somewhat brutal days of George III. (which brutality has descended to our own times) the Park was disgraced by prize-fights, and several duels were fought there, although the place was not so private as Wimbledon Common, Putney, or

Kensington Gravel Pits. One of the favourite places in the Park for these encounters was near the Cheesecake House, or Price's Lodge, for it was there that the celebrated duel between Lord Mohun and the Duke of Hamilton took place in 1712, and it certainly retained its position till 1751, when Fielding wrote *Amelia*, where Colonel Bath and Booth meeting in St. James's Park, the Colonel says, "' I will tell you therefore, Sir, that you have acted like a Scoundrel.'—' If we were not in the Park,' answered *Booth* warmly, 'I would thank you very properly for that Compliment.'—' O Sir !' cries the Colonel, ' we can soon be in a convenient place.' Upon which *Booth* answered he would attend him wherever he pleased.—The Colonel then bid him come along, and strutted forward directly up *Constitution Hill* to *Hyde Park, Booth* following him at first, and afterwards walking before him, till they came to that Place which may be properly called the Field of Blood, being that part a little to the Left of the Ring, which Heroes have chosen for the Scene of their Exit out of this World." Booth ran the Colonel through the body, without seriously injuring him, and a reconciliation took place, ending, "'I bleed a little, but I can walk to the house by the water, (*the Cheesecake House*) and, if you will send me a Chair thither, I shall be obliged to you.'"[1]

I propose to give an account of some authentic duels which have taken place in Hyde Park, commencing with that of Lord Mohun and the Duke of Hamilton, on November 15th, 1712, all the rest being taken from *The Gentleman's Magazine*.

[1] *Amelia*, by Hy. Fielding, ed. 1752. Book 5, ch. vi. p. 132.

DUEL BETWEEN LORD MOHUN AND THE DUKE OF HAMILTON. Page 37.

This duel was invested with a political colouring, the Duke being the leader of the Jacobite faction in Scotland, and Mohun being a violent Whig; so that the Tories, enraged at Hamilton's fall, did not scruple to call it a Whig murder, and denounce Lord Mohun's second, General Macartney, as having unfairly stabbed him; but from the evidence taken at the two inquests,[1] there is not a *scintilla* of truth in the statement.

The story of the duel is, briefly, this. The two noblemen were opposing parties in a lawsuit; and, on Nov. 13, 1712, met in the chambers of a Master in Chancery, when the Duke remarked of a witness —"There is no truth or justice in him." Lord Mohun replied, "I know Mr. Whitworth; he is an honest Man, and has as much truth as your Grace." This, fanned to flame by officious friends, was enough; and, two days afterwards, they fought, early in the morning, in Hyde Park, near Price's Lodge; their seconds, Col. Hamilton and General Macartney, also fighting, as was the custom; or, as they expressed it, "taking their share in the dance."

The duel is shortly described by a witness, " John Reynolds *of* Price's *Lodge in the* Park, Swore, That hearing of a Quarrel, he and one *Nicholson*, got Staves and ran to part them : that he *Reynolds* was within 30 or 40 yards of Duke *Hamilton* and my Lord *Mohun* when they fell. That my Lord *Mohun* fell into the ditch upon his back, and Duke *Hamilton* fell near him, leaning over him. That the two seconds ran in to them; and immediately after them

[1] Brit. Mus. $\frac{515.\ l.\ 2}{215}$

this *John Reynolds*, who demanded the Seconds' Swords, which they gave him, without any Resistance. He then wrested the Duke's Sword out of his Hand, and *Nicholson* took away my Lord *Mohun's*, and gave it to *Reynolds*, who carried the four swords some distance from the parties : He return'd and help'd Duke *Hamilton* up, who still lay on his Face. He got him up, and he walk'd about 30 Yards : they desir'd him to walk farther, and he said he could walk no farther."

By this witness, supported by two others, we see no mention of General Macartney stabbing the Duke, as represented in the illustration, and as it was currently reported at the time. Macartney fled; but Col. Hamilton remained, stood his trial, and was found guilty of manslaughter. He accused Macartney of the foul deed, and great was the hue and cry after him. The Duchess was naturally enraged, and offered a reward of £300 for his apprehension, the Government supplementing her offer by an additional £500, but Macartney got away safely. When things were quieter, he returned, stood his trial at the Queen's Bench, Colonel Hamilton's testimony was contradicted, and he was acquitted of the murder, but found guilty of manslaughter. The punishment for this, by pleading benefit of Clergy, which, of course, was always done, was reduced to a very minimum—something amounting to the supposed burning of the hand with a barely warm, or cold iron—and he was restored to his rank in the army, and had a regiment given him.

CHAPTER V.

Duelling in Hyde Park.

THE first duel in Hyde Park (chronicled in the *Gentleman's Magazine*, which commenced in 1731) is one fought on February 24, 1750, "between Admiral *Knowles* and Captain *Holmes*, with pistols, when two or three shots were exchanged on each side, but no hurt was done. His majesty being informed that more challenges were depending, particularly four Challenges sent to the said Admiral, order'd three officers into Custody." But the bellicose officers under his command did not care for that example, and on March 12 next ensuing, "at 7 in the morning was fought in *Hide Park*, a duel with sword and pistol between Capt. *Clarke* and Capt. *Innes*, belonging to Admiral *Knowles's* squadron; Captain *Clarke* fired first, and the ball went through Capt. *Innes's* breast into his body, of which wound he dy'd at 12 o'clock at night; the Coroner's jury brought it in wilful murder." Captain Clarke was sentenced to be hanged, but was respited. If the facts brought out at the trial were true, he ought to have suffered the extreme penalty of the law, for his pistols were rifled, with barrels 7 inches long, whilst those of his antagonist were only ordinary pocket pistols, with barrels about $3\frac{1}{2}$ inches in length; and they were not more than five yards distant from each other, when they turned about, and Captain Clarke fired before Captain Innes had levelled his pistol.

"Jan. 5, 1762. A duel was fought in *Hyde Park* between an *English* officer and an *Irish* gentleman, when the former was so dangerously wounded in the belly, that his life has been despaired of. He is now, however, in a fair way of doing well. . . . . A lady in *Bond Street,* said to be nearly related to the young officer who was wounded in *Hyde Park,* shot herself through the head with a pistol, and died in great agonies."

"May 13, 1769. A duel was fought between two gentlemen in *Hyde Park,* occasioned by a quarrel at Vauxhall, one of them was run thro' the sword arm, and the other wounded in the thigh, after which they were parted by their seconds."

"July 19, 1769. A duel is said to have been lately fought in Hyde Park between a Captain Douglas and the Rev. Mr. Green, who some time ago was tried for a rape at the Old Bailey, and acquitted. Mr. Green, it seems, disabled the Captain in his sword arm; but, what is the wonderful part of the story, the Captain Douglas, whom the Rev. Mr. Green disabled, cannot be found, so that it is supposed this parson, as the humourous sexton of a neighbouring parish says, never fights with a man but he buries him."

"Mar. 17, 1770. A duel was fought in Hyde Park, between George Garrick Esq^{ro} and Mr. Baddeley, both of Drury Lane Theatre, when the former, having received the other's fire, discharged his pistol in the air, which produced a reconciliation."

George Garrick was the brother of David, the celebrated actor, and Baddeley is notable for two things, one, as being the last of the "King's Servants" (as the actors at the two patent theatres were called) who wore his master's scarlet livery, and the other in leaving a small legacy to provide cake and wine for the green room of Drury Lane Theatre every Twelfth Night ; a custom which, for some time, was in abeyance, but has been revived, in a most liberal and costly manner, by Sir Augustus Harris.

The somewhat bald notice in the *Gentleman's Magazine* of this duel, is supplemented by a more extended one in the *Town and Country Magazine* for March, 1770. " The world have been so ill natured as to suggest that Mrs. B—y had formed a connection with the late Mr. H—d : and that Mr. M—z has since been his happy successor. These reports, whether true or false, occasioned some altercation between Mr. B—y and his wife; and, through resentment, he received her salary, without accounting to her for it.

"Mr. G—e G—k remonstrated with Mr. B—y upon his conduct, which so much displeased him, that he wrote a letter of complaint upon the occasion to Mr. D—d G—k. This epistle being shown to Mr. G—e G—k, he strongly resented it the next time he saw Mr. B—y, who, thereupon, challenged him. In consequence whereof, (after Mr. D—d G—k, had ineffectually endeavoured, for nearly three hours, to dissuade his brother from this hostile design) Mr. G—e G—k engaged Mr. S—s, the attorney, for his second; and Mr. B—y had sufficient influence over his supposed rival, Mr. M—z, to induce that gentleman to become his second.

"These preliminaries being adjusted, they repaired to Hyde Park, and the seconds having marked out the ground, Mr. B—y had already fired at his antagonist, when his wife, who had received intimation of the affair, flew upon the wings of love, (that is, in a hackney coach,) to the field of battle; and, arriving at this critical time, threw herself upon her knees; and, whilst she looked very languishing, (*but whether at her lover, or her husband, is not certain*) cried out ' Oh! spare him! spare him!' which entreaty, it is imagined, induced Mr. G—k to fire his pistol in the air, and a reconciliation took place.

"Mr. Davis, our wooden engraver, passing by at the time, was a spectator of the whole transaction, which enabled him to give our readers so lively and picturesque a representation as that annexed, of this curious and uncommon scene; from which there can, no doubt, remain, but that they were both *left-handed* upon this occasion."

"Oct. 15, 1771. About eight o'clock in the morning, a duel was fought in Hyde Park, between Major B. and T., a gentleman of great fortune in Yorkshire; when, after discharging a pistol each, the latter received a wound in the side, and was immediately carried in a coach to the house of a surgeon near Piccadilly. It is said the dispute arose from Mr. T. having, a few days since, insulted Major B. for shooting upon part of his estate, without being authorized to do so."

Here is a duel caused by what was afterwards called "The War of American Independence," which, however, at the time of its occurrence, had not commenced, although it was imminent.

"Dec. 11, 1773. A duel was fought in Hyde

DUEL BETWEEN GEORGE GARRICK AND MR. BADDELEY, 1770.

Park between Mr. Whateley, banker in Lombard Street, brother to Mr. Whateley, late Secretary to the Treasury, and John Temple Esqre, Lieutenant-Governor of New Hampshire, when the former was dangerously wounded. The cause of the quarrel was the discovery of the confidential letters written by Messrs. Hutchinson, Oliver, Paxton, etc., which were lately laid before the assembly at Boston, and have since been published in most of the London papers."

The next I record has one name well known to literature as a principal, that of " Fighting Parson Bate," otherwise the Reverend Henry Bate—afterwards Sir Henry Bate Dudley—who is mainly remembered as having founded two newspapers of note, namely the *Morning Post* and the *Morning Herald*. " Sep. 14, 1780. A duel was fought in Hyde Park between the Rev. Mr. Bate and Mr. R.,[1] one of the proprietors of the *Morning Post*, occasioned by some reflections cast by the former on the whole body of the proprietors, which was resented by the latter. Mr. Bate fired first, and wounded his antagonist in the muscular part of his arm, the other without effect; and then the seconds interposed, and the matter was accommodated."

One of the most vindictive duels I have read of is that which took place on October 1st, 1797. The principals were Colonel King, afterwards Lord Lorton, and a Colonel Fitzgerald, who, although a married man, had eloped with Colonel King's sister. The following is the account given by the gentleman who acted as second to both parties.

[1] Richardson.

"Agreeable to an arranged plan I accompanied Colonel King to a spot near the Magazine in the Park. Colonel Fitzgerald we met at Grosvenor Gate, unaccompanied by a friend, which, by the way, he told me yesterday, he feared he should not be able to provide, in consequence of the odium which was thrown upon his character; at the same time observing 'that he was so sensible of my honour, that he was perfectly satisfied to meet Colonel King unattended by a friend.' I decidedly refused any interference on his part, informing him 'that had not nearer relations of the ——— been on the spot, he would have seen me as a principal.' He replied, 'he would try to procure a friend;' and withdrew. I addressed him this morning by 'where is your friend, Sir?' Answer (as well as I recollect), 'I have not been able to procure one: I rest assured that you will act fairly.'—I then desired him to apply to his surgeon; which he immediately did, who refused appearing as a second, but said he would be within view. Colonel K. was equally desirous to go on with the business.—I consented. However, I prevailed upon a surgeon, who accompanied Dr. Browne, to be present, as a witness that all was fairly conducted. It was no common business.

"I placed them at ten short paces distance from each other; that distance I thought too far: but I indulged a hope that Colonel F., sensible of the vileness of his conduct, would, after the first fire, have thrown himself on Colonel K.'s humanity. His conduct was quite the reverse; in short, they exchanged six shots each, without effect. K. was cool and determined;—the other, also, determined, and to appearance obstinately bent on blood; after the fourth shot, he said something to me about giving him advice as a friend. I told him I was no friend of his, but that I was a friend to humanity; that if, after what had passed, he possessed firmness enough to acknowledge to Colonel K. that he was the vilest of human beings, and bear, without reply, any language from Colonel K., however harsh, the present business, then, perhaps, might come to a period. He consented to acknowledge that he had acted wrong, but no farther;—that was not enough. He now attempted to address Colonel K., who prevented him, saying 'he was a d—d villain, and that he would not listen to anything he had to offer.' They proceeded. Colonel F.'s powder and balls were now expended; he desired to have one of K.'s pistols. To this I would not consent, though pressed to do so by my friend. Here ended this morning's business—we must meet again; it cannot end here. . . .

"P.S.—On leaving the ground, Col. F. agrees to meet Col. K. at the same hour to-morrow.

"Both the Colonels the same day were put under arrest."

Another duel, which I may almost stigmatize as brutal, occurred on March 11th, 1803. "This morning, a most extraordinary duel took place in Hyde Park, between Lieutenant W. of the Navy, and Captain J. of the Army. The antagonists arrived at the appointed place within a few minutes of each other. Some dispute arose respecting the distance, which the friends of Lieutenant W. insisted should not exceed six paces, while the seconds of Captain J. urged strongly the rashness of so decisive a distance, and insisted on its being extended. At length, the proposal of Lieutenant W.'s friends was agreed to, and the parties fired *per* signal, when Lieutenant W. received the shot of his adversary on the guard of his pistol, which tore away the third and fourth fingers of his right hand. The seconds then interfered, to no purpose; the son of Neptune, apparently callous to pain, wrapped his handkerchief round his hand, and swore he had another which never failed him. Captain J. called his friend aside, and told him it was vain to urge a reconciliation. They again took their ground. On Lieutenant W. receiving his pistol in his left hand, he looked steadfastly at Captain J. for some time, then cast his eyes to Heaven, and said, in a low voice, 'Forgive me.' The parties fired as before, and both fell. Captain J. received the shot through his head, and instantly expired; Lieutenant W. received the ball in his left breast, and immediately inquired of his friend if Captain J.'s wound was mortal. Being answered in the affirmative, he thanked Heaven he had lived thus long; requested a mourning ring on his finger might be given to his sister, and that she might be assured it was the happiest moment he ever knew. He had scarcely finished the words when a quantity of blood burst from his wound, and he expired almost without a struggle. The unfortunate young man was on the eve of being married to a lady in Hampshire, to whom, for some time, he had paid his addresses."

The last duel I find connected with Hyde Park, but was fought at Chalk Farm, is the following: "April 6th, 1803. This morning, as Lieutenant-Colonel Montgomery and Captain Macnamara were riding in Hyde Park, each followed by a Newfoundland dog, the dogs fought; in consequence of which the gentlemen quarrelled, and used such irritating language to each other, that a change of addresses followed, with an appointment to meet at 7 o'clock the same evening near Primrose Hill; the consequences of which proved fatal."

Lord Burghersh, in giving evidence before the coroner's jury, spoke of the triviality of the offence given and received by these two hot-headed idiots. He said, " On coming out of St. James's Park on Wednesday afternoon, he saw a number of horsemen, and Colonel Montgomery among them; he rode up to him; at that time he was about twenty yards from the railing next Hyde Park Gate. On one side of Colonel Montgomery was a gentleman on horseback, whom he believed was Captain Macnamara. The first words he heard were uttered by Colonel Montgomery, who said: 'Well, Sir, and I will repeat what I said, if your dog attacks mine, I will knock him down.' To this, Captain Macnamara replied, 'Well, Sir, but I conceive the language you hold is arrogant, and not to be pardoned.' Colonel Montgomery said: 'This is not the proper place to argue the matter; if you feel yourself injured, and wish for satisfaction, you know where to find me.'"

Montgomery fell, mortally wounded, and Macnamara was tried at the Old Bailey, on 22nd March, for manslaughter. Lords Hood, Nelson, Hotham, and Minto, and a great number of highly respectable gentlemen gave him an excellent character, and, in spite of the judge's summing up, the jury went against his directions, and acquitted the Captain.

Larwood says that the last affair of honour which took place in Hyde Park was in April, 1817, when the Hon. H. C. and a Mr. John T. fired twice at each other and were both wounded; but, as I cannot verify this duel, I give it under all reserve.

The last *fracas* in Hyde Park that I can trace took place on July 12th, 1870, between Majors Gordon and Kane, retired officers in the Indian service, the combatants belabouring each other with their sticks, in retaliation for an affront alleged to have been offered at a private dinner-table.

CHAPTER VI.

Skating on the ponds and Serpentine—The Ring—Many notices thereof—Fireworks in the Park—Bad roads therein, and accidents caused thereby—Regulations in the time of Queen Anne—Making the drive—Riding in the Park.

SOON after the opening of the Park to the public, the water therein was utilized, during a hard frost, for skating, as Pepys tells us in his diary: "Dec. 8th, 1662. Then into the Parke to see them slide with their skeates, which is very pretty. Dec. 15th. Up and to my Lord's, and thence to the Duke,[1] and followed him into the Parke, where, though the ice was broken and dangerous, yet he would go slide upon his scates, which I did not like, but he slides very well."

This must have been, in all probability, on one of the pools in the park—as it was not till 1730 that Queen Caroline, wife of George II., began to make "the Serpentine," as the lake in Hyde Park is called. After that was finished, and a good hard frost came, so that it was frozen hard, it was the resort of the few of the upper classes who could skate. I do not say it was reserved for them, but in those days there were no cheap omnibuses from Whitechapel, and London was but a very small portion of its present overgrown bulk. At all events, in the last century, people could skate without overcrowding, or annoyance from bands of

[1] The Duke of York, afterwards James II.

roughs, such as obtain at the present day, as is well shown in the accompanying illustration of "WINTER AMUSEMENT, a view in Hyde Park, from the Sluice at the East End, 1787." Royalty, in the person of George, Prince of Wales, did not object to disport itself on the lake, and not being overcrowded, we never hear of the ice breaking, or lives being lost until 1794, when a building was erected on the site of the present Receiving House of the Royal Humane Society, wherein those suffering from injuries or immersion could be attended to.

But the chief use of the Park as a place of fashionable relaxation was driving within its precincts, and especially in the "Ring," a small enclosure, which is shown in the 1747 map, just where is the letter "A" in "Park." The practice seems to have obtained as soon as the Park was thrown open to the public, and we have already seen how, in the Commonwealth time, a charge was made for the entrance both of carriages and horses. On May Day, however, was the finest show. Possibly that then, as now, the coaches were renovated, and the horses had new harness. We learn something of this in a very serious tract, published in 1655, with a very long title, a portion of which is: *A serious Letter sent by a Private Christian to the Lady Consideration, the first day of May*, 1655, which commences thus:—

"Lady, I am informed fine Mrs. *Dust*, Madam *Spot*, and my Lady *Paint*, are to meet at *Hide-Park* this afternoon; much of pride will be there: if you will please to take an Hackney, I shall wait upon your Honour in a private way: But, pray, let us not be seen among the foolish ones, that ride round, round,

WINTER AMUSEMENT, 1787.

wheeling of their coaches about and about, laying of the naked breast, neck and shoulders over the boot, with a Lemon and a Fan, shaking it at young Mrs. *Poppet,* crying, *Madam your humble servant, your very humble servant,* while some are doing worse. Young Sir *William Spruce, Mounseir Flash,* and the Lord *Gallant,* will be all on horseback," etc.

But the gossiping pages of Pepys furnish us with a good view of Hyde Park, and I have, therefore, selected some quotations as illustrative.

"April 30, 1661. I am sorry that I am not at London, to be at Hide-Parke to-morrow, among the great gallants and ladies, which will be very fine.

"May 7, 1662. Thence to Paul's Church Yard; where seeing my Ladys Sandwich and Carteret, and my wife (who, this day, made a visit for the first time to my Lady Carteret) come by coach, and going to Hide-Parke, I was resolved to follow them; and so went to Mrs. Turner's: and thence found her out at the Theatre; where I saw the last act of the 'Knight of the burning Pestle,' which pleased me not at all. And so, after the play done, she and The. Turner and Mrs. Lucin and I, in her coach to the Parke; and there found them out, and spoke to them; and observed many fine ladies, and staid till all were gone almost.

"April 4, 1663. After dinner to Hide Parke: my aunt, Mrs. Wight and I in one coach, and all the rest of the women in Mr. Turner's. . . . . At the Parke was the King, and in another coach my Lady Castlemaine, they greeting one another at every tour.[1]

---

[1] Whenever "the tour" is mentioned, the "Ring" is meant which was the most fashionable part.

"April 18, 1664. To Hide Parke, where I had not been since last year; where I saw the King with his periwigg, but not altered at all; and my Lady Castlemaine in a coach by herself, in yellow satin and a pinner on; and many brave persons. And myself being in a hackney and full of people, was ashamed to be seen by the world, many of them knowing me.

"April 22, 1664. I home, and by coach to Mrs. Turner's and there got something to eat, and thence, after reading part of a good play, Mrs. The., my wife and I, in their coach to Hide Parke, where great plenty of gallants, and pleasant it was, only for the dust. Here I saw Mrs. Bendy, my Lady Spillman's faire daughter that was, who continues yet very handsome. Many others I saw with great content, and so home.

"March 19, 1665. Mr. Povy and I in his coach to Hyde Park, being the first day of the tour there. Where many brave ladies; among others, Castlemaine lay impudently upon her back, in her coach, asleep, with her mouth open.

"April 24, 1665. So by coach with my Wife and Mercer to the Parke; but the King being there, and I, now-a-days being doubtfull of being seen in any pleasure, did part from the tour, and away out of the Parke to Knightsbridge, and there eat and drank in the coach, and so home.

"April 21, 1666. Thence with my Lord Brouncker in his coach to Hide Parke, the first time I have been there this year. There the King was; but I was sorry to see my Lady Castlemaine, for the mourning forceing all the ladies to go in black, with their hair plain and without any spots, I find her to be a much more ordinary woman than ever I durst have thought she was; and, indeed, is not so pretty as Mrs. Stewart, whom I saw there also.

"May 1, 1667. Thence Sir W. Pen and I in his coach, Tiburne way, into the Park, where a horrid dust, and number of coaches, without pleasure, or order. That which we, and almost all went for, was to see my Lady Newcastle; which we could not, she being followed and crowded upon by coaches all the way she went, so that nobody could come near her : only I could see she was in a large black coach, adorned with silver instead of gold, and so white curtains, and everything black and white, and herself in her Cap. But that which I did see, and wonder at with reason, was to find Peg Pew in a new coach, with only her husband's pretty sister with her, both patched and very fine, and in much the finest coach in the park, and I think that ever I did see one or other, for neatness and richness in gold and everything that is noble. My Lady Castlemaine, the King, My Lord St. Alban's, Mr. Jermyn, have not so neat a coach that ever I saw. And, Lord ! to have them have this, and nothing else that is correspondent, is, to me, one of the most ridiculous sights that ever I did see, though her present dress was well enough ; but to live in the condition they do at home, and be abroad in this coach astonishes me.

"March 27, 1668. To the Exchange a turn or two, only to show myself, and then home to dinner, where my wife and I had a small squabble, but I first this day tried the effect of my silence, and not provoking her when she is in an ill-humour, and do find it very good, for it prevents its coming to that height on both sides, which used to exceed what was fit between us. So she became calm, by and by, and fond, and so took coach to Hide Park, where many Coaches, but the dust so great that it was troublesome.

"March 31, 1668. So took up my wife and Deb., and to the Park, where, being in a hackney, and they undressed, was ashamed to go into the tour, but went round the Park, and so, with pleasure, home.

"July 10, 1668. Thence in the evening, with my people in a glass hackney-coach to the park, but was ashamed to be seen. So to the lodge, and drank milk, and so home."

But it was not for long that his pride was to be thus hurt, for he started a coach of his own, which came home on the 28th Nov., 1668, and which must have been a very gorgeous turn-out, if we can believe a description of it in a pamphlet called *Plain Truth, or a Private Discourse between P(epys) and H(arbord)*. "There is one thing more you must be mightily sorry for with all speed. Your presumption in your coach, in which you daily ride, as if you had been son and heir to the great Emperor Neptune, or as if you had been infallibly to have succeeded him in his government of the Ocean, all which was presumption in the highest degree. First, you had upon the fore part of your Chariot, tempestuous waves and wrecks of ships; on your left hand, forts and great guns, and ships a fighting; on your right hand was a fair harbour and galleys riding, with their flags and pennants spread, kindly saluting each other, just like P(epys) and H(ewer). Behind it were high curled waves and ships a sinking, and here and there an appearance of some bits of land."

Now he could ride in the Park with pleasure, as he notes, "March 18, 1669. So my wife and I to Dancre's to see the pictures; and thence to Hyde Park, the first time we were there this year, or ever in our own coach, when with mighty pride rode up and down, and many coaches there; and I thought our horses and coach as pretty as any there, and observed to be so by others."

But this coach evidently was not grand enough for him, for we read: "April 30, 1669. This done, I to my coachmaker's, and there vexed to see nothing yet done to my coach, at three in the afternoon; but I set it in doing, and stood by it till eight at night, and saw the painter varnish it, which is pretty to see how every doing it over, do make it more and more yellow : and it dries as fast in the sun as it can be laid on almost; and most coaches are, now-a-days, done so, and it is very pretty when laid on well, and not too pale, as some are, even to show the silver."

Of course he must needs show this off at once, and on May Day, he duly made his appearance in the Park. "At noon, home to dinner, and there find my wife extraordinary fine, with her flowered tabby gown that she made two years ago, now laced exceeding pretty; and, indeed, was fine all over; and mighty earnest to go, though the day was very lowering; and she would have me put on my fine suit, which I did. And so, anon, we went alone through the town with our new liveries of serge, and the horses' manes and tails tied with red ribbons, and the standards gilt with varnish, and all clean, and green reines, that people did mightily look upon us; and the truth is, I did not see any coach more pretty, though more gay, than our's all the day . . . . . . the day being unpleasing, though the Park full of Coaches, but dusty, and windy, and cold, and now and then, a little dribbling of rain; and, what made it worse, there were so many hackney coaches, as spoiled the sight of the gentlemen's; and so we had little pleasure. But here was W. Batelier and his sister in a borrowed coach by themselves, and I took them and we to the lodge: and, at the door, did give them a syllabub and other things, cost me 12s., and pretty merry."

Next day, he went again. "After dinner, got my wife to read, and then by coach, she and I, to the Park, and there spent the evening with much pleasure, it proving clear after a little shower, and we mighty fine, as yesterday, and people mightily pleased with our Coach, as I perceived; but I had not on my fine suit, being really afraid to wear it, it being so fine with the gold lace, though not gay."

But he was destined to undergo the humiliation of hearing his friends' criticisms on his new-born finery. "May 10th, 1669. Thence walked a little with Creed, who tells me he hears how fine my horses and coach are, and advises me to avoid being noted for it, which I was vexed to hear taken notice of, being what I feared: and Povy told me of my gold laced sleeves in the park yesterday, which vexed me also, so as to resolve never to appear in Court with them, but presently to have them taken off, as it is fit I should, and so called at my tailor's for that purpose."

One more quotation, to show that fireworks were exhibited in the Park, and I have done with Pepys. " May 29th, 1669. Home to dinner, and then with my wife to Hyde Park, where all the evening; great store of company, and great preparations by the Prince of Tuscany to celebrate the night with fireworks, for the King's birthday."

From that time to the present the Park has always been a fashionable drive, not always attended with safety to its frequenters: witness two accidents there in 1739. *The London Daily Post*, of Sept. 19, 1739, says: "On Monday evening last, as their Royal Highnesses the four Princesses [daughters of George II.] were coming to town from Kensington, a single Horse Chaise, with a Gentleman and his daughter in it, drove against the leading Coach in Hyde Park; the Chaise at length overturned, and the Horse falling under the Horses of the leading Coach, put them into such confusion, that four of them came down, and trampled for some time on the Horse and Chaise; the Gentleman and his daughter were much hurt, and the Postillion to the leading Coach had his Thigh broke by his fall; the Princesses were extreamly frightened, and cry'd out for Help. Several Persons came up to their Assistance; they returned to Kensington and were blooded: the Postillion is attended by the King's Surgeons."

Closely following on this was another accident, as we read in *The Weekly Miscellany* of Oct. 20, 1739. "Sunday night last his Grace the Duke of Grafton, coming from Kensington, and ordering his Coachman to drive to the New Gate in Hyde Park, in order to make some Visits towards Grosvenor Square, the Chariot, through the Darkness of the Night, was overset in driving along the Road, and, falling into a large, deep Pit, the Duke slipt his Collar bone, and the Coachman broke his Leg, which was splintered in many Places: and on Monday, the Limb was taken off by Amputation. One of his Grace's Footmen was, also, much hurt."

Even in Queen Anne's reign it was found necessary to issue some rules and directions (July 1, 1712) "For the better keeping Hyde Park in good Order." The gatekeepers were to be always on duty, and not to sell ale, brandy, or other liquors. No one should leap over the ditches or fences, or break the latter down. "No person to ride over the grass on the South side of the Gravelled Coach Road . . . . . excepting Henry Wise, who is permitted to pass cross that Part of the Park leading from the Door in the Park Wall, next his Plantation." No grooms nor others were to ride over the banks, or slopes, of any pond. No stage coach, hackney coach, chaise with one horse, cart, waggon, nor funeral should pass through the Park, and no one cut or lop any of the trees.

Henri Misson came over to England in the reign of James II., and published his experiences, which were translated by John Ozell, in 1719. Speaking of Hyde Park, he says, "The King has a Park so call'd at the end of one of the suburbs of *London*. Here the People of Fashion take the Diversion of the Ring: In a pretty high place, which lies very open, they have surrounded a Circumference of two or three hundred Paces Diameter with a sorry kind of Ballustrade, or rather with Poles plac'd upon Stakes, but three Foot from the ground; and the Coaches drive round and round this; when they have turn'd for some Time round one Way, they face about and turn t'other; So rowls the World."

On the completion of the Serpentine, and the consequent road on its north bank, the cramped and confined Ring went out of fashion, as we learn in No. 56 of *The London Spy Revived*, December 6, 1736. "The Ring in Hyde Park being quite disused by the Quality and Gentry, we hear that the ground will be taken in for enlarging the Royal Gardens at Kensington in the next Spring." But this was probably either only a rumour, or else Queen Caroline was better advised. The old name, however, still clung to the new road, and the carriage ride round the Park is still indifferently called the Ring or the Drive.

In the Library of the British Museum are two copies of an old ballad (circa 1670-5) entitled "News from *Hide-Park*,"[1] a portion of which gives a graphic description of the Park at that time.

"One Evening, a little before it was dark,
 Sing tan tara rara tantivee,
I called for my Gelding and rid to *Hide-Parke*
 On tan tara rara tantivee:
It was in the merry Month of *May*,
When Meadows and Fields were gaudy and gay,
And Flowers apparell'd as bright as the day,
 I got upon my tantivee.

"The *Park* shone brighter than the Skyes,
 Sing tan tara rara tantivee:
With jewels and gold, and Ladies' eyes,
 That sparkled and cry'd come see me:
Of all parts of *England*, *Hide-park* hath the name,
For Coaches and Horses, and Persons of fame,
It looked at first sight, like a field full of flame,
 Which made me ride up tan-tivee.

---

[1] Rox. ii. 379.—Lutt. ii. 147.

"There hath not been seen such a sight since *Adam's*.
  For Perriwig, Ribbon and Feather,
Hide-park may be term'd the Market of *Madams*,
  Or *Lady-Fair*, chuse you whether:
Their gowns were a yard too long for their legs,
They shew'd like the Rainbow cut into rags,
A Garden of Flowers, or a Navy of Flags,
  When they all did mingle together.

" We talke away time until it grew dark,
  The place did begin to grow privee;
The Gallants began to draw out of the Park:
  Their horses did gallop tantivee,
But, finding my courage a little to come,
I sent my bay Gelding away by my Groom,
And proffered my service to wait on her home.
  In her coach we went both tantivee."

CHAPTER VII.

Rotten Row, the King's Old Road—The New King's Road made and lighted—The Allied Sovereigns in the Park—The Park after the Peninsular War—The Duke of Wellington in the Park—The Queen and Royal Family in the Park.

IF we look at the old map of Hyde Park, we shall find that what is now called *Rotten Row* was then termed *The King's Old Road* and *The King's New Road*, whence the generally accepted derivation of *Rotten Row*, from *Route du Roi*. Soon after the accession of William III., and his purchase of Kensington Palace, his route from St. James's Palace to his residence lay through the Green Park and the King's Road in Hyde Park, and, finding it dark at night, he had it lit by three hundred lamps, which, for the time, rendered it a fairyland of brilliancy; so much so, that Thoresby, in his diary (June 15, 1712), "could not but observe that all the way, quite through Hyde Park to the Queen's Palace at Kensington, has lanterns for illuminating the road in the dark nights, for the Coaches."

As we see, the New King's Road was a trifle more direct than the old one, and skirted the Park. It was finished in 1737, as we find in *The London Spy Revived* (No. 183, September 23, 1737). "The King's Road in Hyde Park is almost gravell'd and finished, and the Lamp Posts are fixed up; it will soon be open'd, and the old Road level'd with the Park." The original intention was to do so, returf it, and once again make it a portion of the Park, but it was never carried out.

It would be absurd to chronicle even a portion of the people who have appeared in the Row and Ring : the list would simply consist of every person of note that lived in or visited London. It was used as a place for exercise and social intercourse, as we see in the two accompanying illustrations of the Row in 1793.

Another social group, date 1834, may also be given, but although they were well-known dandies of their day, they are unknown now, and their names are not worth recapitulating.

But never-to-be-forgotten visitors were the Allied Sovereigns, the Emperor of Russia and the King of Prussia, who were present at a grand review of all the regular troops, and most of the volunteers who resided in or near the metropolis, in Hyde Park on 20th June, 1814. With them were their brilliant staffs, while the Prince Regent, attended by the Duke of York, etc., acted as host to his Royal and Imperial guests.

Captain Gronow, in his *Anecdotes and Reminiscences*,[1] gives the following description of " Hyde Park after the Peninsular War. That extensive district of park land, the entrances of which are in Piccadilly and Oxford Street, was far more rural in appearance in 1815 than at the present day. Under the trees cows and deer were grazing ; the paths were fewer, and none told of that perpetual tread of human feet which now destroys all idea of

[1] 1st Series, 2nd edition, 1862, p. 71.

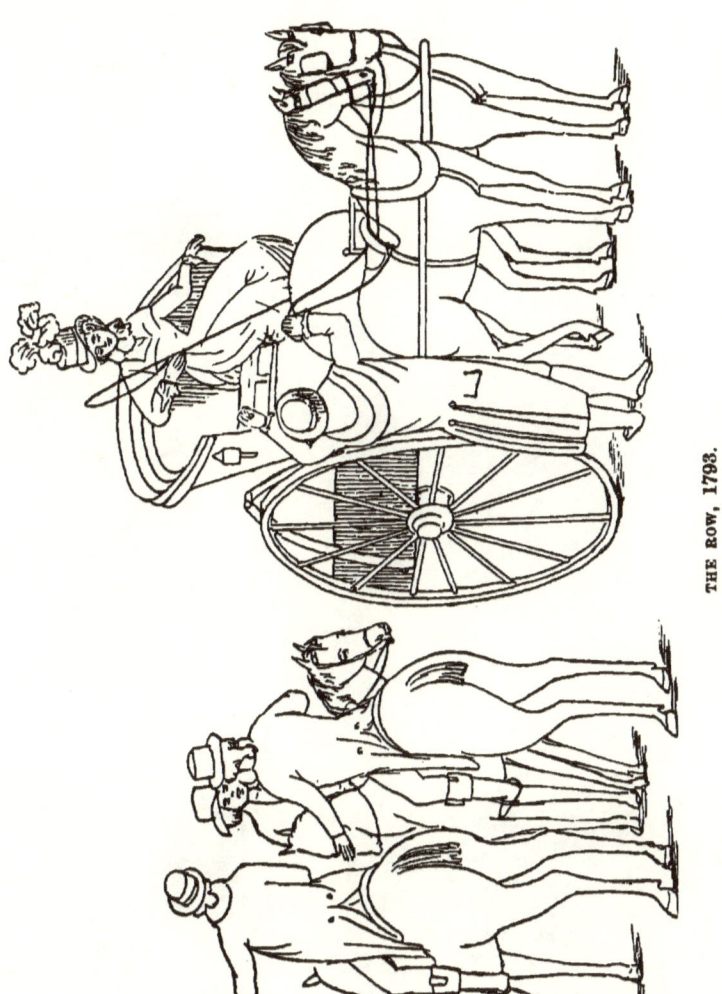

THE ROW, 1793.

THE ROW, 1793.

THE ROW, 1814. THE ALLIED SOVEREIGNS.

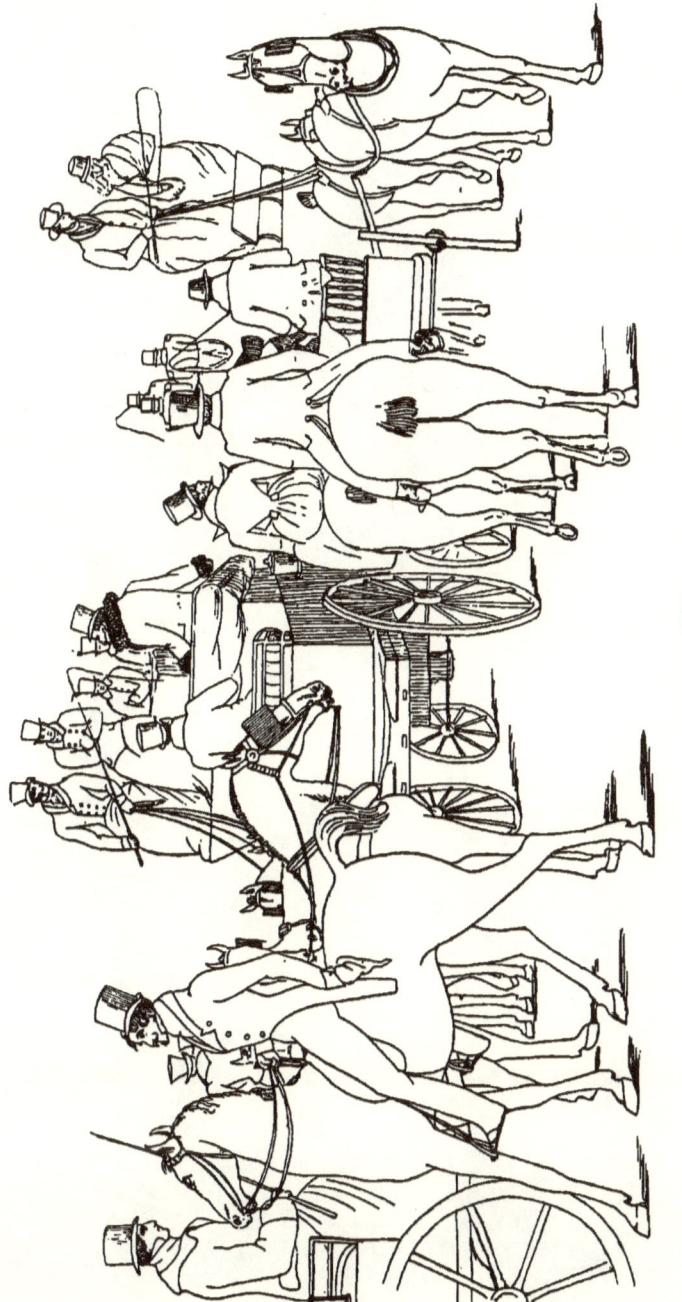

THE BOW, 1834.

country charms and illusions. As you gazed from an eminence, no rows of monotonous houses reminded you of the vicinity of a large city, and the atmosphere of Hyde Park was then much more like what God has made it, than the hazy, gray, coal-darkened half twilight of the London of to-day. The company, which then congregated daily about five, was composed of dandies and women in the best society, the men mounted on such horses as England alone then could produce. The dandy's dress consisted of a blue coat with brass buttons, leather breeches, and top boots; and it was the fashion to wear a deep, stiff, white cravat, which prevented you from seeing your boots while standing. All the world watched Brummell to imitate him, and order their clothes of the tradesman who dressed that sublime dandy. One day, a youthful beau approached Brummell, and said, 'Permit me to ask you where you get your blacking?' 'Ah!' replied Brummell, gazing complacently at his boots, 'my blacking positively ruins me. I will tell you in confidence; it is made with the finest champagne!'

"Many of the ladies used to drive into the Park in a carriage called a *vis-à-vis*, which held only two people. The hammer-cloth, rich in heraldic designs, the powdered footmen in smart liveries, and a coachman who assumed all the gravity and appearance of a wigged archbishop, were indispensable. The equipages were, generally, much more gorgeous than at a later period, when democracy invaded the parks, and introduced what may be termed a 'Brummagem society,' with shabby-genteel carriages and servants. The carriage company consisted of the most celebrated beauties, amongst whom were remarked the Duchesses of Rutland, Argyle, Gordon, and Bedford, Ladies Cowper, Foley, Heathcote, Louisa Lambton, Hertford and Mountjoy. The most conspicuous horsemen were the Prince Regent (accompanied by Sir Benjamin Bloomfield); the Duke of York, and his old friend Warwick Lake; the Duke of Dorset, on his white horse; the Marquis of Anglesea and his lovely daughters; Lord Harrowby and the Ladies Ryder; the Earl of Sefton and the Ladies Molyneux; and the eccentric Earl of Morton on his long-tailed grey. In those days, 'pretty horsebreakers' would not have dared to show themselves in Hyde Park; nor did you see any of the lower, or middle classes of London intruding themselves in regions which, with a sort of tacit understanding, were then given up, exclusively, to persons of rank and fashion."

But there was one constant visitor well within the memory of man, belonging both to 1814 and the Park, which he used almost daily until his death. I mean the first Duke of Wellington, with whose sharply-defined features, blue frock coat, and white trousers, every Londoner was familiar.

The Queen, too, until the great grief of her life fell upon her, was a pretty constant visitor to the Park—in her younger days on horseback; and who has not seen the Princess of Wales and her children there? Although, as Captain Gronow justly observes, the frequenters of the Park are not so aristocratic as they used to be, and society generally is much more mixed.

THE DUKE OF WELLINGTON.

Page 64.

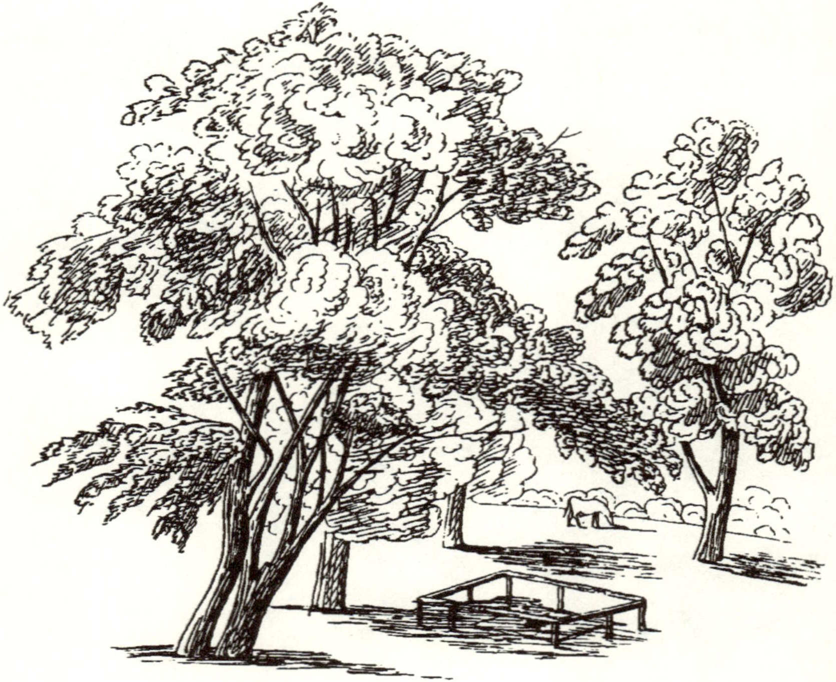

A SPRING IN THE PARK, 1794.

CHAPTER VIII.

The springs in Hyde Park—Used as water supply for Westminster—Horses in the Park—The Westbourne—Making the Serpentine—The "Naumachia" thereon—Satires about it—The Jubilee Fair.

HYDE PARK has several springs of water, one of which was said to have been slightly mineral. The one shown in this illustration still exists, and the author of "The Morning Walk" thus eulogizes one :—

> " But let my footsteps first pursue their course
> To yon clear fountain, hid in shady grove,
> And quaff the clear salubrious crystal brook,
> Emblem of purity ! when innocence
> Partakes, and all the wakened sense restores.
> O blessed *Jordan!* at thy limpid stream,
> Gladly I mingle with the cheerful throng,
> And drink the cup, and then renew my walk,
> With strengthen'd nerves, down the delightful shade."

Some of these springs were utilized for the supply of water outside the Park—but the larger quantity came from the Westbourne. Still, in 1620, the Dean and Chapter of Westminster had permission given them to use the water of four springs in Hyde Park for their benefit, and letters patent were granted to " Thomas Day, Gent. of Chelsea, to enable him to take the water from Hyde Park to the City of Westminster." This, I take it, meant to utilize the Westbourne, as the Dean and Chapter had the springs: but both their privileges were annulled

F

by the King's Bench, as it was alleged that the ponds in the Park were, by these means, so drained that there was not enough water left for the wants of the King's deer.

In the time of James I. there were eleven pools in the Park, and a glance at Roque's map of 1747 will show that many were then still remaining; indeed, in the accompanying illustration of the Bathing House in 1794, we see a horse drinking at one of them. By this, we see that horses were turned out to grass in the Park. In 1751, grooms used to exercise their horses there, as did also a riding master named Faubert.

> "See, too, the jolly courser, with his groom,
> Expert, not like to him who *Persia's* crown
> Obtained, yet skill'd with upright crest and arm,
> Compacted knee, to give the rein and bitt
> Their motion due, his flight retarding not.
> —— Next *Faubert* view with graces of menage,
> And troops of horse in strictest motion wheel."

From the heights of Hampstead spring several small streams, such as the Fleet, the Brent, and the West Bourne, probably so called to distinguish it from St. Mary le bourne, which was further east. Roque's map shows its position with regard to the Serpentine, but, before that misnamed lake was made, it ran right through the Park from north to south, leaving the Park about Albert Gate, where was a bridge, from which Knightsbridge takes its name. Then it flowed by what are now William Street, Lowndes Square, and Chesham Street, falling into the Thames near Ranelagh.

Queen Caroline, wife to George II., conceived the idea of utilizing this little stream, and making it into a lake, and, as it was supposed that she was

HORSES IN THE PARK, 1794.

expending her own money on this work, no objection was raised to her so doing, but it is said that at her death she left the King to pay a sum of no less than £20,000 on account of it. We learn when it was commenced from *Read's Weekly Journal, or British Gazetteer*, Saturday, September 26th, 1730. "Next Monday, they begin upon the Serpentine River, and Royal Mansion in Hide-Park: Mr. Ripley is to build the House, and Mr. Jepherson to make the River under the Directions of Charles Withers, Esqre." This latter gentleman, who was Surveyor General of Woods and Forests, died shortly before the Serpentine was finished, probably in 1733, when his successor was appointed; and in May, 1731, it was deep enough, in part, to allow two small yachts upon it. Its cost was estimated at £6000—but a portion of that (£2500) had to go as compensation to the Chelsea Water Works Company, who held a 99 years' lease, granted to one Thomas Haines, in 1663, whereby, on annual payment of 6s. 8d., he had command of all the springs and conduits in the Park.

The water supply for the Serpentine came from the Westbourne, until, in the course of time, owing to the extension of building, the houses around draining into it, its water became too foul for the purpose, and, in 1834, it was cut off, and connected with the sewer in the Bayswater Road; and the supply thus lost is made good by the Chelsea Water Works, who pump in water at the Kensington Gardens end, and the overflow at the very pretty Dell forms a striking feature in the landscape gardening of the Park. Formerly, as we see in Roque's map, the overflow was conducted into a pool, which was bridged over by the King's Old Road.

The Serpentine was not utilized for any purpose until August 1st, 1814, when a national rejoicing called "The Jubilee" was held in the Park, to celebrate the conclusion of peace with France, and the celebration of the centenary of the accession of George I. There were to be illuminations, fireworks, and balloon ascents in St. James's and the Green Parks, and in Hyde Park a fair, and a "Naumachia," or sea-fight, which was somewhat appropriate, as the famous Battle of the Nile was fought on August 1st, 1798.

The mimic three-deckers and frigates were necessarily small, and they were made out of ships' barges at Woolwich, and great was the chaff made about this "liliputian navy." Here are some skits thereon :—

"*John Bull*, the other day, in pensive mood,
　Near to the Serpentine Flotilla stood ;
His hands were thrust into his emptied pockets,
And much of ships he muttered, and of rockets ;
Of silly Fêtes—and Jubilees unthrifty—
And babies overgrown, of *two and fifty* ;[1]
I guess'd the train of thought which then possess'd him,
And deem'd th' occasion fit, and thus address'd him :

" ' Be generous to a fallen foe,
　　With gratulations meet,
　On Elba's *Emperor* bestow
　　Thy Liliputian fleet :

" ' For, with his Island's narrow bounds,
　　That Navy might agree,
　Which, laugh'd at daily here—redounds
　　In ridicule to thee.'

" Says John, ' Right readily I'll part
　　With these, and all the gay things,
　But it would break the R——'s heart
　　To take away his play things.' "

---

[1] The age of the Prince Regent.

Or take the two following distiches :—

"A simple Angler, throwing flies for trout,
Hauled the main mast, and lugg'd a First Rate out.

"A crow in his *fright*, flying over the Fleet,
Dropped something, that covered it all, like a sheet."

In contemporary accounts, the "Naumachia" was generally very summarily dismissed, and the following is, perhaps, one of the best of them.

"Between eight and nine o'clock, the Grand Sea Fight took place on the Serpentine River, where ships of the line, in miniature, manœuvred and engaged, and the Battle of the Nile was represented in little. Of this mock naval engagement on the great Serpentine Ocean, it would be extremely difficult to give any adequate description. It is, perhaps, sufficient to observe that it was about on a par with spectacles of a similar nature, which have been frequently exhibited at the Theatres. . . . We were as heartily glad when the cockle-shell fight was over, as we had been tired of waiting for it. We were afraid, at one time, whether it would have neither beginning nor end. Indeed, there had been a wretched skirmish between four and five in the afternoon, between an American and an English frigate,[1] at the conclusion of which, the English colours were triumphantly hoisted on the rebel Yankee. . . . At a signal given, the fireworks in the Green Park were let off, and four of the little fleet in the Serpentine were set on fire. The Swans screamed, and fluttered round the affrighted lake."

Such an opportunity for his satirical pen could

---

[1] Technically we were then at war with America—a war which began June 18th, 1812, and was ended by the Peace of Ghent, December 24th, 1814.

not be missed by C. F. Lawler, the then *pseudo* Peter Pindar, and he wrote thereon: "Liliputian Navy!!! The R——t's Fleet, or John Bull at the Serpentine."—"The P——e's Jubilee." "The R——l Showman." "The R——l Fair, or Grande Galante Show." And, on the sale of the Temple of Concord, which had been erected in the Green Park: "The Temple knock'd down: or R——l Auction. The last lay of the Jubilee." They are mostly scurrilous and spiteful, but from the first of them I take the following :—

"Now to Hyde Park the crowds repair,
To mark the wonders of the fair;
To view the long extended line,
The glory of the Serpentine.

"Now sounds the Cannon, near and far,
The signal for the naval war,
The cockle fleet their flounder sails
Now spread to catch the whisp'ring gales.

"Now meet the rival ships; now rave
The echoing thunders o'er the wave;
Within the banks the eels retire,
To shun the fury of the fire.

"The startled pike lifts up his head,
Curious, tho' paralyz'd with dread;
Snatches a momentary peep,
Then dives below the nether deep.

"And all the realm of fish—roach, dace,
Perch, minnow, chub, and tench, and plaice,
Far from the scene of havoc fly,
And seek the stream's extremity.

"Whisking his tail a flying eel
Struck a three decker's cockle's keel
(The vessel was the navy's boast,
And lay at anchor near the coast).

"Ungovernable from the stroke,
Quick from her *netting-pin* she broke;
With rude concussion struck the shore,
Then bilged, and sank, to ride no more.

Satires on the Naumachia.

"Boats from the cockle-shells at hand
Were quickly lower'd down and mann'd,
The gallant mariners to save—
To snatch them from a wat'ry grave.

"Scar'd at a spectacle so shocking,
Each 'prentice boy doff'd shoe and stocking,
Wading knee-deep, with shorten'd breath,
To snatch the struggling tars from death.

"An angler threw his fishing-line
Into the ruffled Serpentine;
Hook'd up the ship with no small pain,
And dragg'd her from the mimic main.

"See the tri-coloured cockles run,
The gaping crowd enjoy the fun;
Some still maintain a running fight
Some strike, some sink to endless night!

"'Lord! 'twas a glorious fight,' says Dick;
'Monsieur at last got devilish sick!'
'Then 'twas a real fight,' cry'd Sam;
'Why, lad, I thought it all a sham!'

"'Real! no, no!' says Jack, 'you fool!
'Twas all a bit of *ridicule;*
To show us lubbers, I've a notion,
How things are done upon the ocean.'"

There was another satirical poem on this Naumachia, entitled "AN EXTRAORDINARY GAZETTE, containing dispatches from ADMIRAL SQUIB, giving a detailed account of A GREAT NAVAL VICTORY obtained over the combined fleets of *France* and *America*, in the GREAT SERPENTINE SEA, on the 1st August, 1814,"—a small portion of which I transcribe.

"Now since, as you will understand,
This mighty *Sea* is quite inland,
It to their Lordships will appear
Strange, how the d——l we got here.

. . . . . .

A council call'd, some doubts were made,
Whether the ships could be convey'd;
Which I, who knew my men, dispell'd,
And every thought of failure quell'd.

Then quickly issued my command
The men should take them *overland;*
And such as were too large to drag on,
Should be convey'd upon a *waggon.*
The plan was hail'd with rapt'rous glee,
With *double grog,* and *three times three.*

 "Our topmasts struck—the rigging stow'd—
The guns were sent off on the road—
And, as for *shot* and *Congreve rockets,*
The sailors took them in their pockets.
All hands were now put to the oar,
To tow the *men-of-war* ashore;
Which done—it cost but little pains—
The great exertion yet remains,
To lift their vast and pond'rous keels,
And *ship* them safely on the *wheels;*
Which, after much fatigue, at length
Was done by dint of manual strength.
All this achiev'd, they mov'd away
By help of *horse-artillery.*[1]
In future times 'twill scarce be creded
How well this novel plan succeeded.
And oh! the sight was worth a treasure,
And would have given their Lordships pleasure,
To see with what determined zeal
The sailors strove for the public weal.
Some took a *bowsprit*—some a *mast*—
Some held a *hull* by *handspikes* fast;
While others, not less glad than able,
Lash'd it safely with a *cable.*
But one, than all the rest much bolder,
Carried a *fire-ship* on his *shoulder.*
The whole arriving on the strand,
Without an accident on land,
Our fetter'd barks were soon untied,
And launch'd into the *ocean* wide;
With masts and rigging re-equipp'd,
And guns and ammunition shipp'd;
We now were fit to put to sea,
And meet the dastard enemy.
And for long time we sail'd about,
To find the slinking *Frenchmen* out;
Until we met near *Rotten* shore,
As I have said herein before."

The accompanying illustration is from a satirical

---

[1] These mimic ships were drawn by artillery horses from the Thames side to the Serpentine.

A MAN OF WAR, 1814.

print by George Cruikshank, *re* the Jubilee, called "The Modern Don Quixote, or the Fire King."

There were pictorial caricatures of this Naumachia, of course, but, judging from two contemporary prints of it in the Crace collection (Port. ix. 96, 97), in the British Museum, it must have been a very pretty sight, only, naturally, on a very small scale.

Another attraction in Hyde Park, at this Jubilee, was a fair, with its shows by Richardson, Reede, Saunders, and Gingel;—also Polito's wild beasts were on exhibition. There were drinking booths, with taking signs, such as " The Duke of Wellington," " The Vetteran Prince Blucher," " The Prince Regent," etc.; dancing, singing and refreshment booths, and—being warm weather—eating and drinking could be indulged in in the open air. This fair was kept up after the Jubilee with the additional attractions of *E.O. tables—black and white cocks—dice tables*, and a game with dice called *under and over seven:* nor did the police even make a show of stopping this gambling. There were donkey racing, jumping in sacks, running for smocks, etc., and there were printing presses, where, on payment, people had the privilege of themselves pulling off a typographical *souvenir* of the fair. Nay, it was even contemplated to print a *Jubilee Fair Journal.*

It was anticipated that this fair would last until the 12th, and so it possibly might have done, had it been conducted with anything like decency and order; but, as these were conspicuously absent, Lord Sidmouth, Secretary of State for the Home Department, ordered it to be closed on the night of

Saturday the 6th. This order the booth keepers petitioned against, on the plea that, on the strength of its being open for a longer time, they had laid in a large stock of provisions, liquor, toys, etc., which would be thrown upon their hands. Lord Sidmouth's order not being enforced, they kept on, so that it was found necessary to issue another—which was acted on—and the fair came to an end on the night of the 11th.

A contemporary newspaper, speaking of it, says: " Never, within the memory of man, has there been witnessed such scenes of drunkenness and dissipation as these fooleries have given rise to, and the misery they have brought upon thousands is extreme. A report from the pawnbrokers would be an awful lesson to governments, how they encourage such riot. Since the delirium, from the example of the highest quarter, began, the pawnbrokers have more than trebled their businesses; clothes, furniture, and, worst of all, *tools*, have been sacrificed for the sake of momentary enjoyment; industry of every kind has been interrupted, and many hundreds of starving families will long have to remember the *æra* of the Park Fêtes."

A notice of this Jubilee may well close with an " Epigram on the P—— R——'s expressing a wish for the continuance of the Fair in Hyde Park.

" The R——, we have oft been told,
Prefers the *Fair* when *stout* and *old;*
Now, here we've cause to think him wrong,
For liking *any Fair too long.*"

CHAPTER IX.

Coronation of George IV.—Boat-racing on the Serpentine—
Illumination of the Park—Fireworks—Coronation of Queen
Victoria—Fair in the Park—Fireworks in Hyde Park, at
"Peace rejoicing," May, 1856.

THE next jollification in Hyde Park was on July 19, 1821, at the Coronation of George the Magnificent. According to *The Morning Chronicle* of that date, " The preparations for the amusements of the populace are extensive. Boats were conveyed to the Serpentine River, and the arrangements for the fireworks and other diversions are on the most extensive and magnificent scale. It is expected that a sort of Coronation Fair will be established in Hyde Park, and that oxen and sheep will be roasted whole. Many hogsheads of Ale and Porter have been transported thither for distribution."

In the next day's number the same journal gives the following description :—

" On the slight view we had on Tuesday evening of the preparations making in Hyde Park, we had no conception they were of such an extensive nature as we found them to be yesterday. The machinery erected for letting the fireworks off was on a larger scale than any thing of that kind which has hitherto been produced in this country ; the number of rockets for explosion exceeded 3000.

The workmen were most actively employed during the day, to complete the work within the railing. It was placed on a piece of ground on a height on the north side of the Serpentine River, and the view from the river, on the south side of it, only prevented by the scattered trees on the bank of the river, and they were illuminated with Chinese lamps nearly to Hyde Park Corner. On the right and left of the enclosure were the designs for the fireworks, and, in the centre, were several marquees scattered, to about the number of 30, which had the appearance of a camp. The back of the enclosure was completed by transparencies; the centre one was Neptune on his car, drawn by sea-horses, followed by the usual group of figures. Above that, in another transparency, was the figure of Britannia, with an olive-leaf in her hand.

" On the border of the river stands a small house, for the purpose of containing the necessary articles to preserve persons from accident, who venture to bathe in the river. This was fitted up for the purpose of displaying some elegant devices in the way of illuminations. At the east end of the River, near the Bridge, preparations were made for the fireworks and illuminations. There were not less than 500 hampers of lamps in the Park in the morning, and people busily employed in cleaning and trimming them. The Park itself during the day had a most beautiful appearance, which was assisted by the assemblage of several persons of the first distinction; and, to enliven the scene, there were more than a hundred wherries and barges on the river, some of them covered with awnings. The novelty of the scene pleased, and we saw many families alight from their carriages, and take boat. At one time there were not less than 30 boats rowing up and down the river, filled by most elegantly dressed ladies. The surface of the water was unruffled, the sky was clear, and the sun shone most brilliantly, and its lustre was not diminished by the beauty of Britannia's daughters.

" The fireworks were of the most splendid description, the ample space of ground allotted for the purpose enabled those who had the management of this description of amusement to render it peculiarly gratifying to an immense crowd of spectators."

The description of this fête in *The Times* of July 20th, 1821, is somewhat more meagre, but it supplies some deficiencies in the foregoing.

"The crowd moved forward to Hyde Park to witness a boat-race, which took place, a little before two o'clock, on the Serpentine River. Upon this occasion four boats started, and were obliged to double a standard, erected at either extremity of the river, twice. The race was won by about two lengths of the winner's boat. The river was crowded with boats filled with ladies and gentlemen regaling themselves upon the water; and its banks lined with carriages and well dressed persons, who appeared to derive much enjoyment from the scene before them. But what excited the greatest share of attention from the spectators, was a splendid triumphal car drawn by two elephants, one before the other, as large as life, and caparisoned after the eastern manner, with a young woman, dressed as a slave, seated on the back of each, and affecting to guide the animals with an iron rod. The machine was constructed on a large raft, and was towed by three or four boats, manned by watermen in blue uniforms."

The Crace collection (Port. ix. 98) has a few small water-colour drawings of this fête, but they are so sketchy as to be practically valueless.

At the Coronation of William IV. and Queen Adelaide, on September 8th, 1831, Hyde Park was only utilized for a display of fireworks, at which many were more or less hurt by the falling rocket sticks; six so seriously as to have to be taken to St. George's Hospital.

In the Crace collection (Port. ix. 99) there is a very fair lithograph of a bird's-eye view of the fair in Hyde Park on the occasion of the coronation of Queen Victoria, on June 28, 1838, and *The Morning Chronicle* of the following day has the best and fullest account of this fair I can find; and, as it is so intimately connected with one of the most joyful events in the reign of our good and beloved Queen, I may, perhaps, be pardoned if I give it *in extenso*.

"THE FAIR IN HYDE PARK.

"Of all the scenes which we witnessed connected with the Coronation, probably this was the most lively, and that in which there was the least confusion, considering the mass of persons collected together. Our readers are already aware that the fair was permitted to take place by the Government, on the petition of the present holders of the show which formerly belonged to the celebrated Richardson; and it was to their care, together with that of Mr. Mallalieu, the Superintendent of Police, that its general management was entrusted. In justice to those gentlemen, we must say that the arrangements made for the accommodation of the public were admirable, while they were carried out with the very greatest success. The booths were arranged in a square form, and covered a space of ground about 1400 feet long, and about 1000 feet broad.

" They were arranged in regular rows, ample space being allowed between them for the free passage of the people; and they consisted of every variety of shape, while they were decked with flags of all colours and nations. One portion of the fair was set apart exclusively for gingerbread and fancy booths, while those rows by which these were surrounded were appropriated to the use of showmen, and of persons who dealt in the more substantial articles of refreshment. Of the latter description, however, our readers would recognize many as regular frequenters of such scenes; but, probably, the booth which attracted the greatest attention, from its magnitude, was that erected by Williams, the celebrated boiled beef-monger of the Old Bailey. This was pitched in the broadest part of the fair, and immediately adjoining Richardson's show; and at the top of it was erected a gallery for the use of those who were desirous of witnessing the fireworks in the evening, and to which access was to be procured by payment of a small sum.

" While this person, and the no less celebrated Alger, the proprietor of the Crown and Anchor, were astonishing the visitors with the enormous extent of the accommodation which they could afford the public, others set up claims of a character more agreeable to the age, in the exceedingly tasty mode in which they had decorated their temporary houses. Of these, that which struck us as most to be admired, was a tent erected by a person named Bull, of Hackney, the interior of which, decorated with fluted pillars of glazed calico, had a really beautiful appearance. It would be useless, however, to attempt to particularize every booth, for each held out its alluring attractions to the gaping crowd with equal force, and each appeared to be sufficiently patronized by the friends of its proprietor.

"Not a few, in addition to the solid attractions of eating and drinking, held out others of a more 'airy' description, and in many it was announced that a 'grand ball' would be held in the evening, 'to commence at six o'clock'; whilst, in others, bands of music were heard 'in full play,' joining their sweet sounds to the melodious beating of gongs and shoutings through the trumpets of the adjoining shows. In attractions of this kind we need only say that the fair was, in most respects, fully equal to any other at which we ever had the good fortune to be present, whether at Greenwich, or Croydon, or in any other of the suburban or metropolitan districts. Beef and ham, beer and wine, chickens and salad, were all equally plentiful, and the taste of the most fastidious might be pleased as to the quality or the quantity of the provisions provided for him. In the pastry-cook's booths, the usual variety of gingerbread nuts and gilt cocks in breeches, and kings and queens were to be procured; while, in some of them, the more refined luxury of ices was advertised, an innovation upon the ancient style of refreshment which we certainly had never expected to see introduced into the canvas shops of the fair pastry-cooks.

"While these *marchands* were holding out their various attractions to the physical tastes of the assembled multitude, the showkeepers were not less actively engaged in endeavouring to please the eye of those who were willing to enjoy their buffooneries or their wonders. Fat boys and living skeletons, Irish giants and Welsh dwarfs, children with two heads, and animals without heads at all, were among the least of the wonders to be seen: while the more rational exhibition of wild beasts, joined with the mysterious wonders of the conjuror and the athletic performances of tumblers, in calling forth expressions of surprise and delight from the old, as well as from the young, who were induced to contribute their pennies 'to see the show.'

"Nor were these the only modes of procuring amusement which presented themselves. On the Serpentine River a number of boats had been launched, which had been procured from the Thames, and watermen were employed, during the whole day, in rowing about those who were anxious to enjoy the refreshing coolness of the water, after the turmoil and heat of the fair. Ponies and donkeys were, in the outskirts of the fair, plentiful, for the use of the young who were inclined for equestrian exercise, while archery-grounds and throw-sticks held out their attractions to the adepts in such practices, and roundabouts and swings were ready to gratify the tastes of the adventurous. Kensington Gardens were, as usual, open to the public, and not a few who were fearful of joining in the crowd contented themselves here in viewing the gay scene from a distance. Timorous, however, though they might be, of personal inconvenience, they did not fail to enjoy the opportunities which were afforded them, of looking into the book of fate; and we observed many of the fairest parts of the creation busily engaged in deep and private confabulations with those renowned seers, the gypsies.

"With regard to those persons who visited the fair, we must say we never saw a more orderly body. From an early hour the visitors were flocking in; but it was not until Her Majesty had gone to Westminster Abbey, that the avenues approaching Hyde Park became crowded. Then, indeed, the countless thousands of London appeared to be poured forth, and all seemed to be bound for the same point of destination. Thousands who had taken up their standing places at Hyde Park Corner, poured through the gate; whilst many who had assumed positions at a greater distance from the Parks, passed through the squares and through Grosvenor Gate. Every avenue was soon filled, every booth was soon crammed full of persons desirous of procuring refreshment and rest after the fatigue of standing so long in the crowd to view the procession.

"These, however, were not the only persons who joined the throng. Every cab, coach, or omnibus which had been left disengaged, appeared to be driving to the same point, full of passengers. Fulham, Putney, Mile End, and Brixton alike contributed their vehicles to carry the people to the Parks, and thousands from the very extremities of the City were to be seen flocking towards the fair. All seemed bent on the same object, that of procuring amusement, and work seemed to have been suspended, as if by common consent. While the east end thrust forth her less aristocratic workmen, the west end was not altogether idle in furnishing its quota to the throng, and we noticed many really elegantly dressed ladies and gentlemen alight from their carriages to view the enlivening scene; and many of them, who were, apparently, strangers to such exhibitions, were, evidently, not a little amused at the grotesque imitations of those amusements in which the aristocracy delight.

" Carriages of every description were admitted into the parks, and the splendid carriage of an aristocrat was not unfrequently followed by the tilted waggon of some remover of furniture, with its load of men, women and children, who had come to 'see the fun.' All seemed, alike, bent on amusement: all, alike, appeared to throw aside those restraints which rank, or fashion, or station had placed upon them, and to enter fully into the enjoyment of the pleasure of the busy scene in which they were actors. The delightful locality of the fair, the bright sunbeams playing upon the many-coloured tents, the joyous laughter of the people, untouched by debauchery, and unseduced by the gross pleasures of the appetite; the gay dresses of the women, all in their best, joined in making the scene one which must live long in the recollection of those who witnessed it. All appeared to remember that this was the day of the Coronation of a Queen, so youthful, so beautiful, so pure, and all appeared to be determined that no act of insubordination, or of disorder on their part, should sully the bright opening of a reign so hopeful, and from which so much happiness is to be expected.

" We have already said that the arrangements of

the fair were excellent; but, while these called forth our admiration, the exceeding attention paid to the public by the police force, appeared to prevent the possibility of accident or robbery. All gambling-booths and thimble-riggers had, of course, been necessarily excluded, but we fear it was not possible to shut out all those persons whose recollection of the laws of *meum et tuum* was somewhat blunted. We heard of numerous losses of small sums, and of handkerchiefs and other trifles, but, throughout the day, we gained no information of any robbery which was of sufficient extent to produce more than a temporary inconvenience to the person robbed. A temporary police-station was erected in the grounds, in which Mr. Mallalieu and a considerable portion of his men were in attendance during the day; but, although there were, necessarily, some cases in which slight acts of intemperance were visible, nothing of any serious importance occurred during the whole of the early part of the day.

" The orderly conduct of the people, which we have already described as having been observable during the morning, was maintained during the rest of the day. Notwithstanding that the crowd at three o'clock had increased tenfold, no disturbance nor riot occurred. The return of her Majesty attracted a few from the crowd, but nearly every one returned, and all remained for the grand attraction of this part of the day's amusements—the fireworks. As evening closed in, the fatigue of the people rendered rest, as well as refreshment, necessary, and every booth was in a short time crowded with eager inquiries for eatables and drinkables. The dancing booths were crowded to suffocation, and the viands of the purveyors of grog were soon put into requisition."

The fireworks, which were to have been let off at nine o'clock, were, owing to the light night, postponed till eleven, and were very noisy and effective, and "One o'clock having arrived, the people separated in a quiet, orderly manner, but it was not till a very late hour that the fair was quite cleared of visitors. Like all such scenes, some irregularities were observable, but on the whole, we never, at any time or in any place, saw a crowd so orderly disposed. No accidents of any importance, we believe, occurred during the day in the fair. Fears were, at one time, entertained that some of the crowd might have sustained injury from the fall of the rocket sticks and other fireworks, and a troop of horse was suggested as a proper means of keeping them at a proper distance from the ground. The excellent arrangements of the police, however, rendered such a step unnecessary; and, although the crowd advanced until within a yard or two of the ground, forcing their way through the *cheveaux de frise*, we believe no serious injury was inflicted on any person."

The fair was, at the solicitation of Mr. Hawes, M.P. for Lambeth, permitted to be held for two days, the Coronation Day, and that following—but it was further extended for two more days. The area allotted to it comprised nearly one-third of the park, extending from near the margin of the Serpentine, to within a short distance of Grosvenor Gate.

Of course, the next day's fair was not so thronged as that on Coronation Day, still, "By three o'clock a vast number of people were in the parks, and thousands were hourly arriving, but the fair was not crowded. At the time just stated, a heavy thunderstorm came on, in the first instance accompanied by hail, which lasted nearly an hour. To those who were in the fair, the drenching rain was a most unwelcome visitor. Some of the unlucky holiday makers who had ventured in the vertical roundabouts, were in a woful plight; the rain was pelting on them while they were dangling in the air, and the men to whom the machines belonged coolly got under shelter till the worst part of the storm was over, utterly regardless of their patrons aloft, several of whom, at the risk of their necks, slid down the beam to *terra firma*, and good, stout exhortations soon relieved their aerial aquatic companions. The storm was a godsend, in more senses than one, to the victualling booths, for more was disposed of in the shape of ham, beef and stout during its continuance than, perhaps, would have been if the good things were to be given away in fine weather. People dined whether they were in want of that meal or not, and, no doubt, took credit for their patronage.

"When the rain ceased, the fair-going gentry crept from their canvas coverings, and made for the spot where the clown's gibes and jeers were wont to set his auditors in a roar. But the rain had made the ground so wet and sloppy, that a melancholy seemed to have come over all, the clown included. As for the poor boats on the Serpentine, they clung to the shore, as if they had taken a dislike to an aquatic life, and few were there disposed to navigate them. The gipsy tribe, of which there were hundreds in the fair, crept to their blanket hovels, to bewail the loss of the silver crossings of which the previous day had furnished an abundant supply. Into one of these miserable cabins upwards of thirty were seen to go in the space of an hour, whose appearance and manners would denote that they should know better than to put faith in the trash of the walnut-dyed impostors."

The day afterwards turned out fine, and the fair was crowded. On the third day a booth caught fire, but no great damage was done. On the fourth and last day, the Queen drove as close to it as she well could do, and all the booths were cleared away that night.

Shirley Hibberd, writing in *Notes and Queries* (7s. vi. 105), says: " The many interesting papers that have of late appeared recalling scenes and incidents of the Queen's Coronation, are (so far as I have seen) defective in making no mention of the morris-dancers in Hyde Park. My recollections of the event have been delightfully revived by recent readings, and once more the joyous celebration is before me. I see the park a dusty field, with not a blade of grass upon it, and I hear my father say, in accordance with the belief prevailing, that the grass would grow all the better for being thus destroyed. And, amongst the things that then surprised me, were the morris-dancers, that I had read of, and had never, till then, seen. There could be no mistake, I should now say, about their genuineness, for they were clad as peasants, and all their ways consorted with their new and nicely trimmed smocks, and their well tanned faces. The dancers had, at least, two distinct styles, which I now conjecture were representative of two far-removed provinces, for the two styles were accompanied with distinctive habiliments. In each case the music consisted of pipe and tabor. One set struck short staves at a certain turn in the dance, when the dancers stood in two ranks face to face. The other set struck white handkerchiefs, which were thrown out by a trick of the hand so as to acquire momentary rigidity."

The police charges from Hyde Park on Coronation Day seem to have consisted of small gamblers and thimble-riggers, and the following is given as an example.

"MARYLEBONE.[1] Three men and one woman, who gave their names *John Scullie, Edward Clegg, Lewis Joseph*, and *Ellen Taylor*, were brought before the magistrates, charged with having been found gambling in Hyde Park, in the thickest of the fair.

" The male prisoners were detected by the special constable on duty at the above spot, in the act of playing at a most deceptive game, called ' prick-in-the-garter,' at which each of them had contrived to fill his pockets at the expense of the deluded multitude, many of whom, being countrymen, were not at all aware of the artful dodge. The female was found rattling the dice in one of the booths, and had, also, contrived to line her pockets very well. On being taken, she declared she was an innocent country servant out of place, and most vehemently denied that the dice belonged to her.

" They were all four despatched to the treadmill for one month, the magistrates at the same time informing them that the money found on them would go to their support in prison.

[1] *Morning Chronicle*, June 30, 1838 ; p. 4, c. 3.

"Clegg, on hearing this, exclaimed, 'Dang it, that is hard, too, that I should have to pay the Governor for punishing me on the wheel, a sort of caper wot I arn't at all accustomed to. Do let me have a few bob, good luck to your honour, to spend when I comes out.'

"Mr. Rawlinson. 'Not one farthing. The fair is meant for the recreation of honest people, and not for the advantage of blacklegs and gamblers.'

"Clegg. 'Vell, if this 'ere arn't a vicked robbery, I never seed one in my life; but the Queen, God bless her, shall know how her subjects are treated, for, if I don't publish it in all the papers, my name's not Edward Clegg.'

"The prisoners were then removed."

There was no demonstration of joy in Hyde Park to celebrate the marriage of the Queen and Prince Albert on Feb. 10, 1840; and the next occasion when any public entertainment took place therein was in thankfulness for the Treaty of Peace between Russia, France and England, signed at Paris in April, 1856. This "Peace Rejoicing," as it was called, took place on May 29th following, and took the form of a display of fireworks in Hyde, Green and Victoria Parks and on Primrose Hill. We have only to deal with those in Hyde Park, and the best contemporary account of them that I can find is in *The Morning Chronicle* of May 30, 1856, as follows:—

"Whatever may have been the sentiments with which the conclusion of peace was received, there can be no doubt, whatever, but that the fireworks displayed to celebrate that important event were highly popular. In delaying the period for public rejoicings until several weeks after the exchange of the ratifications of peace, it would almost appear that the Government were anxious that all the conditions of the peace should be fully and fairly discussed, and thoroughly understood, before calling upon the nation to celebrate its rejoicings. It may be, that by postponing the event, we may have appeared to have ignored altogether the existence of electric telegraphs, and those other means of rapid communication and intercourse which were unknown at the last celebration of peace, and professed ourselves unable to believe any news which had not travelled through the old time-honoured channels of official routine.

" It may have been fitting that we should, as was done at Paris, command an illumination, and indulged in our fêtes, immediately the electric spark had conveyed to us the intelligence of the signature of the treaty. But there can be no doubt but that the public rejoicings of last night had more of real value and greater significance, because time had been allowed for calm reflection, and the people thoroughly understood what it was for which they were called upon to rejoice. A grand display of fireworks, such as that which has been for some time past announced, could hardly fail to draw together an immense number of spectators ; and, while we would not confound the desire to witness a magnificent spectacle with an assent to the terms of the treaty of peace ; still any person who mingled among the crowds would have abundant opportunities of learning from the general tone of the conversation that there was little or no dissatisfaction with the conditions upon which the peace had been obtained, which they were assembled to celebrate.

"Long before the shades of evening began to fall, the immense area of Hyde Park set apart for the public was crowded with a dense mass of individuals, the majority of whom, without, perhaps, either knowing or caring much about the occasion which had called them together, were resolved to be in time to secure good places to see the fireworks. Thousands had already congregated by two or three in the afternoon.

"Towards seven o'clock, all trees commanding a view of the enclosure where the fireworks were prepared had received their share of venturous climbers, whose good positions excited envy, and made them excellent marks, not merely for the jokes, but for the missiles of the vulgar crowd below. A perfect storm of turfs and sods, torn from the grass, was hurled at the people who swarmed the trees, many of whom were speedily dislodged; but others, who had secured the uppermost branches, remained possessors of their positions to the end. Foiled in their attempt to dislodge the arboreal class of spectators, the roughs commenced an indiscriminate assault on the crowd, hurling clods and pieces of turf among the more densely packed masses. The assailants became, in turn, the assailed, and many a long and annoying battle was waged, and no small share of angry feeling created by these discreditable proceedings. Any person with a decent coat or hat was sure to become a mark for the mischievous young urchins who indulged in those freaks, and it was only when some two or three persons had the good sense to administer a little wholesome chastisement to the young rascals, that temporary peace was secured.

"At length the hour of nine o'clock arrived, and a signal rocket sent up announced that the long expected display was about to commence, and it was immediately followed by a grand display of white, red, green and yellow fires, with a continuous discharge of maroons. Scarcely had the brilliant colours ceased, when 100 rockets went screeching and screaming through the air in their graceful course, and shell after shell exploded in rapid succession. Then came wheel pieces and gold streamers, and blue and yellow rockets and green and yellow shells; then pearl streamers, blue and yellow rockets, and serpents and yellow shells, and numbers of fixed pieces and tailed stars, and rocket wheels and Scotch stars, and parachutes and pearl rain, and twelve-pointed stars and crackers, and Saxon hoops and silver rain, and diamond pieces and looking glasses, and kaleidoscopes and Maltese crosses, and turning suns and tourbillons, and five-pointed lances and ten-stars, and a variety of other things known only to the initiated in the mystery of the pyrotechnic art.

"The beauty of the varied coloured showers of fire, the bold careering of the rockets, the graceful curves of the jerbes falling over like sheaves of wheat, formed a scene such as falls to the lot of a generation to witness but once only. The grand tableau, by some strange arrangement, instead of coming as a grand finale to the whole, was discharged about the middle of the proceedings; its effect was grand and effective in the extreme. By far the most imposing part of the spectacle was the aerial portion. The fixed pieces presented but little of novelty or grandeur, and several of them were scarcely worthy of the occasion. Two colossal fountains, showering around a golden shower, were remarkable for their splendour, and were among the most successful of any of the displays.

"Notwithstanding the enormous masses of people present, there was no vast pressure from the crowds except at the conclusion of the display, when the attempts made to pass through Grosvenor Gate, and the other outlets of the park, were attended with some of those fearful crushes which, somehow or other, appear to be inseparable from a London gathering. The houses of the nobility and others, looking on to the park, were illuminated in splendid style, and conspicuous among the whole of the adjoining mansions was that of Lord Ward, the whole front of the house being literally a blaze of gas jets, formed by lines following the architectural details of the building."

Being present, I can vouch for the good behaviour of the crowd, also to the general harmlessness of the rocket-sticks, which fell among us in showers. But the light-fingered gentry reaped a great harvest. I, and all our party, lost our scarf-pins, and, on going to Bow Street next day to try and recover mine, a large iron tea-tray full of pins, taken from captured thieves, was brought, and I was told to pick out my own, but I could not find it. The fireworks were made at the Laboratory, Woolwich, and in such profusion that it was said there were enough over for another display.

CHAPTER X.

The Great Exhibition of 1851.

But what has rendered Hyde Park historically immortal is the choice of it as the site of the "GREAT EXHIBITION OF THE INDUSTRY OF ALL NATIONS," in 1851, an institution which was claimed to have been foreseen by Chaucer, as evidenced by portions scattered at wide intervals over his *Book of Fame*.[1]

> " But as I slepte / me mette I was
> Wythin a temple y made of glas
> In whyche / there were mo ymages
> Of gold / standyng in dyuers stages
> And mo ryche tabernacles
> And with perle / mo pynnacles
> And mo ryche portretures
> And quaynt maner of fygures
> Of gold werke / than I sawe euer
> . . . . .
> Tho sawe I stonde on thother syde
> Strayt doun to the doris wyde
> From the deys [2] many a pyler
> Of metal that shone not ful cleer
> . . . . .
> Tho gan I loke aboute me and see
> That ther come entryng in to the halle
> A ryght grete company wyth alle
> And that of sondry regyons
> Of alle kyns condicions
> That dwelle in erthe under the mone
> Poure and ryche.

---

[1] The "Book of Fame," by Geoffrey Chaucer; printed by Caxton, 1486 (?)
[2] Dais.

> But whyche a grete congregacioun
> Of folke / as I sawe come aboute
> Some wythin and some wythoute
> Nas never seen ne shal be ofte."

The Society of Arts organized a small exhibition of manufactures in 1847, at their rooms, which attracted much attention, so much, indeed, that in 1848 they had an exhibition of pottery, and in 1849 one chiefly of works in the precious metals. These shows were so successful, that it was felt that something should be attempted on a far larger scale, and it is now, I believe, generally conceded that the conception of the Great Exhibition of 1851 was due to Mr. F. Wishaw. Secretary to the Society of Arts. True it is that Prince Albert is generally credited with the idea, but this arose from the fact that he took a leading part in the movement, as President of the Society.

In this capacity he was kept fully informed of what the Society were doing; but immediately after the termination of the Session of 1849 he took the subject under his own personal superintendence. He proceeded to settle the general principles on which the proposed exhibition of 1851 should be conducted, and to consider the mode in which it should be carried out. On the 29th June, 1849, the general outlines of the Exhibition were discussed by his Royal Highness, and a portion of the minutes of a meeting of several members of the Society of Arts, held at Buckingham Palace on the 30th of June, is as follows:—

"His Royal Highness communicated his views regarding the formation of a Great Collection of Works of Industry and Art in London in 1851, for the purpose of exhibition, and of competition and encouragement.

"His Royal Highness considered that such Collection and Exhibition should consist of the following divisions:
 Raw Materials.
 Machinery and Mechanical Inventions.
 Manufactures.
 Sculpture and Plastic Art generally.

"It was a matter of consideration whether such divisions should be made subjects of simultaneous exhibition, or to be taken separately. It was ultimately settled that, on the first occasion, at least, they should be simultaneous.

"Various sites were suggested as most suitable to the building, which it was settled must be, on the first occasion at least, a temporary one. The Government had offered the area of Somerset House; or, if that were unfit, a more suitable site on the property of the Crown. His Royal Highness pointed out the vacant ground in Hyde Park on the south side, parallel with, and between the Kensington drive and the ride commonly called Rotten Row, as affording advantages which few other places might be found to possess. Application for this site could be made to the Crown."

Besides Somerset House, the Commissioners had to consider the merits of other sites proposed for the Exhibition, among which may be named Leicester Square, Trafalgar Square, the Isle of Dogs, Battersea Fields, and Regent's Park; but they selected, after the most careful consideration, that of Hyde Park, and the building occupied a site between the two roads, the eastern end of the

The Great Exhibition of 1851.

building being exactly in the centre oft he Knightsbridge Barracks, and its western end reached very nearly to Exhibition Road ; and possession of this ground was given to the contractors on 30th July, 1850.

On January 3rd, 1850, a Royal Commission was appointed to carry out the proposed Exhibition, and the following were the members. The Prince Consort, Duke of Buccleugh, Earls of Rosse, Granville and Ellesmere, Lords Stanley and John Russell, Sir Robert Peel, Henry Labouchere, W. E. Gladstone, Sir A. Galloway (or the Chairman of the Court of Directors of the East India Company for the time being), Sir R. Westmacott, Sir Charles Lyell (or the President of the Geological Society for the time being), Charles L. Eastlake, Thomas F. Gibson, Richard Cobden, William Cubitt (or the President of the Institution of Civil Engineers for the time being), John Gott, Samuel Jones Loyd, P. Pusey and William Thompson. They were "to make full and diligent inquiry into the best mode by which the productions of our Colonies, and of foreign countries may be introduced into our Kingdom ; as respects the most suitable site for the said Exhibition ; the general conduct of the said Exhibition ; and, also, the best mode of determining the prizes, and of securing the most impartial distribution of them." John Scott Russell and Stafford Henry Northcote were appointed joint secretaries, and an executive committee was formed, consisting of Henry Cole, Charles Wentworth Dilke, George Drew, Francis Fuller, and Robert Stephenson, with Matthew Digby Wyatt as secretary.

The story of the building is succinctly told by Sir Henry Cole in his Introduction to the Official Catalogue. " The Committee ventured at once to recommend that upwards of 16 acres should be covered in ; a bold step at that time (Feb. 21) when no data whatever of the space likely to be filled had been received. It was their opinion that it was desirable to obtain suggestions, by public competition, as to the general arrangements of the ground-plan of the building, and public invitations were accordingly issued. . . . . In answer to the invitation to send in plans, upwards of 245 designs and specifications were submitted. . . . . All these plans were publicly exhibited during a month, from the 10th of June, at the Institution of Civil Engineers, Great George Street, Westminster. . . . . . The Committee reported that, in their opinion, there was no 'single plan so accordant with the peculiar objects in view, either in the principle, or detail of its arrangement, as to warrant them in recommending it for adoption.'

" They, therefore, submitted a plan of their own ; and, assisted by Mr. Digby Wyatt, Mr. Charles Heard Wild, and Mr. Owen Jones, they prepared extensive working drawings, which were lithographed. . . . . The Building Committee published in detail the reasons, both of economy and taste, which had induced them to prepare plans for a structure of brick, the principle feature of which was a dome two hundred feet in diameter. Public opinion did not coincide in the propriety of such a building, on such a site, and the residents in the neighbourhood raised especial objections. The subject was brought before both Houses of Parliament; and, in the House of Commons, on the 4th July, 1850, two divisions took place on the question, whether the proposed site should be used at all for any building for the Exhibition. In the one division the numbers in favour of the site were 166 to 47, and, in the second, 166 to 46. The Commissioners published at considerable length a statement of the reasons which had induced them to prefer the site, and there can be no doubt that the force of this document mainly influenced the large majority in both divisions.

"Whilst the plan of the Building Committee was under discussion, Mr. Paxton was led, by the hostility which it had incurred, to submit a plan for a structure chiefly of glass and iron, on principles similar to those which had been adopted and successfully tried by him at Chatsworth. Messrs. Fox, Henderson, and Company tendered for the erection of the Building Committee's plan, and strictly in accordance with the conditions of tender: they also submitted estimates for the construction of the building suggested by Mr. Paxton, and adapted in form to the official ground-plan. An engraving of Mr. Paxton's original design was published in the *Illustrated London News*, 6th July, 1850, which, when compared with the building that has actually been erected, will show what changes were subsequently made. The Commissioners having fully investigated the subject, finally adopted, on the 26th July, Messrs. Fox, Henderson and Company's tender to construct Mr. Paxton's building as then proposed, for the sum of £79,800."

The first iron column was fixed as early as the

26th September, 1850, and the building was ready for opening on May 1st, 1851. It covered an area of 18 acres, was 1850 feet long, 408 feet wide, and 64 feet high, irrespective of the arched roof of the transept; and in order to put it familiarly before people, Mr. Fox, at a dinner given to him at Derby, June 28th, 1851, said, " I walked out one evening into Portland Place; and there, setting off the 1850 feet upon the pavement, found it the same length within a few yards; and then, considering that the building would be three times the width of that fine street, and the nave as high as the houses on either side, I had presented to my mind a pretty good idea of what we were about to undertake."

It was also part of the contract that the building was removed and the site given up within seven months after the close of the Exhibition, namely before the 1st of June, 1852; which was duly done, and the building re-erected at Norwood, where it still is in existence under the name of the Crystal Palace.

The Mr. (afterwards Sir) Joseph Paxton, who designed the building, was head gardener to the Duke of Devonshire at Chatsworth, where the glass-houses are the wonder and admiration of all who behold them; and he may as well tell the story of how he came to be mixed up with the Great Exhibition, in the same words as he told it at a meeting of the Derby Institute.

"It was not," said he, "until one morning, when I was present with my friend, Mr. Ellis, at an early sitting in the House of Commons, that the idea of sending in a design occurred to me. A conversation took place between us with reference to the construction of the New House of Commons, in the course of which I observed that I was afraid they would also commit a blunder in the building for the Industrial Exhibition. I told him that I had a notion in my head, and that if he would accompany me to the Board of Trade, I would ascertain whether it was too late to send in a design. I asked the Executive Committee whether they were so far committed to the plans as to be precluded from receiving another; the reply was, 'Certainly not; the specifications will be out in a fortnight, but there is no reason why a clause should not be introduced allowing of the reception of another design.' I said, 'Well, if you will introduce such a clause, I will go home; and, in nine days hence, I will bring you my plans all complete.' No doubt the Executive thought me a conceited fellow, and that what I said was nearer akin to romance than to common sense.

"Well! this was on Friday, the 11th of June. From London I went to the Menai Straits, to see the third tube of the Britannia Bridge placed, and on my return to Derby, I had to attend to some business in the Board Room, during which time, however, my whole mind was devoted to this project; and whilst the business proceeded, I sketched the outline of my design on a large sheet of blotting paper. Well! having sketched this design, I sat up all night, until I had worked it out to my own satisfaction; and, by the aid of my friend, Mr. Barlow, on the 15th, I was enabled to complete the whole of the plans by the Saturday following, on which day I left Rowsley for London.

"On arriving at the Derby Station, I met Mr.

Robert Stephenson, a member of the Building Committee, who was also on his way to the Metropolis. Mr. Stephenson minutely examined the plans, and became thoroughly engrossed with them, until, at length, he exclaimed that the design was just the thing, and he only wished that it had been submitted to the Committee in time. Mr. Stephenson, however, laid the plans before the Committee, and at first the idea was rather pooh-poohed; but the plans gradually grew in favour, and by publishing the design in the *Illustrated London News*, and showing the advantage of such an erection over one composed of fifteen millions of bricks and other materials, which would have to be removed at a great loss, the Committee did, in the end, reject the abortion of a child of their own, and unanimously recommended my bantling. I am bound to say that I have been treated by the Committee with great fairness.

"Mr. Brunel, the author of the great dome, I believe was, at first, so wedded to his own plan, that he would hardly look at mine. But Mr. Brunel was a gentleman, and a man of fairness, and listened with every attention to all that could be urged in favour of my plans. As an instance of that gentleman's very creditable conduct, I will mention, that a difficulty presented itself to the Committee as to what should be done with the large trees, and it was gravely suggested that they should be walled in. I remarked that I could cover the trees without any difficulty; when Mr. Brunel asked, 'Do you know their height?' I acknowledged that I did not. On the following morning, Mr. Brunel called at Devonshire House, and gave

"ALBERT! SPARE THOSE TREES."

me the measurement of the trees, which he had taken early in the morning, adding, 'Although I mean to try to win with my own plan, I will give you all the information I can.'"

These trees caused a happy modification of Paxton's plan, and to them we owe the transept, which redeemed the building from being a long and ugly glass shed. As it was, the trees suffered no damage, and really were a very effective feature in the Exhibition. Some other and smaller trees were cut down, which were thus bemoaned by *Punch*.[1]

"ALBERT! SPARE THOSE TREES.

"Albert! spare those trees,
   Mind where you fix your show;
For mercy's sake, don't, please,
   Go spoiling Rotten Row.

"That Ride, that famous ride,
   We must not have destroyed,
For, ne'er to be supplied,
   Its loss will leave a void.

"Oh! certainly there might
   Be for your purpose found
A more congenial site
   Than Hyde Park's hallowed ground.

"Where Fashion rides and drives,
   House not Industrial Art;
But, 'mid the busy hives
   Right in the City's heart.

"And, is it thy request
   The place that I'd point out?
Then I should say the best
   Were Smithfield, without doubt.

"There, by all votes approved,
   The wide world's wares display,
The Market first removed
   For ever and a day."

---

[1] *Punch*, June 29, 1850.

Prince Albert's academic cap is typical of his being LL.D. and Chancellor of Cambridge; and the singular-looking being addressing him is a staunch and bigoted Tory, whom *Punch* delighted to caricature, Colonel Charles de Laet Waldo Sibthorp, M.P. for Lincoln, whose opposition to the Exhibition of 1851 amounted almost to mania. Take, for instance, the following quotation from a speech of his in the House of Commons on the subject (26 July, 1850):—

"Hyde Park was emphatically the Park of the People, and it was now proposed to be devoted to purposes which he must hold to be prejudicial to the people in a moral, religious, and social point of view. It was sought to appropriate it to the encouragement of—what? To the encouragement of everything calculated to be prejudicial to the interests of the people. An exhibition of the industry of all nations, forsooth! An exhibition of the trumpery and trash of foreign countries, to the detriment of our own already too much oppressed manufacturers. . . . . They were flying in the face of the rights of the public merely to gratify the foreigner, who had no right to be here at all."

On another occasion he said, "They might call it success, but he called it failure. He did not wish to see that building destroyed by any acts of violence, but would to God that some hailstorm, or some visitation of lightning, might descend to defeat the ill-advised project." For this he had to sit for his portrait once again. *Punch*, 15th February, 1851.

On the opening day of the Exhibition, Parliament sat afterwards, at 6 p.m., and, in the course of a debate on the "Oath of Abjuration (Jews) Bill," Colonel Sibthorp told the House that "He was not present at the Crystal Palace. He felt that his duty to God and his country demanded of him that he should not go there, and he deeply regretted that an eminent prelate of the Church should have been induced to invoke a blessing on that which he (Colonel S.) considered most injurious to the interests of the country and an insult to Almighty God."

But if Colonel Sibthorp took a pessimistic view of the Exhibition, others held equally optimistic opinions respecting it. It was going to inaugurate a sort of Millennium and a general brotherhood of nations: war was to cease, and all countries were to vie with each other in cultivating the arts of peace. The following song will show the drivel they used to sing about it in the streets.

CRYSTAL PALACE.

Britannia's sons an attentive ear
One moment lend to me,
Whether tillers of our fruitful soil,
Or lords of high degree.
Mechanic too, and artizan,
Old England's pride and boast,
Whose wondrous skill has spread around
Far, far from Britain's coast.

Chorus.

For the World's great Exhibition,
Let's shout with loud huzza,
All nations can never forget
The glorious first of May.

From every quarter of the globe
They come across the sea,
And to the Crystal Palace
The wonders for to see;

Raised by the handiwork of men
Born on British ground,
A challenge to the Universe
Its equal to be found.

Each friendly nation in the world
Have their assistance lent,
And to this Exhibition
Have their productions sent;
And with honest zeal and ardour,
With pleasure do repair,
With hands outstretch'd, and gait erect,
To the World's Great National Fair.

The sons of England and of France,
And America likewise,
With other nations to contend
To bear away the prize,
With pride depicted in their eyes,
View the offspring of their hand:
O, surely England's greatest wealth
Is an honest working man.

It is a glorious sight to see
So many thousands meet,
Not heeding creed or country,
Each other friendly greet.
Like children of one mighty sire,
May that sacred tie ne'er cease;
May the blood-stained sword of War give way
To the Olive-branch of peace.

But, hark! the trumpets flourish,
Victoria does approach,
That she may long be spared to us
Shall be our reigning toast.
I trust each heart it will respond
To what I now propose—
Good-will and plenty to her friends,
And confusion to her foes.

Great praise is due to Albert,
For the good that he has done,
May others follow in his steps
The work he has begun;
Then let us all, with one accord,
His name give with three cheers,
Shout huzza for the Crystal Palace,
And the World's great National Fair!

The Exhibition was opened on the first of May, and, as over forty years have passed since then, a good account of the ceremony will, doubtless, be grateful to very many of my readers, whilst to those who are old enough to remember it, it will be a pleasing reminiscence. *Forsan et hæc olim meminisse juvabit.* The following is condensed from *The Times* of May 2nd, 1851.

" That the ceremonial of the opening may be distinctly understood, let us sketch, as rapidly as possible, the appearance of the interior about half-past 11 o'clock, when the doors closed and admission ceased. In the north half of the transept, and grouped around the throne, were assembled the Royal Commission, Her Majesty's Ministers, the Executive Committee, the Diplomatic Corps, the Lord Mayor, Sheriffs, and Aldermen of the City, the Commissioners of Foreign Powers, the Special Commissioners, Dr. Lyon Playfair and Colonel Lloyd, the architect, Mr. Paxton, the contractors, Messrs. Fox and Henderson, and the principal officers of the Executive, including Messrs. Digby Wyatt, Owen Jones and C. H. Wild. A list of the great and distinguished persons present would only be a repetition to the public of names with which they are familiar, and we, who have watched, from the commencement, the progress of this great undertaking, think it only justice, in describing an event such as that which occurred yesterday, that those who, by their energy and skill, have contributed to the success which has been accomplished, should chiefly be remembered.

" Let us look at that assemblage for a few minutes, and see what meaning we can gather from their movements. They are nearly all in Court dresses, and, in some instances, the experienced eye can detect the awkwardness of manner which such unwonted habiliments superinduce. While they chat together, other characters appear on the scene.

"The Heralds come—a curious mixture of the ancient and modern; one half of their *personelle* strictly *à la mode*, the rest, a tabard covered with mediæval escutcheons and devices. Notwithstanding recent retrenchments, the Beef-eaters showed themselves yesterday in great strength, health and corpulence; and some of them, for size, might bear comparison with the giant porter of 'Queen Bess.' Officers of the Household troops appeared on the scene at an early hour, their showy uniforms heightening the effect, and giving brilliancy to the whole assemblage. The galleries which run along the northern half of the transept had been, to some extent, reserved for choristers and for families of distinction.

"Almost the first person who arrived here was the Duke of Devonshire. His name is closely connected with the design and progress of the Exhibition, and his presence was recognized by a large number of persons. The next arrival that attracted any interest was that of the Duke of Wellington. It was his 82nd birthday. As usual, he came early, and the loud cheers which announced his coming outside were enthusiastic and protracted as he took his place in the north-eastern gallery of the transept. Thence, after a short interval, he descended to the area below, and, again, his presence was hailed with repeated acclamations.

After conversing for some time with the Marquis of Anglesey, he turned his attention to the practical men, to whose well-directed skill and energy the magnificent display before him must be attributed. He complimented Mr. Fox and Mr. Paxton, and talked with them both for some time. He conversed with Mr. Cobden, and was engaged in close confabulation with the Marquis of Anglesey, when, to the immense amusement of everybody, a Chinese mandarin, with a tail of fabulous length, appeared before them.[1] He saluted them both in the Oriental style, and, though he did not venture to exchange one observation with them, he hovered around their chairs for some time, expressing, by his looks, the interest which he felt in the presence of persons so distinguished. This live importation from the Celestial Empire managed to render himself extremely conspicuous, and one could not help admiring the perfect composure and nonchalance of manner which distinguished him. He talked with nobody, yet he seemed perfectly at home, and on the most friendly terms with all. The great variety of uniforms and costumes worn by the assemblage collected in the space around the throne, and the remarkable manner in which the proportions and decorative arrangements of the building brought out their position, rendered the spectacle which the north side of the transept presented a very imposing one.

"Seated apart from the throng, and accompanied by his chaplains, might be observed the Archbishop

[1] This was no mandarin, but the skipper of a Chinese junk, then on exhibition, who had dressed himself gorgeously, and obtained admission somehow.

of Canterbury, and, not far off, the Bishop of Winchester, who, in the absence of the Bishop of London, appeared as senior suffragan of the province. The Lord Chancellor was also conspicuous in the assemblage, and our Civic dignitaries, in their flaunting scarlet robes, enjoyed their full share of public attention.

"A chair, selected from the Indian collection, and over which a magnificent scarlet velvet elephant cloth, richly brocaded, was placed as a covering, served as a throne. In front of the raised dais on which it was placed rose the splendid crystal fountain of Mr. Osler, the appropriate centrepiece of a Palace of Glass. This object had, previously, been concealed from public view, and its beauty and artistic design captivated everybody. It is 27 feet high, contains four tons of crystal, and is a work of which its exhibitor may well be proud.

"And now let us turn from the scene which the area of the north transept presented, to the aspect of the building generally. After all, there is no decoration which a building can possess which equals that presented by a vast and well arranged assemblage of people. Living masses convey to a great structure a character of animation, which no inanimate objects, however beautiful, can supply. The long lines of faces lighted up with excitement, the diversities of dress and ornament, of themselves furnish subjects for inexhaustible reflection; and when they are so disposed that the fairer portions of humanity have the precedence, and occupy the first rank, the scene presented appeals directly to the gallantry and enthusiasm of the spectator. So it was yesterday. The seats, which on either side lined the nave and its galleries, were reserved exclusively for ladies; and thus, standing in the centre of the building, one could see stretching from that point, east and west, north and south, long lines of elegantly dressed women, the verge and binding of an assemblage which comprised not less than 25,000 people.

"It was originally contemplated that the centre of the nave should remain entirely unoccupied; but, as we anticipated, this arrangement was found, at the last moment, impracticable; and thus her Majesty and the State procession were left to make their progress between living walls of loyal subjects and admiring foreigners, extending in long lines from one end of the buildings to the other.

"The hour hands of the clocks with which the Crystal Palace is decorated were approaching 12 when the faint huzzahs of crowds outside announced that the Queen had arrived; the booming sound of a Royal Salute from across the Serpentine struck faintly on the ear, and then a loud flourish of trumpets from the north gallery of the transept told that her Majesty had entered the building. She was conducted, at once, to the robing room. Thence, after a short pause, and attended by her Court, she proceeded, between flower-stands and tropical plants, past the Colebrook Dale gates, and the fountains and statuary with which that part of the edifice is adorned, to the throne in the centre.

"On her appearance, the vast assemblage rose to welcome her, a burst of enthusiastic cheering broke forth from every side—ladies waved their handkerchiefs, gentlemen their hats, and the whole scene presented was of unusual splendour. The sun, too, for a moment, emerged from the envious clouds that for some time previously had dimmed his lustre, and a flood of light pouring in through the glistening dome of the transept, illuminated this imposing spectacle of loyalty. When her Majesty ascended the throne, attended by the Royal family and the distinguished visitors of her Court, the organ of Messrs. Grey and Davison pealed forth the notes of the National Anthem, and the immense choir, collected for the occasion, accompanied the strain. This produced a grand effect, and not a heart present could remain unmoved at a scene so touching and so sublime. His Royal Highness Prince Albert, when the music had ceased, joined the Royal Commissioners, who drew near to the throne, and read to her Majesty a long report of the proceedings of the Commissioners, to which the Queen suitably, but briefly, replied. His Grace the Archbishop of Canterbury then approached the throne, and, with great fervency of manner, offered a prayer, invoking God's blessing on the undertaking.

"At the close of this prayer the choir joined in singing the Hallelujah Chorus, and the effect of this performance may be estimated from the fact that the Chapel Royal, St. Paul's Cathedral, Westminster Abbey, and St. George's Chapel, Windsor, contributed their entire vocal strength, while there were also present pupils of the Royal Academy of Music, part of the band of the Sacred Harmonic Society, and many other performers, both foreign and English. The vast area of the building left free scope for the volume of sound poured forth, and the assembled multitudes, their feelings already elevated by the grandeur of the spectacle before them, listened with becoming reverence to the triumphant music of the great German composer.

"It was at this stage of the proceedings that the Chinese already alluded to, and whom we discover to be no less a person than the Mandarin He-sing, of the Chinese junk, unable any longer to control his feelings, made his way through foreign diplomatists, Ministers of State, and the distinguished circle with which Court etiquette had surrounded the throne, and, advancing close to her Majesty, saluted her by a grand salaam, which she most graciously acknowledged.

"A procession was then formed, which, turning to the right, moved to the west end of the nave on the north side, and, as it passed, the glazed roof of the building vibrated with enthusiastic cheers. Down a deep lane of human beings, full of loyal expectancy, it passed—her Majesty and the Prince, preceded by the Lord Steward and the Lord Chamberlain, their faces turned towards the Royal personages, and their feet performing that curious movement, known only at Courts—namely, advancing backwards.

"The *coup d'œil* varied at every step, yet was always picturesque and beautiful. The foreign Commissioners, whose labours had hitherto confined them to their own department of the Exhibition, gazed with wonder at the development of British industry by which they found themselves surrounded. Even those most acquainted with the objects that lay on either side the route, were surprised by the new and undiscovered attractions which everywhere presented themselves. The

Indian and Colonial collections were left behind, the Fine Arts Courts passed, and the procession, cheered incessantly in its progress, moved into the area devoted to our many featured manufacturing products. Glimpses were caught, over the heads of the spectators, on the right, of the Furniture Court, and the massive forms of the fixed machinery beyond it. On the left, the Colebrook Dale dome, the gigantic statues of Lords Eldon and Stowell, the well known form of our great dramatist, and many other objects which adorn the centre aisle, were left behind.

"Past the furs of bears and other wild animals, suspended from many a girder, and carpets lending their brilliant colours to complete the decorations, and clothe the narrow lines of the interior, the pageant swept on its way. It reached the western entrance, and saw itself reflected in the immense mirror exhibited at this point. Then wheeling round the model of the Liverpool Docks, it was returning on the south side of the nave, when the gigantic organ, by Willis, suddenly hurled forth its immense volume of sound. The effect was extremely fine, but there was so much to think of, so many points to observe, and the admiration of all had already been so largely taxed, that each new, telling characteristic of the progress scarcely produced its deserved impression.

"At length the procession reached the transept, round the south end of which it proceeded, and then swept into the foreign department of the Exhibition. Here, immense efforts had been made to prepare for its suitable reception. France had collected the choicest specimens of her manufactures; and, though only two days ago her division was in confusion, and the possibility of her taking a suitable part in the opening pageant doubtful, one could not help admiring the tasteful manner in which her exhibitors had decorated the portion of their collection which was within sight. Other countries, more forward in their preparations, were, of course, able to make a more satisfactory appearance. The great attention which the industrial communities of Europe bestow on matters of artistic design and of ornamental manufactures, enabled them to decorate their divisions of the nave in a manner more effective than we, with our utilitarian tendencies, could hope to achieve.

"Amid a rare collection of various objects, the procession moved forward, received everywhere with loud acclamations. The French organ, by Du Croquet, and that from Erfurt, by Schulze, each in turn poured forth its music : and, as the pageant rounded the eastern end of the building, the bands of the Coldstream and Scots Fusileer Guards varied the performance by their spirit-stirring strains. The return along the north side of the nave renewed the enthusiasm of the foreigners and visitors assembled there. The cheering and waving of hats and handkerchiefs went on continuously around the building; and at last, having completed a progress more triumphant in its peacefulness and spirit of goodwill than the proudest warlike pageant that ever ascended the Capitol of ancient Rome, the Queen returned once more to the position in the transept where her throne was placed. She looked exceedingly well, and bore the excitement of the occasion with a firmness worthy of herself and of the people she governs. The applause of the assemblage was acknowledged both by herself and the Prince in the most gracious manner.

"His Royal Highness appeared less composed than her Majesty, and his emotion was visible when the ceremony and the procession had been happily conducted to its close. It was natural that he should feel strongly the termination of a spectacle, the grandest, perhaps, that the world ever saw, and with which his name and reputation are, henceforth, inseparably associated. He wore a field marshal's uniform, and the Prince of Wales the Highland dress. The Queen wore a dress of pink watered silk, brocaded with silver, trimmed with pink ribands and blonde, and ornamented with diamonds. Diamonds and feathers formed the head-dress. Her Majesty wore the riband and George of the Order of the Garter, and the Garter of the Order as an armlet. Her Royal Highness, the Princess Royal, wore a white satin slip, with two skirts of Nottingham lace, and had round her head a wreath of pale pink wild roses. The Royal children were objects of great attention, and the Prince of Wales received special cheers from the assemblage.

"And now the last act of the ceremonial remains to be recorded. The Marquis of Breadalbane, in a loud tone of voice, announced that the Queen declared 'the Exhibition open.' A flourish of trumpets proclaimed the fact to the assembled multitudes. The Royal family, attended by the Court, withdrew from the building; the choir once more took up the strains of the National Anthem;

the barriers, which had hitherto restrained the spectators within certain limits, were withdrawn, and the long pent-up masses poured over every part of the building, unrestrained by policemen, and eager to gratify their curiosity."

Thus was opened the Great Exhibition of 1851—and it speaks volumes for the good behaviour of the crowd, that, at Westminster Police Court, in which district the Crystal Palace was, there was, next day, only one charge having the least reference to the Exhibition, in which a London artizan was fined 10s. for a trifling assault upon the police, for which he expressed his contrition.

There must have been an especial glamour about this Exhibition, probably because it was the first of its kind, but I have never yet met with anybody who saw it, and all succeeding ones, but who, like myself, awards it the palm above all.

After having been open to the public for 141 days, it was closed on the 11th October. There was no ceremony, the only incident which marked the event being that, at 5 p.m., all the organs in the building played "God save the Queen," accompanied by many voices in all parts of the crowded avenues; after which, a bell was rung, warning the visitors to depart. On the 13th and 14th it was open to exhibitors and their friends, who were admitted by tickets, without charge. On the 15th the history of the Great Exhibition was brought to an end, with a slight business-like ceremony, in which Prince Albert, as the President, received the reports of the juries, and made a speech in reply. This took place on a temporary dais, in the middle of the transept (the crystal fountain having been previously removed), and the whole building was crowded with exhibitors and others, admitted by tickets. This little ceremony over, the National Anthem was sung; after which the Bishop of London read a prayer of thanksgiving. This was followed by the Hallelujah Chorus, at the close of which the Prince and commissioners left the platform, and the business of the day terminated.

In a pecuniary point of view, it was a great success, the grand total of cash received being, according to a report of the Royal Commissioners, 6th November, £505,000, leaving an available surplus, after defraying all expenses, of £150,000. This was invested in land at South Kensington, where it provided a site for the Albert Hall, several exhibitions, the Natural History Department of the British Museum, the Imperial Institute, etc.

Concerning this money there are some curious facts. Of the money received at the doors £275,000 was in silver, and £81,000 in gold. The weight of the silver coin so taken (at the rate of 28 lbs. per £100) would be 35 tons, and its bulk 900 cubic feet. The rapid flow of the coin into the hands of the money-takers prevented an examination of each piece as it was received, and £90 of bad silver was taken, but only one piece of bad gold, and that was a half-sovereign. The half-crown was the most usual bad coin, but a much more noticeable fact is that nearly all the bad money was taken on the half-crown and five shilling days. The cash was received by eighteen money-takers; on the very heavy days six extra ones being employed during the busiest hours. From them it was gathered by three

Statistics of the Exhibition.

or four money porters, who carried it to four collectors, charged with the task of counting it. From them it went to two tellers, who verified the sums, and handed it to the final custody of the chief financial officer, who locked each day's amount in his peculiar iron chests, in the building, till next morning, when, in boxes, each holding £600, it was borne off in a hackney cab, in charge of a Bank of England clerk and a bank porter. The money was received in all forms, ranging between farthings and ten pound notes. Contrary to the notices exhibited, change was given. Occasionally foreigners gave Napoleons, and these coins being mistaken for sovereigns, they received nineteen shillings out, and liberty of admission into the bargain. The moneys of America, Hamburg, and France were often tendered and taken.

To wind up this notice of the Great Exhibition, I may say that the total number of visitors, from the 1st of May to the 11th of October, was 6,063,986.

See page 104.

CHAPTER XI.

Royal Humane Society's Receiving House—Boats and bathing—The Dell—Chelsea Water Works reservoir—Walnut-trees—Flower-walk—Military executions—The Magazine, Whip, Four in Hand and Coaching Clubs—Their dress—Satire on coaching—The Park as a military centre—The first review—Fort at Hyde Park Corner—Guard-house—Camp in Hyde Park—Insubordinate troops.

On the north bank of the Serpentine, nearly on the site of the Cheesecake House, is the Receiving House of the Royal Humane Society, built in 1834 (the Duke of Wellington laying the first stone), on the site of a former one, which was erected forty years previously, George III. having given the Society a piece of ground for the purpose. Needless to say, it is a very useful institution, especially during severe frosts, being a convenient place where fractures, contusions and immersions can be properly attended to.

Near the Receiving House, boats can be hired for diversion on the lake, and on the opposite, or southern side, is a very fine bathing place, which is most extensively patronized, both in early morning and late evening, in the summer—nay, all the year round come some bathers, be the weather what it will, regardless of rain or frost. A boat rows up and down to rescue any swimmer who should be suddenly seized with cramp. On the same side,

FROM "ROQUE'S SURVEY," 1741-1745.

Face page 120.

but nearer the eastern end, is the favourite place for sailing miniature vessels, some of them being beautiful models, exquisitely fitted and very costly.

At the eastern end of the Serpentine, its water overflows in a minature cascade into a very pretty little dell, in which are rabbits disporting themselves, together with pheasants, and in 1890 there was a squirrel. As the public are not allowed to invade this portion, but only to look at it, the small zoological domain increases and multiplies, and the animals become exceedingly tame. In this dell is a monolith, which came from Moorswater, in the parish of Liskeard, Cornwall, where it was quarried on Jan. 3, 1862. One of the excavators employed in the work was accidentally killed, and his death was the cause of the publication of two books, *William Sandy, who died by an accident at Moorswater, etc.,* and *The grace of God manifested in the life and death of William Sandy, etc.* This monolith, although obviously only placed in the Dell for ornamental purposes, was, by a correspondent in *Notes and Queries*,[1] declared to be a phallic symbol.

Between Stanhope Gate and Grosvenor Gate, close by the flower-walk, may be noticed a circular basin having in its centre a fountain. This, which is shown in Roque's Map, was a reservoir of the Chelsea Water Works Company, and it stood, as the same map well shows, in a double avenue of walnut-trees. These, ultimately, became very decayed, and about 1811 they were cut down, and their timber made into gun-stocks for the army. The flower-walk is a worthy successor to the avenue, and gives great scope to the gardener's skill and

[1] 6s. iv. 172.

sense of colour, from early spring, with its hyacinths, daffodils, narcissi and tulips, to late autumn, when the bedding out plants, which have afforded innocent delight to hundreds of thousands, are distributed among the poor, and thus continue their sphere of usefulness by brightening the homes of the recipients.

If the reader will turn to Roque's Map, he will see, just where the Marble Arch now stands, a "Stone where soldiers are shot." And it was a place for military executions, and the shooting of two sergeants for desertion, etc., is thus described by Draper in 1751 :—

> "Avaunt *Silenus!* thy lewd revels vile!
> Cold *Russia's* troops, in a more Northern clime,
> Are disciplined far better than to waste
> Their strength in fev'rish *Gin;* is this the scene
> Of execution military? more
> It seems *Silenus'* Banquet. Ah! 'tis done,
> No mercy meets the wretch; it is not due
> If *George* can give it not, whose royal breast
> Glows with forgiveness." [1]

The *Gentleman's Magazine* for 1747 gives an account of a military execution here. "Thursday, 26th Nov. A court-martial was held at *Whitehall*, general *Wade* president, on the trial of Sergeant *Smith*, who was lately bought from *Scotland*, for deserting into the service of the *French*, and, afterwards, to that of the rebels; and after hearing, and the facts being proved, he was found guilty.

"Friday, Dec. 11. Sergeant *Smith* was conducted from the Savoy to the Parade in *St. James's Park*, and from thence by a party of the Foot-guards, commanded by Col. *Dury*, attended by the minister of

---

[1] The writer saw the messenger returning from the King at *Kensington*, and the execution.

the Savoy, to *Hyde Park*, where he was hang'd on a gibbet erected for that purpose, and bury'd near it: he seemed not much concerned, and professed himself a protestant. He had been in the service of several princes, and abus'd them all by desertion. Having thus acquir'd divers languages, he was of great service to our officers in *Germany*, as interpreter, who treated him as a companion, and promoted him to be paymaster sergeant, by which, and other perquisites, he had above £200 per annum; but he could not overcome his propensity to change."

Anent this stone, Larwood says, that when Cumberland Gate was built, and the ground prepared for that purpose, this stone was found so deeply imbedded in the earth, that it was thought more convenient to cover than to remove it. The earth was consequently thrown over it, and it now lies buried in its original resting-place.

On the north-west side of the Serpentine, and close by the bridge, which there crosses it, is a magazine for gunpowder, generally known as "The Magazine," a singularly exposed position for the storage of such destructive material. It now forms the starting place, at the commencement of the season, of the "Four-in-Hand" and "Coaching" Clubs, either of which, if the weather is propitious, is a very pretty sight.

The first of these clubs was started as the "Whip Club," and in the *Morning Post*, June 9, 1808, is a description of a "Meet."

"The *Whip Club* met on Monday morning in Park Lane, and proceeded from thence to dine at Harrow-on-the-Hill. There were fifteen barouche-landaus, with four horses to each; the drivers were all men of known skill in the science of charioteering. Lord Hawke, Mr. Buxton, and the Hon. Lincoln Stanhope were among the leaders.

"The following was the style of the set out: Yellow bodied carriages, with whip springs and dickey boxes; cattle of a bright bay colour, with plain silver ornaments on the harness, and rosettes to the ears. Costume of the drivers: a light drab colour cloth coat made full, single breast, with three tiers of pockets, the skirts reaching to the ankles: a mother-of-pearl button of the size of a crown piece. Waistcoat blue and yellow stripe, each stripe an inch in depth. Small clothes corded with silk plush, made to button over the calf of the leg, with sixteen strings and rosettes to each knee. The boots very short, and finished with very broad straps, which hung over the tops and down to the ankle. A hat three inches and a half deep in the crown only, and the same depth in the brim exactly. Each wore a large bouquet at the breast, thus resembling the coachmen of our nobility, who, on the natal day of our beloved sovereign, appear, in that respect, so peculiarly distinguished. The party moved along the road at a smart trot; the first whip gave some specimens of superiority at the outset, by 'cutting a fly off a leader's ear.'"

In the *Annual Register*, vol. 51, p. 883 (1809), is the following satire "ON THE WHIP CLUB:—

"Two varying races are in Britain born,
One courts a nation's praises, one, her scorn;
Those pant her sons o'er tented fields to guide,
Or steer her thunders thro' the foaming tide;
Whilst these, disgraceful born in luckless hour,
Burn but to guide with skill a coach-and-four.
To guess their sires each a sure clue affords,
These are the coachman's sons, and those, my Lord's!

> Both follow fame, pursuing different courses;
> Those, Britain, scourge thy foes—and these, thy horses;
> Give them their due, nor let occasion slip;
> On those, thy laurels lay—on these, the whip!"

The *Morning Post*, April 3rd, 1809, says that the title of the "Whip Club," had then been changed to the "Four-in-Hand-Club," and their first meet took place in Cavendish Square on April 28th of that year. The dress of the drivers was altered, and was as follows. A single-breasted blue coat, with a long waist, and brass buttons, on which were engraved the words "Four-in-Hand-Club," waistcoat of kerseymere, ornamented with stripes alternately of blue and yellow; small clothes of white corduroy, made moderately high, and very long over the knee, buttoning in front over the shin-bone. Boots very short, with long tops, only one outside strap to each, and one at the back; the latter were employed to keep the breeches in their proper longitudinal shape. Hat with a conical crown, and the *Allen* brim (?); box, or driving coat of white drab cloth, with fifteen capes, two tiers of pockets, and an inside one for the Belcher handkerchief; cravat of white muslin spotted with black. Bouquets of myrtle, pink and yellow geraniums were worn. In May of the same year, the club button had already gone out of fashion, and "Lord Hawke sported yesterday, *as buttons*, Queen Anne's shillings; Mr. Ashurst displayed crown pieces."

Possibly this "Four-in-Hand-Club" was dissolved, for Captain Gronow says[1] that amongst his papers he found a list of the original members of the club, which met at Richmond on Saturday,

[1] "Celebrities of London and Paris." 3rd Series, 1865.

June 2nd, 1838, and passed a series of resolutions, that formed the basis of the regulations which were observed during its existence : and he relates how "In the days of which I speak there were amateur coachmen, who drove with unflinching regularity, and in all weathers, the public stage-coaches, and delighted in the opportunity of assimilating themselves with professional jehus. Some young men then, heirs of large landed proprietors, mounted the box, handled the ribbons, and bowled along the high road ; they touched their hats to their passengers, and some among them did not disdain even the tip of a shilling or half-crown, with which it was the custom to remunerate the coachman.

"Many persons liked travelling to Brighton in 'The Age,' which was tooled along by Sir Vincent Cotton, whilst others preferred Charley Tyrrwhit. On the Holyhead, Oxford, and the Bath and Bristol roads, Lord Harborough, Lord Clonmel, Sir Thomas Mostyn, Sir Charles Bamfylde, Sir Felix Agar, Sir Henry Parnell, Sir Bellingham Graham, Mr. Clutterbuck, Sir John Lade, and other members of the Four-in-Hand-Club, were seen, either driving the coach, or sitting cheek-by-jowl with the coachman, talking about horses and matters relating to 'life upon the road.' One of the members of the Four-in-Hand-Club, Mr. Akers, was so determined to be looked upon as a regular coachman, that he had his front teeth so filed, that a division between them might enable him to expel his spittle in the true fashion of some of the most knowing stage-coach drivers."

In the Park, and close by the path which leads

from Grosvenor Gate to the Magazine, are some small barracks for the use of the guards of the Magazine—but Hyde Park has been for more than two centuries the *Campus Martius* of London, and the first review recorded as having been held there was by Lord Hunsdon, the then Ranger, when as Stow says in his *Annales*, on the 28th of March, 1569, "The Pensioners well appointed in armour on horsebacke, mustered before the Queen's Maiestie in Hide Park beside Westminster."

In *The Bow-man's Glory*, 1682, is "A Brief Relation of the several appearances of Archers, since His Majesties Restauration.—On March the 21st *Anno Domini*, 1661. Four hundred archers, with their bows and arrows, made a splendid and glorious show in *Hide Park*, with flying colours, and cross-bows to guard them. *Sir Gilbert Talbot*, Baronet, was their Colonel, Sir *Edward Hungerford*, Knight of the Bath, their Lieutenant-Colonel; Mr. *Donne* was their Major. Great was the appearance both of the nobility, gentry and commonalty: several of the archers shot near twenty score yards within the compass of a hat with their cross-bows; and many of them, to the amazement of the spectators, hit the mark; there were, likewise, three showers of whistling arrows. So great was the delight, and so pleasing the exercise, that three Regiments of Foot laid down their arms to come and see it."

In the early days of the Commonwealth, London was fortified by the Parliament, and so urgent were they on this matter that we read in *A Perfect Diurnall of the Passages in Parliament*, April 24th to May 1st, 1643, "An order was made by the common Councell of London, that the Ministers in the severall Parishes of the Citie should stir up the Parishioners in their severall churches the next day to send such of their servants and children as are fit to labour, with spades, shovells and other necessary tooles to helpe and assist the raising of the out-workes for the defence of the Citie, which is very needeful to be finished with all expedition, in regard two great Armies are now on foote near the Citie, and that they would begin the work by Wednesday next."

Nay, the very women helped in this work, as Butler tells us in *Hudibras* (part ii. cant. 2.) :—

> "Women, who were our first Apostles,
> Without whose aid we 'ad all been lost else;
> Women, that left no stone unturn'd
> In which the cause might be concern'd;
> Brought in their children's spoons and whistles,
> To purchase swords, carbines and pistols.
>
> . . . . . .
>
> What have they done, or what left undone,
> That might advance the cause at London?
> March'd rank and file, with drum and ensign,
> T' intrench the City for defence in;
> Rais'd Rampiers with their own soft hands,
> To put th' Enemy to stands;
> From Ladies down to Oyster-wenches,
> Labour'd like Pioneers in Trenches,
> Fall'n to their pickaxes, and tools,
> And help'd the Men to dig like Moles."

In a very fine copy of *Hudibras* (ed. 1793), with voluminous notes by T. R. Nash, he thus elucidates the line "Rais'd Rampiers with their own soft hands." "When London was expected to be attacked, and in several sieges during the civil war, the women, and even the ladies of rank and fortune, not only encouraged the men, but worked with their own hands. Lady Middlesex, Lady Foster, Lady Anne Waller, and Mrs. Dunch, have been particularly celebrated for their activity."

The probability is that he took the names of these ladies from a not very scarce satirical tract printed in 1647, called *The Parliament of Ladies, or Divers remarkable passages of Ladies* in Spring Gardens; in *Parliament Assembled*, etc., which was never meant to be taken seriously. They are mentioned in the following resolution :—

"The House considered in the next place, that divers weake persons have crept into places beyond their abilities, and to the end that men of greater parts might be put into their rooms, they appointed the Lady *Middlesex*, Mistris *Dunce*, the Lady *Foster*, and the Lady *Anne Waller*, by reason of their great experience in Souldery in this Kingdome, to be a Committee of Tryers for the businesse."

When London was fortified, in 1643, a large fort, with four bastions, was raised at Hyde Park Corner, where Hamilton Place now stands, and there it remained for four years, being pulled down in 1647. There was also at the north-east corner of the Park, where now stands the Marble Arch, a Guard House, to watch travellers on the Oxford Road, which was also defended by a large fort with four bulwarks, at the corner of Wardour Street. There was also in the neighbourhood of Hyde Park a small redoubt and battery on Constitution Hill; whilst another gives its name to Mount Street.

The guard at Cumberland Gate were especially watchful, for we read in *A Perfect Diurnall of the Passages in Parliament*, of 28th January, 1643: "There was also a Gentleman this day intercepted by the Courts of Guard of Hyde Parke, going to Oxford to the King, and being searched, there was

K

divers letters found about him, which were brought to the Parliament and read, and found to be of very dangerous consequence, making a discovery of the state of things here, and the proceedings of the Lord Generall's army." And, also, in *A Continuation of certain Speciall and Remarkable Passages from both Houses of Parliament, and other parts of the Kingdome*, March 2-9, 1643. "Wednesday (8th March): a hat-full of Letters being intercepted by the Court of Guard at Hide Parke Corner, which came out of *Wiltshire*, (some of them being directed to persons disaffected to the Parliament,) they were brought to the House, and ordered that the Committee should take a view of them, that if any were of ill consequence, the same might be discovered, and the party found out."

On August 6, 1647, Fairfax and the Parliamentary army marched, with laurel branches in their hats, through Hyde Park, where they were met by the Lord Mayor and Aldermen, to the City.

In December, 1648, there was a camp of the Parliamentarians in Hyde Park; and Cromwell there reviewed two regiments of horse, on 9th May, 1649, which is thus described in *Perfect Occurrences of every Daie iournall in Parliament*, etc., May 4-11, 1649: "The Lord Generall commanding a Randezvous this day (9th May) in *Hide-parke*, of his Regiment, and the Lieutenant-Generalls of Horse. The Lieutenant Generall made Speeches, declaring the Parliament's great care and paines : 1. In execution of Justice against the grand Delinquents. 2. In their Declaration and Resolution to put an end to this and future Parliaments. 3. Their care for settling trade, by setting forth a gallant Navy at

Sea. And 4. Their proceedings for payment of Souldiers Arreares. And as for Martiall law, those that thought it a burden, should have liberty to lay down their Armes, receive their Tickets, and bee payd as those that stay. There was one Trooper made some objections, and was bold, for which he was committed, but at the solicitations of some of his followers, the Lieut.-Gen. ordered his freedome, and to be received in againe. The Levelers colours were pulled out of three or four of their hats."

This was the Parliamentary account—now let us see the other side, as expressed in *Mercurius Pragmaticus (for King Charles II.)*, May 8-15, 1649, which is specially jocose on the Lord Protector's red nose. " Newes at *London* this *Wednesday* Generall *Tom* (Fairfax) drew his Regiment and *Cromwel's* to a Randevouz in *Hide-Parke*, where Lieutenant-Gen. *Nose* made a Speech to them, setting forth very eloquently the good *Acts* his *brethren* were now about to doe for the destruction of the *Subject*: the particulars of his *Oration* would be too tedious to relate. *Fairfax* sayd nothing, save *nodded* with the *head*, and made *mouths* at the Souldiers. There was one *Trooper* made some bold demands and objections against *Rubinose*, for which he was committed, whereupon there began to be some grudging, or shew of *mutiny*, which made *Nol* to pull in his *Nose*, and give *Liberty* to the *Trooper* againe; yet those who had *Sea greene* Colours received some affronts, having their fancies taken from them, to which they said little, whatever they thought."

CHAPTER XII.

Grand Reviews in 1660-1661-1668, 1682-1695-1699—Camps in 1715-1716-1722—Poem on the latter—Reviews in 1755-1759-1760.

A FEW weeks before the restoration of Charles II. Hyde Park was the scene of a very grand review, which is thus described in *The Parliamentary Intelligencer*, April 23-30, 1660. "On Tuesday, April 24, the Militia forces of the City Trained Bands and Auxiliaries, according to an Order of the council, marched into Hide-Park, the Maior in his Collar of S's, with the Mace, Sword, Cap of Maintenance, the Aldermen in Scarlet, and the Commissioners of the Militia in handsome equipage going before them to a place erected for their entertainment. Each *Colonel* had his Tent and their Regiments very full, several of the Nobility and Gentry of great quality going as Volunteers. In Alderman *Robinson's* Regiment were 250, the rest very many. The Regiments were all so numerous and so gallantly accoutred, as did sufficiently speak the strength and riches of the City, there being very little visible difference betwixt the Trained Bands and Auxiliaries, but only in their age."

Strype, in his Continuation of Stow's Survey, tells us that at this review there were six Regiments of Trained Bands, six of Auxiliaries, and one Regiment of Horse. The twelve Regiments of Foot consisted of 80 Companies, and each Company consisted of not less than 250 men—which would give a total of 18,000 men; and the Regiment of Horse numbered 600.

On March 21, 1661, there was a parade in Hyde Park of 400 archers, and, on Sept. 27, 1662, Charles II. here reviewed his Life Guards. The 4th July, 1663, saw another muster of the King's Guards, which Pepys, who was present, thus records:— " Thence with Creed to hire a coach to carry us to Hyde Parke to-day, there being a general muster of the King's Guards, horse and foot; but they demand so high, that I, spying Mr. Cutler, the merchant, did take notice of him, and he, going into his coach, and telling me that he was going to the muster, I asked, and went along with him; where a goodly sight to see so many fine horses and officers, and the King, Duke and others came a-horse-back, and the two Queens in the Queene-Mother's coach, My Lady Castlemaine not being there. After a long time being there, I light, and walk to the place where the King, Duke, etc. did stand to see the horse and foot march by, and discharge their guns, to show a French Marquisse (for whom this muster was caused,) the goodness of our firemen, which, indeed, was very good, though not without a slip now and then; and one broadside close to our coach we had going out of the Park, even to the nearnesse as to be ready to burn our hairs. Yet, methought, all these gay men are not the Soldiers that must do the King's business, it being such as these that lost the old King all he had, and were beat by the most ordinary fellows that could be."

We have seen how, in the year of the Great Plague, the Guards were encamped in Hyde Park, and how miserably some of them died there: and it does not seem to have been again used for military display till Sept. 16, 1668, which Pepys saw. "When I come to St. James's I find the Duke of York gone with the King to see the muster of the Guards in Hyde Park; and their Colonel, the Duke of Monmouth to take his command this day, of the King's Life Guard, by surrender of my Lord Gerard. So I took a hackney coach, and saw it all; and, indeed, it was mighty noble, and their firing mighty fine, and the Duke of Monmouth in mighty rich clothes; but the well ordering of the men I understand not." Evelyn, also, speaks of these reviews.

On Jan. 28, 1682, the Guards were again reviewed in Hyde Park, this time for the gratification, and in honour of the Ambassadors of the Sultan of Morocco, whose followers afterwards performed a *fantasia*, after the manner of their country. Queen Mary reviewed troops in the Park on the 9th and 10th of May, 1692, and there was a very grand parade of troops previous to their departure for Flanders on Dec. 23, 1695. *The London Post*, Nov. 8-10, 1699, says that on Nov. 9 "The King reviewed the 3 Troops of Guards in Hide-Park. They appeared all in their new Cloaths, and fine accoutrements, with Feathers in their Hats, and made an extraordinary show. His Majesty rid through every Rank, and was very well pleased to see them in so good an Appearance; after which, he placed himself on the left of the Front, till the whole marched by him in File; then they took their ground again, and afterwards were ordered to pass

Man by Man before his Majesty; and a detachment was made out of all the 3 Troops, for His Majesty's Guards, who attended His Majesty to Kensington. There was an incredible Crowd in the Park to see the Show, some computing that there could not be less than 10,000 People, and 600 Coaches."

In 1715, King George I. being newly set upon the throne, there were Jacobite riots in many parts of England, and, in July of that year, a camp was formed in Hyde Park, for the protection of London, of a very strong body of troops, together with twelve pieces of artillery. The camp occupied the site of the Exhibition of 1851, and, according to the *St. James's Evening Post*, July 23-26, 1715, "The three Battalions of Foot Guards on 23rd July marched to their Encampment in Hyde Park, and the Horse and Grenadier Guards took their Post there next day, and the Regiment of the Duke of Argyle is expected there this day." The same paper says that "This Day His Royal Highness the Prince of Wales went to view the Camp in Hyde Park." In the copy for July 30-Aug. 2 we read that on the anniversary of the King's accession, Aug. 1, "There were likewise Rejoycings in the Camp at Hyde Park, where the King's and other loyal healths were drank by the Officer and Soldiers, and a Discharge was made of their Artillery and Small-Arms. The first Regiment of Guards received their new cloathing, and made a very fine appearance." The King, on Aug. 8th, "went to Kensington, view'd the Camp on his way, and return'd at Night to St. James's." *The Flying Post, or The Postmaster*, Nov. 1-3, 1715, gives an account of the celebration of the birthday of the Prince of Wales (Oct. 30) in the camp. It says : "It was solemnized with extraordinary Demonstrations of Joy, the Army being wonderfully pleas'd with his Royal Highness, because he inherits the Military, as well as the other Virtues of his Royal Father and other Great Ancestors. His Grace the Duke of Montague signaliz'd his Bounty on that Occasion, by giving an Ox to his Troop, which was roasted whole at the head of the Standard. His Grace gave them, likewise, 50 lbs. weight of Pudding, a Hogshead of Wine, and 2 of Strong Beer, with which they drank the Healths of His Majesty, their Highnesses the Prince and Princess, and of their Royal Issue, with those of the Dukes of Marlborough and Montague, and other loyal Healths. They had, also, Illuminations in Circles, throughout the Camp, and there were incredible Numbers of People, who came to see those Novelties, without committing any Disorder."

Another newspaper, the *St. James's Evening Post*, Nov. 1-3, 1715, supplements this account thus : "After the triple Salvo of the Artillery and Small Arms that was made in the Evening, Col. Oughton, one of the Grooms of His Royal Highness's Bed Chamber, and Major of the first Regiment of Guards, invited all the Foot Officers to an Entertainment in his Tent ; and, that the Soldiers might Share in the Universal Joy on this Occasion, distributed a Guinea per Company among the private Men, to drink the Prince's Health, etc., which they did with repeated Huzzahs and Acclamations of Joy, under great illuminated Circles erected for that purpose at the head of every Company." The same paper, of Dec. 10-13, tells us that on Dec. 10, " the

Army decamped from Hyde Park, and the Artillery, etc., were sent back to the Tower."

There was another camp in the Park next year, when the Prince of Wales reviewed the troops, and yet another in 1722, of which *The Daily Post* of May 9 records : " Yesterday, all the Foot Guards that were not upon duty, march'd to the Camp mark'd out in Hide Park ; his Majesty and Royal Highness view'd them from the Terrass Walk in the Privy Garden at St. James's as they passed by." Every newspaper of the day had an account of the Royal Review of the troops in camp on June 11, 1722, but the best was in *The Flying Post*, June 12-14. "The Forces which were review'd by the King last Monday in Hyde Park, were only the three Regiments of Foot Guards, the Horse being to be review'd another time. His Majesty having rode round the three Regiments, the first of which was on the Right, the Second on the Left (the Posts of Honour), and the Scots Regiment in the center; his Majesty made a stand, afterwards, near the Ring, the Prince at some small distance from him, where all the Regiments passed by in review, Earl Cadogan standing on his Right, and General Withers on his Left, with each his half-pike.

"His Majesty and his Royal Highness, after having dined in one of the Earl of Cadogan's tents, went into another, which Prince Eugene took from the Prime Vizier of the Turks, who presented it to the Duke of Marlborough, who afterwards made a present of it to my Lord Cadogan. There was an appearance of about sixty Dukes and other Peers, besides abundance of other persons of distinction, particularly the Bishop of Durham, who was finely mounted, in a lay habit of purple,[1] with jack-boots, and hat cock'd, and black wig ty'd behind him, like a militant officer. But, above all, the eyes of the numerous spectators were on his Majesty, whom they admired for that graceful, easy mien with which he sat on horseback and returned the salutes of the officers, and for the wonderful agility with which he dismounted."

This camp was so famous, that there was a long poem published about it,[2] of which I extract some short portions, as it brings the place, its times and manners, very vividly before us.

> "Before the Camp, the Cannon find a Place,
> (Ready to stare the Enemy in the Face,)
> Mounted, Charg'd, Prim'd, and all things *Toujours Prêt*,
> To give the daring Rebels an *Arrêt*.
> Where watchfull Centinells stand (full of Ire,)
> With Match or Halberts, ready to give Fire.
> The Warning-Piece, too, stands not far before,
> Whose harsh Report is watch'd by many a Score,
> Not only of Drums and Trumpets, for *Tattou*,
> But of the Mobb, who come to see this Show:
> And gaping, stand in Crowds on either side,
> And, in the Firing it, take a mighty Pride.
> Behind, are plac'd the *Powder-Carriages*,
> The Cannon's necessary Equipages;
> T' th' Right is Pitch'd the Master-Gunner's Tent,
> Set out with Match, for Use, or Ornament.
> Facing the Front, are set the Quarter Guard,
> To give th' Alarm, in case they shou'd be scar'd.
> Whose constant Watch, for some strange Enterprize
> Does (tho' the Rest are all at play) suffice,
> And takes away all fear of a Surprise.
> The Right and the Left wings, are form'd by th' Horse,
> And in the centre, stand the Foot, of course.
> The Field-Colours, each Squadron's Ground mark out,
> The Gay *Bell-tents* are plac'd before the Foot;

---

[1] The Bishop of Durham is a Prince Palatine, as well as a Bishop, and on entering his palatinate used to be, and may be now, girt with a sword.

[2] "A ramble thro' Hyde Park; or, the Humours of the Camp." London, 1722.

In Gaudy Line, they're ranged along the Plain,
To keep their Arms from Rust, by Dew or Rain.
At either regiments Head of Horse are rear'd,
Their several Standards, with their careful Guard:
Betwixt the Horse, are stretched the *Picket Ropes*,
Where the Horses stand, to fill their Hungry Chops;
Some of which sure, find Provender but scanty,
They look so near akin to *Rosinante*.
I' th' Rear, (and that, indeed's, the fittest for 'em,)
Are plac'd the Officers, in nice Decorum.

Their airy Tents are sprucely Neat and Clean,
And all is there disposed with a *Bonne Mine*,
Each strives to shew his Genius to be *Brilliant*,
In the Composure of his gay Pavillion.
The spacious Avenue that leads to th' Door,
Is with red Gravel (rolled) all cover'd o'er;
A Grassy Turf each Walk emborders round,
And greatly beautifies the golden Ground;
In various Forms their Fancies are exprest,
One Walk, on either side, with Flowers is drest:
Another entrench'd, some strew'd with Cockle-Shells,
(And each think, doubtless, that his own excels.)
While others, who're, perhaps, more negligent,
Have nought but rugged Earth before their Tent.
The noble H——'s Pavilion's in the Centre,
A Guard is at the Door, that none should enter
But whom he bids, and lest it be expos'd,
With platted Boughs 'tis all round enclosed:
So thick they stand, so loftily they rise,
Secure he's kept from view of Vulgar Eyes.
  "The Tops o' th' Tents and Borders differ too,
Some are adorn'd with Red, and some with Blue;
This, has its flaming Swords, and that, its Arms,
And each the Eye with various Figures charms.
But leave we this, my Muse, and let's begin,
To shew what Furniture's contain'd within.
(Lest they take Cold) Some boarded are all o'er,
Others have only Two, that lead to th' Door,
But most have painted Cloths [1] upon the Floor.
Facing the Entrance is set up the Bed,
Of what's lik'd best, of Green, or Blue, or Red:
Some, too, are lac'd, some wrought, others are plain,
And, from the Bed, there is a kind of Train,
Of the same sort, stretch'd out on either side,
Which Masters' and the Valets' Rooms divide,
And does the necessary Lumber hide.

---

[1] Oil-cloth.

> The Table and the Chairs are some o' th' rest,
> Set to accommodate th' expected Guest;
> Near the Bed, hangs (in a convenient Place,)
> That necessary Utensil, the Looking Glass,
> Where Mr. *Smart* may see his Monkey Face.
> But, hold, let not the Tea-Table be forgot,
> O'er which they hold many a luscious Chat,
> With Generous She's; and make a *Prose Lampoon*,
> (By way of Dialogue) upon half the Town.
> An useful Copper Kitchin stands just by,
> From whence whene'er the Tea-pot's almost dry,
> Of Boiling Water they've a fresh Supply."

In 1755, the King several times reviewed his Light Horse Cavalry in Hyde Park. *Read's Weekly Journal* tells us how on 17th July, 1759, "the regiment of Norfolk Militia march'd to Kensington, where His Majesty stood under the Piazza in front of the Palace, and saw them file off in ranks of eight deep; the Earl of Orford, Colonel, march'd at the head of the first battalion, with drums beating and fifes playing; the second battalion had Sir Armine Woodhouse, Bart., Lieut.-Col., at their head, and were look'd on as a fine corps. His Majesty seem'd greatly pleas'd with their appearance. Their uniform is scarlet turn'd up with black. They march'd on Kingston, and other towns contiguous, on their way to Portsmouth." Walpole, in his letters (19th July, 1759), says, "The crowds in Hyde Park, when the King reviewed them, were unimaginable."

On 20th November, 1760, George II. held his last review in Hyde Park, for he died suddenly on the 26th. The following account of it is given in *Read's Weekly Journal*, of 25th November. " Exactly at a quarter before ten, at the review of Colonel Burgoyne's regiment of Light Horse, in Hyde Park, his Majesty entered the grand pavillion or tent, erected under the garden wall, where were likewise present their Royal Highnesses the Prince and Princess of Wales, the Duke of York, Princess Augusta, and some other of the young princes and princesses ; Lord Viscount Ligonier, Lord Anson, and a great number of other noblemen, etc. As soon as his Majesty entered the pavillion, the whole regiment, before they began their exercise, passed before him, four in a rank; after which they all dismounted, and drew up before the tent. His Majesty expressed the greatest satisfaction at seeing their manner of exercising, and retired at half-past ten ; there were near 20,000 spectators present. As soon as the review was over, some pieces of a new construction, and of a globular form, were set on fire, which occasioned such a smoke, as to render all persons within a considerable distance invisible, and thereby, the better enabled, in time of action, to secure a retreat."

CHAPTER XIII.

Reviews in 1763-1764—Shooting-butts in 1778—Camp in 1780—Severe Sentence of a Court-martial—Volunteer reviews, 1799-1800—The ruin at the latter.

IT would be wearisome to chronicle every review, except grand ones such as the following, which is thus described in the *St. James's Chronicle*, June 25-28, 1763. " On the morning of the 27th inst. at half-past eight, his Majesty, the Duke of York, and Prince William Henry, attended by Earl Delawar, and escorted by the first troop of Horse Guards, mounted their horses at the Queen's Palace,[1] and proceeded up Constitution Hill to Hyde Park. They were received at their entry into St. James's Park by Lord Ligonier, the Marquis of Granby, Earl Talbot and Earl Harcourt, with their attendants and their led horses. At the gate of the Green Park they were received by Lord Orford, Ranger of the Parks, on Horseback; and, on their entry into Hyde Park, his Majesty received a Royal Salute from the Artillery. The manner of the three Regiments of Foot Guards going through their new method of exercise, need not be repeated; it is sufficient to observe that never men went through their discipline with greater exactness, which reflected the highest honour on their Officers, and filled the numerous spectators with admiration.

[1] Then called Buckingham House.

VOLUNTEER REVIEW BY GEORGE III., 1799.

Besides the illustrious personages above mentioned, his Majesty's two younger Brothers, and a great number of the First Persons of Distinction of both Sexes, and near One Hundred Thousand other People, were present. It is remarkable that Elliot's Light Horse, the *Matrosses*,[1] who managed the artillery with such inimitable skill, and those of the Guards, who served abroad in Germany, wore in their Caps and Hats Sprigs of Laurel and Oak, emblematical of the Immortality and never-dying Fame of their late glorious Achievements."

On July 25 following, the King again reviewed Elliot's Light Horse in the Park, and the same newspaper (July 23-26) records the following accidents. " Colonel Elliot, in putting up his sword into the Scabbard, by the prancing of his Horse wounded himself in the Thigh, but not so dangerously but that he went through the whole Exercise of his Regiment, with great Composure and Exactness. A large arm of a Tree broke down, by which accident a Sergeant in the Guards had his Skull fractured, and several others were terribly bruised."

George III. held many reviews in Hyde Park, especially during the early days of the American War of Independence, and the Park was a veritable *Champ de Mars* for military exercises. In 1778, an earthen rampart, twenty feet high and three feet wide at its base, was erected as butts for musket practice. It began at Cumberland Gate, and ran westwards towards Bayswater. Being near the high road, it was very dangerous, although at that time the other side of the road was all fields.

[1] Next in rank to gunners.

On June 2nd, 1780, broke out the fanatical riots generally known as the "Lord George Gordon Riots," with which we have nothing to do, other than to chronicle the fact that the troops in and near London being considered insufficient to cope with the rioters, others were summoned from different parts of the country. Lodging must be found for these on their arrival, and we read in *The London Chronicle*, June 6-8, 1780, that " Orders are given from the War Office for a Camp to be formed in Hyde Park, and the several regiments that are to compose the same are now on their march ; and, yesterday, the Hampshire Militia pitched their tents there for that purpose." Also, later on in the same paper (p. 552), " Seven battalions of militia marched into Hyde-Park yesterday afternoon, where they immediately encamped. A large detachment of the Hampshire militia are doing duty at the President Lord Bathurst's house in Piccadilly. The Park Gates are all shut, and no person suffered to pass through on any account whatever."

The Morning Chronicle of June 10 says : " Thursday (June 8), six regiments of Militia were encamped in Hyde Park; they are to be joined by several other regiments, which will make their number 10,000 men " : and the same journal, June 13, tells us that, " The Grand Camp in Hyde Park consists of the nine following regiments: the Queen's, the Royal Irish, the Twenty-second, Cambridge, South Hants, North Hants, Oxford, Northumberland, One of York." On the 14th June, the King, Prince of Wales, and " the Bishop of Osnaburgh" (Duke of York) visited the Camp—and so he did on several other occasions. But the riots came to an end, and

THE SOLDIERS' TOILET, 1780.

the news of the taking of Charlestown drove everything else out of people's heads, so that we do not hear much more of this Camp; but Paul Sandby painted a series of views of the Camp, and exhibited them at the next Royal Academy. He also engraved them. "*The Great Encampment in Hyde Park.*" "*The Encampment in Hyde Park—The Filbert Merchant.*" "Ditto—*Marshall Sax's Tent.*" "Ditto—*The Soldier's Toilet*" (which is here reproduced), and several others. In "*The Soldier's Toilet*" we get rather more than a peep into the domestic life of the Camp, and in the background we see St. George's Row, and the chapel attached to the burial ground in the Bayswater Road, now rebuilt. After the scare was over, and martial law in London was abolished, the Camp was much visited; but when it had fulfilled its needs it had to come to an end, and on the 10th of August the Camp broke up, after having earned golden opinions from the Londoners.

After this Camp the King held frequent reviews, of which nothing need be said, nor indeed is there anything military to chronicle with regard to Hyde Park until May 1, 1787, on which date (*Gent.'s Mag.*) "His Majesty having sent down the sentence of a Court-martial held upon a private of the Life Guards (for rude and improper behaviour to his officer) to the Colonels of the four troops, for their consideration, it was returned by them, and the purport was as follows:

Sentence.—" That the prisoner Lloyd, private in the first troop of Horse Guards, shall receive one thousand lashes, and then be publicly dismissed the troop.

"His Majesty, we understand, but not in pity to the prisoner, whose demerits deserve a severer punishment, has remitted that part of the sentence which orders the *thousand lashes*, as corporal punishment was never inflicted on his own Body Guard ; and has ordered him to be dismissed the troop, with every public mark of infamy.

"May 14. This day Lloyd, the Life Guardsman, convicted by a Court-martial, as mentioned in a former article, was publicly trumpeted out of the regiment, on the reviewing ground in Hyde Park. After the ceremony was over, the populace carried off the man in triumph, in sight of the whole regiment."

Reviews by the Prince of Wales, the Duke of York, and the Duke of Gloucester were frequent ; and, after 1793, were much increased by the Volunteers, who were then generally enrolled. There had been Volunteers previously, notably the "Royal London and Middlesex Light Horse Volunteers," which ranked as the oldest corps, having been enrolled in 1779, during a violent French scare. Next year, they materially helped to put down the Lord George Gordon Riots, and were rewarded by the King and the City of London with standards. Disbanded in 1783, they were again enrolled in 1794, and reviewed in Hyde Park, with their old standards proudly flying, in July of that year.

But the grandest review in the Park at this time was on the 4th of June, 1799, the 62nd birthday of George III., when the "Armed Associations" passed before him. The illustration is taken from a portion of a contemporary engraving, and the following account is taken from *The Annual Register* :—

" June 4th. Being his Majesty's birthday, the several associations of the metropolis and its neighbourhood, consisting of sixty-five well-equipped corps, and amounting to upwards of 8000 effective men,[1] assembled in Hyde Park, where they were reviewed by the King. The Temple Association, commanded by Captain Graham, was the first that entered the Park; it arrived at seven o'clock, during a heavy shower of rain, which continued incessantly from the time it left the Temple Gardens. Several other corps followed soon after; and, at half past eight, the whole were on the ground. The necessary dispositions, agreeable to the official regulations, were then made; and, about ten minutes past nine, his Majesty appeared, attended by the Prince of Wales, the Dukes of York, Kent, Cumberland and Gloucester, a number of general officers, and a formidable detachment of the Life Guards.

" The line being formed, a cannon was fired, to announce the approach of the King; on which all the corps immediately shouldered in perfect order, and the artillery then fired a royal salute of twenty-one guns. A second gun was fired on his Majesty's arrival in front of the line, and each corps immediately presented arms, with drums beating and music playing. A third cannon was fired as the signal for shouldering, which was promptly obeyed. His Majesty having passed along the line, and returned by a central point in front, a fourth cannon was fired as a signal to load; and, upon the fifth gun being fired, the different corps began to fire volleys, in

[1] Really, 841 cavalry and 7351 infantry.

succession, from right to left. The same loading and firing were repeated upon the sixth and seventh cannons being fired; in all fifty-nine rounds.

"On the eighth cannon being fired, three cheers were given, and the music played, "God save the King." The corps then passed his Majesty in grand divisions, in a most excellent manner, under the direction of General Dundas, who headed them on horseback; after which, they filed off to the stations respectively allotted for them. The whole of the evolutions pointed out to them in the general orders having been performed, and another royal salute of twenty-one guns fired, his Majesty, after expressing the highest satisfaction at the martial appearance and excellent conduct of this loyal and patriotic army, departed from the ground at a quarter before one, amidst the joyous shouts and affectionate greetings of the people, who assembled, on this occasion, to the amount of upwards of 100,000, including all the beauty and fashion of the metropolis.

"The sight was truly grand and highly gratifying; and notwithstanding the evolutions were considerably impeded by the high wind and some rain, the whole were performed in a manner that reflects much credit upon every corps present, whose conduct fully entitles them to the very handsome compliment of his Royal Highness the Commander-in-Chief, paid them by order of his Majesty, in the *Gazette* of that evening. The ground was kept clear by the London and Westminster, and Southwark Volunteer corps of cavalry, who preserved the lines from being infringed by the immense multitude who crowded the Park."

Another review in the Park on 15th May, 1800, did not pass off so quietly. The Grenadier battalion of the Guards were being exercised, when a gentleman named Ongley, a clerk in the Navy Office, was shot by a musket ball during the volley firing, whilst standing but twenty-three feet from the King. The wound was not dangerous—through the fleshy part of the thigh—and it was immediately dressed; and very little might have been heard of it, had not the King, that same night, been shot at in Drury Lane Theatre. The cartouch-boxes of the soldiers were examined, but none but blank cartridges were found. So little, indeed, was thought of it, that the King, who said it was an accident, stopped on the ground for half an hour afterwards, and four more volleys were fired by the same company before he left.

The next birthday review of Volunteers (4th June, 1800) was not a happy one. It was a larger affair than that of the previous year, some 12,000 men being under arms; but they had to stand in soaking rain for eight hours, as did the majority of the spectators. The following is from the pen of an eye-witness:—

" So early as four o'clock, the drums beat to arms in every quarter, and various other music summoned the reviewers and the reviewed to the field. Even then the clouds were surcharged with rain, which soon began to fall; but no unfavourableness of the weather could damp the ardour of even the most delicate of the fair. So early as six o'clock, all the avenues were crowded with elegantly dressed women escorted by their beaux; and the assemblage was so great, that, when the King entered the Park, it was thought advisable to shut several of the gates, to avoid too much pressure.

"The circumstance of the weather, which, from the personal inconvenience it produced, might be considered the most inauspicious of the day, proved, in fact, the most favourable for a display of beauty, for variety of scene, and number of incidents. From the constant rain, and the constant motion, the whole Park could be compared only to a new-ploughed field. The gates being locked, there was no possibility of retreating, and there was no shelter but an old tree or an umbrella. In this situation you might behold an elegant woman, with a neat yellow slipper, delicate ankle, and white silk stockings, stepping up to her garter in the mire, with as little dissatisfaction as she would into her coach—there, another, making the first *faux pas*, perhaps, she ever did, and seated, reluctantly, on the moistened clay.

"Here is a whole group assembled under the hospitable roof of an umbrella, whilst the exterior circle, for the advantage of having one shoulder dry, is content to receive its dripping contents on the other. The antiquated virgin laments the hour in which, more fearful of a speckle than a wetting, she preferred the dwarfish parasol to the capacious umbrella. The lover regrets there is no shady bower to which he might lead his mistress, 'nothing loath.' Happy she, who, following fast, finds in the crowd a pretence for closer pressure. Alas, there were but few grottos, a few caverns—how many Didos—how many Æneas's? Such was the state of the spectators. That of the troops was still worse—to lay exposed to a pelting rain; their

RETURNING FROM THE REVIEW, 1800.
Page 150.

arms had changed their mirror-like [1] brilliancy to a dirty brown; their new clothes lost all their gloss, the smoke of a whole campaign could not have more discoloured them. Where the ground was hard, they slipped; where soft, they sunk up to the knee. The water ran out at their cuffs as from a spout, and, filling their half boots, a squash at every step proclaimed that the Austrian buckets could contain no more."

[1] The barrels and locks of the muskets of that date were bright and burnished. Browning military gun-barrels were not introduced till 1808.

CHAPTER XIV.

Volunteer reviews of 1803—Review in honour of the Allied Sovereigns, 1814—Popularity of Blücher—Review by the Queen in 1838—Volunteer review, 1860.

As far as I can learn, there were no more grand Volunteer reviews in Hyde Park, until 26th Oct., 1803, and this, I think, is borne out by the " gush " of the *Annual Register* on the occasion, which would hardly have occurred had they been frequent. " This was a truly proud day for the country. It presented the sublime spectacle of a patriot Monarch, who reigns no less distinguished in the hearts of his people than on his throne, meeting the brave citizens of his metropolis, armed in defence of his crown and of the British Constitution ; and, with the characteristic virtue of the sons of Albion, resolved to continue free, or gloriously to fall with the liberty and independence of their country. Such a spectacle is worthy of such a people: such a people are deserving of the superior blessings they possess."

The Volunteers mustered 12,401, and they were reviewed by the King. With the exception of the Prince of Wales, all the Royal Princes were present, the Duke of Clarence " in the uniform of the Teddington Association." The Queen was present, as were also the Princesses, and the royal party was joined by the refugee French Princes,

Monsieur (afterwards Louis XVIII.) being dressed in green with red facings, the Prince de Condé, in white, faced with blue; the Duc de Bourbon in white, faced with red; and the Duc de Berri in green. There were no accidents, although there were some 200,000 spectators; "every person who could come from within a circle of twenty miles being collected. Many came to town from a distance of above a hundred miles to be present at the sight."

"The *éclat* with which the grand review of the London district of volunteers went off on Wednesday, excited a laudable ambition in the breasts of the Westminster, Lambeth and Southwark corps, to surpass, if possible, their brethren in arms, in discipline, in zeal, and military appearance." They mustered 14,676 men, but the total Volunteer force in the vicinity of the metropolis was then reckoned at 46,000. The morning of 28th October opened very dispiritingly, even worse than on the 26th.

"The fog, however, not content with equalling that of Wednesday, increased to such a degree, that, at half past seven, not a single object could be seen in the park, and several Corps would have passed by Oxford Street Gate, had they not been stopped there by a party of Life Guards stationed there to guard the entrance. The eager expectation which ushered in the morning now changed to fearful anxiety. It was too dark to observe the expression of the countenance; but everybody, in tones of despondency, began to express their apprehensions that all the beauty of the military spectacle would be lost, and that a glimpse of the troops could not be obtained, much less a full view of them, and the embellishments of the scene. The houses, scaffolds, carts, caravans, and carriages of all descriptions, drawn up for the accommodation of spectators along the Bayswater Road, instantly began to drop their prices; and would have fallen still lower, had not the fog fortunately begun to clear away about half past eight, when the business of the day again assumed a cheerful aspect, and the spectators eagerly assembled in amazing crowds, and to a still greater extent than on Wednesday."

The King, Queen, and all the Royal family were present, but on this occasion there were no foreign visitors.

Although there were perpetual drills and inspections in Hyde Park, there does not seem to have been a grand review until the one which took place in honour, and in the presence of the Allied Sovereigns, the Emperor of Russia, and the King of Prussia, who were then on a visit to the Prince Regent, and it took place on Sunday, June 20, 1814. The following is *The Times* account of it.

"Yesterday, at an early hour, all the regular troops, together with most of the Volunteer Corps in the metropolis and its vicinity, were in motion to proceed to Hyde Park, for the purpose of being reviewed by the Prince Regent, and his Imperial and Royal visitants. Immense crowds of people, of all ranks, were at the same time seen flocking thither in every direction; and, in consequence of an excellent regulation, by which all carriages, except those of the Royal family, and all horsemen, except military officers, were prohibited from

The Allied Sovereigns in 1814. 155

entering the Park, these spacious grounds afforded ample room and accommodation for the multitudes of spectators.

"By half past eight o'clock, all the different troops of the line, together with the corps of Yeomanry and Volunteers, had taken up the positions assigned to them. The line, which partly ran parallel with the wall of Kensington Gardens, extended from Buckden Hill to the Piccadilly gate of Hyde Park; a brigade of horse artillery formed the extreme right of the whole; next to them were drawn up successively in line, several regiments of Dragoons, the Royal Horse Guards, the Blues, the Queen's Bays, and the Scots Greys; next followed two regiments of Light Horse, we believe the 9th and 13th; the Surrey Yeomanry, with the London Light Horse, and several other minor corps, completed the whole of the cavalry.

"The different battalions of the three regiments of Guards not at present employed on foreign service, headed the line of infantry. We did not observe any other regiment of regular troops, and the rest of the ground was occupied by battalions of Volunteers. They comprised most of the Volunteer Corps still existing in the metropolis; and though, in general, they did not muster very strong, yet, even in point of numbers, their appearance was respectable. These troops are not again likely to meet under arms for some time to come, and the close of their patriotic military career well merited the distinguished honour of this day's review, by three of the most powerful Sovereigns in Europe.

"About ten o'clock, the Duke of York, accompanied by a numerous staff, rode down the line. Soon after, the firing of a gun announced that the Royal personages had entered the Park. They were preceded by a detachment of the 10th Hussars : the Prince Regent had, on his left, the Emperor of Russia, and on his right, the King of Prussia. The *cortège* of the sovereigns was extremely numerous, and of the most brilliant description, comprising all the distinguished military characters at present in London. Among others, Marshal Blücher, Prince Platoff, Lords Hill and Beresford were recognized and cheered by the spectators. The effect of the whole was impressive, from the richness and variety of the uniforms; but, above all, from that singular combination of august and powerful Sovereigns, and of men who had conferred the greatest benefits on Europe by their military talents.

" The Royal party, commencing with the extreme right, rode along the whole of the line, and were received with presented arms, by the different corps. They then took their stations near the centre of the Park, when a *feu-de-joie*, in three successive rounds, was fired from right to left. The effect of this continuous fire was exceedingly fine, from the rapidity and precision with which it was executed. The different corps then defiled by companies in front of the Royal personages, and in this order marched off the ground, which concluded the business of the review. We cannot, accurately, estimate the number of troops on the ground; but, from the time occupied in their marching in review, we should suppose that they must have amounted to 15,000. The Dragoons, in particular, were

POPULARITY OF BLÜCHER, 1814.

Page 157.

admirable for their equipments and martial appearance. The day, though lowering at times, and rather cool, was, upon the whole, extremely favourable to the spectacle. We did not hear of any serious accident happening; though some of the lower orders, who perversely mounted on the trees in the Park, met with some falls by the breaking down of the branches. We were sorry to observe that some of the younger plantations were injured by the mob climbing upon trees insufficient to sustain their weight. It was a pity this wanton mischief had not been prevented."

One person, at all events, who was present, must have carried away with him, when he left England, a curious recollection of Hyde Park; for as old "Vorwärts," as Marshal Blücher was familiarly termed, (used, as he must have been to being mobbed whenever he appeared in public,) was walking one day in Hyde Park, it is said that the crowd went so far as to investigate his person, and that the veteran was fain to put his back against a tree for protection; a scene thus humorously caricatured.

There were no reviews of particular importance in Hyde Park until we come to the present reign—when the Queen, soon after her Coronation, reviewed a small but select body, about 5000, of artillery, cavalry, and infantry, for the delectation of her foreign guests.

The following account is condensed from *The Times* of July 10, 1838 :—

"It was at one time proposed to hold a review of a much larger number on Wormwood Scrubs, but considerations of expense interfered, and it was settled that a smaller number of picked troops should be reviewed, as we could not vie with the vast assemblages of troops which were sometimes called together at Töplitz and elsewhere on the Continent. But the foreign critics were loud in their praises of the appearance of all the troops they saw, as regarded their perfect order and discipline, and the admirable way in which the manœuvres and evolutions were executed, and declared that they would have borne advantageous comparison, in their different branches, with any troops in the world—but perhaps, this was only their natural politeness.

" The Duke of Wellington, Lord Hill (Commander of the Forces), Lord Combermere, with a host of distinguished officers, received the Special Ambassadors from foreign States, the Duc de Nemours, Marshal Soult (Duc de Dalmatie) and others— whilst the Duke of Cambridge (the Queen's uncle) arrived with a crowd of Continental Princes. The Queen took up her position on the ground at twenty-five minutes to twelve; and, after the Staff and noble and illustrious foreigners had paid their respects to her, she proceeded in her carriage down the lines, each body of troops presenting arms as she passed, and the bands striking up the National Anthem.

" Then, returning to the flag, the troops marched past in slow time—went through some evolutions, burnt a great quantity of powder; and, finally, both lines advanced in parade order, headed by the Marquis of Anglesey, and saluted her Majesty, who then retired. The Duke of Wellington and Marshal Soult were vociferously cheered, and, as for the latter, many persons not only cheered him as he moved on, but came beside his horse, and grasped the veteran cordially by the hand, a freedom with which he seemed rather pleased. During the review one of his stirrup leathers broke and it was afterwards found that it was one of a pair much used by Napoleon in his campaigns, and which had been furnished to the Marshal by Messrs. Laurie and Marner, the saddlers."

The next great review held in the Park takes a long stride in point of time, and took place on 23rd June, 1860, when the Queen reviewed some 18,450 Volunteers. These had been called into existence by a circular letter from General Jonathan Peel on 12th May, 1859, and the movement became so popular, that about a year afterwards sufficient were enrolled to enable this review to be held, and the result fully bore out the wisdom of the experiment.

The following account is extracted from *The Times* of June 25th, 1860 :—

" The galloping about of the Staff was equal to a series of races, the object of the running being an utter mystery to the uninitiated. Something dreadful always appears to be happening at the end of the line where the Staff is not, and away the group of uniforms tear to rectify it ; it is important perhaps, but to the public inexplicable. Everybody felt grateful for the amusement furnished by a trumpeter of the Life Guards, in the heavily laced coat and jockey cap, which favoured the racing theory. He was attached to the Duke of Cambridge, and occasionally blew a screech on his trumpet—a most wretched and unwarlike sound, though it was, we believe, a signal of some kind ; certainly, it was a signal for laughter whenever it was heard. Another source of amusement was the rather Lucretian and selfish enjoyment of the perplexities of the dense crowd of officers and military personages of various grades, in the railed space below the galleries. Ten feet more of ground might have been given, and the want of it caused confusion. The pressure at last was too great, and there was a rush under the rail into the open. The police could then do nothing against the plumes and epaulets. The disorder gave the Staff two or three gallops to the spot. The Commander-in-Chief himself remonstrated, but the disorder, which was not very serious after all, could not be retrieved. The ground gained was kept; but, as a compromise, the front ranks were directed to sit down, which they did, and Policeman 209 was released from his responsibility. There was much speculation as to some of the most gorgeous uniforms in this military miscellany which were quite new to English eyes. Very wild guesses were made, but opinion settled down on East Indian Horse Artillery and Cavalry, regular and irregular. A magnificent Lord Lieutenant, whose place was near the Queen, but who had lost his pass ticket, was sternly refused ingress, and remained in the crowd undistinguished.

"At 4 o'clock, the first gun of the Royal salute apprised all that her Majesty was entering the Park. A succession of cheers from the extreme left announced it also. A detachment of Life Guards headed the procession, which passed from left to right along the front of the galleries. Her Majesty was in an open carriage, with the King of the Belgians, the Princess Alice, and Prince Arthur.

His Royal Highness Prince Albert, in uniform, rode by the side of the carriage, near which also were the Prince of Wales, and Prince Jules of Holstein-Glucksburg. Aides de Camp, Equerries, the Adjutant-General, and other high military officials preceded the carriage. It was immediately followed by the venerable Lord Combermere, who was old in service before most of the soldiers on the ground were born, for he counts 70 years, not of age, but of service. His horse was led, and every attention was paid to the veteran warrior. He wore the Order of the Bath, and the uniform of his regiment, the Life Guards. In the two other carriages were the Princess Louise, the Princess Mary of Cambridge and the Grand Duchess of Mecklenburg Strelitz. In the line of procession followed the Lords Lieutenant of the counties to which the several corps of Volunteers belong.

" The *cortège* passed nearly to the extreme left of the line of Volunteers, then turned and proceeded slowly along the front of the extreme right, and, turning again, drew up on the open ground in front of the Royal Standard. The three bands of the Household Brigade were stationed opposite the Royal carriages; through the intervening space the Volunteer companies marched, those on the right of the line of columns coming up first. It was half-past four when the 1st Huntingdonshire Mounted Rifles passed her Majesty; and, at a few minutes to six o'clock the 25th Cheshire closed the review, which lasted without intermission for quite an hour and a half.

" Her Majesty left the ground at six o'clock, in the same order as she arrived, but some time elapsed before the public could get clear of the enclosures. The difficulty of getting a large body of troops out of the Park has almost become a military axiom, but the difficulty is not insuperable. The Volunteer officers solved the problem without confusion, except a little crushing at the gates; but the crushing was more among the spectators than the troops."

CHAPTER XV.

Volunteer Reviews, 1864, 1876—Mobs in the Park—Funeral of Queen Caroline.

THE next review in the Park was also of Volunteers, 21,743 in number, who were inspected by the Prince of Wales on 28th May, 1864. After the inspection, the Prince, who wore the uniform of the Honourable Artillery Company, took his place at the head of his corps. The following is from *The Times*, 30th May, 1864 :—

"The Royal carriages, meanwhile, had drawn up close to the flagstaff, and, as they took their position, His Royal Highness Prince Arthur, accompanied by Major Elphinstone, R.E., came forward and joined the party. Shortly afterwards, the Duc d'Aumale and the two gentlemen by whom he was accompanied, were perceived in the reserved seats by His Royal Highness the Duke of Cambridge. They were at once conducted within the enclosure, and, having paid their respects to the Princess of Wales, remained to witness the march past.

"First in order came the Hon. Artillery Company, a body which can trace its pedigree back to a time when there was no standing army in England; and whose ancestors, the old Train Bands, ranged themselves sometimes on the side of the sovereign, and sometimes against it, but always on the side of liberty. Next, marched the representative corps of Oxford and Cambridge Universities, and the brigade closed with a battalion raised from those distinguished Civil servants who act as the wheels on which our social machinery revolves. The Prince, wearing the uniform of Colonel of the Hon. Artillery Company, with the blue riband of the Garter, was warmly cheered, as he rode past in advance of his brigade; and, having gracefully saluted the Commander-in-Chief, took up his post on the left of General Pennefather, where he could be seen to advantage by the different regiments as they passed.

"It is no new thing to say of the Hon. Artillery Company that they are hardly to be distinguished from the *corps d'élite*, to whose uniforms their own so narrowly approximate; but, on Saturday, conscious of their added dignity, they put forth special efforts to justify their ancient renown. Oxford University came tripping along merrily, to the music of *Faust*—a little short in the step perhaps, but that may have been the fault of the band—with a somewhat novel look imparted to their ranks by the bright blue colour of their caps and stockings. The Cambridge men enjoyed the advantage, as far as appearance is concerned, of those knowing Zouave gaiters, which, on parade, replace the 'cardinal' stockings. In other respects the University Corps were on a footing of perfect equality, and, in every respect, worthy to be included in the new formation of infantry of the guard. Lord Bury, the Lieutenant-Colonel of the Civil Service Regiment, was warmly greeted—a tribute apparently personal, as well as complimentary to the fine regiment under his command.

"The Cavalry Brigade, composed of the 1st Surrey Light Horse, the 1st Middlesex, and the 1st Hertford Volunteer Cavalry, formed, in the aggregate, a squadron of nearly one hundred. The horses, for the most part, were exceedingly good, but many of them had either not been accustomed to march in line, or were disconcerted by the music of the band. Cavalry, at present, is scarcely one of the elements of strength in the Volunteer Service, and it would be well if, occasionally, means could be taken of enlisting the co-operation of the Yeomanry. The military effect of Volunteer reviews would be much heightened by their presence.

"The Artillery display was very imposing. This has always been a favourite branch of the service; but, in spite of their previous knowledge of the subject, the public were surprised to find how large a proportion the Artillerists bore to the general force under arms. In addition to the six light guns which had gone past with the Hon. Artillery Company, in the Prince of Wales's Brigade, 20 others of heavier calibre were now paraded in charge of the 1st Administrative Brigade, the Middlesex Artillery Volunteers, commanded by Col. Creed, and the 3rd Middlesex Artillery Volunteers. The bearing of the men and their general equipments were highly creditable to all concerned; and, not content with mere efficiency, some of the batteries borrowed a hint, as to style, from the Royal Horse Artillery, and horsed their guns exclusively with animals of one colour. In addition to what may be called, for the sake of distinction, the Service Artillery, there was a complete Brigade of Artillery Volunteers, armed with carbines only, numbering close upon 2000 men.

"When these had passed, the infantry divisions came up, and continued to move along in unbroken order for nearly an hour and a half. The public are, by this time, such keen critics at Volunteer reviews, and the regiments themselves, by the earnestness they threw into the movement at the outset, have accustomed spectators to such a standard of efficiency, that anything in the nature of shortcoming is sure to be detected. It is, therefore, paying no small compliment to the force upon the ground, to say that, at the conclusion of the proceedings, the general voice declared the display to have been attended with complete success. From first to last, as far as the Volunteers were concerned, there was not a single hitch: on the contrary, the improvement in discipline since the last great display in Hyde Park is too palpable to admit of question. A fact, to which attention cannot be too strongly pointed, is, that the battalions from various parts of the country, taking part in the review, were, if anything, in advance of those in the metropolis. It has been the fashion to speak—not slightingly, for it was never possible to do that—but in a careless off-hand manner, of the performances of 'country corps,' and to assume that, in 1864, as in 1860, London is still giving the tone to the provinces in all matters connected with volunteering. But, if the regiments sent up from Lancashire, Nottingham, Warwick, and Derbyshire, are average specimens of those in other parts of England, the metropolis must look to its laurels, and that without delay.

"It is true that all the established favourites of the London Volunteer garrison were on the field on

Saturday afternoon, and in no degree lessened their former high repute. The South Middlesex, for example, were present in large numbers, and the perfect evenness, as to merit, of the companies, shewed the good results of the internal competitive examinations instituted in that corps. The London Scottish, steady and precise, repaid the trouble taken by Lord Elcho, while the London Rifle Brigade, solid and sombre, upheld the credit of the City of London. The Inns of Court, neatly dressed and smartly handled, as Rifles should be, elicited frequent remarks of ' We've not seen any like this, yet,' and, from one old gentleman, the plaintive soliloquy: 'Fine fellows, very fine fellows; what a pity there are such rogues among them!' The Victoria Rifles, under the Duke of Wellington, did credit to their long and careful training, but, rating the merit of these and other corps as high as possible, the fact cannot be got rid of that, without exception, the finest Brigade upon the field was that commanded by Lord Grosvenor, and composed exclusively of country corps.

" The 6th Lancashire, better known as the 1st Manchester, led the van of this Brigade, followed by the celebrated ' Robin Hoods.' The late Lord Herbert once coveted an Irish Militia regiment so much, that he almost infringed the rules of the Service, in the hope of transferring it bodily into the Queen's army. The Commander-in-Chief must be more than mortal, or less than a soldier, if he did not cast a longing eye on those serried files of Lincoln green. So great was the interest excited by their appearance, that the Volunteer corps which had just made the circuit of the field, and returned to their former positions, cheered them enthusiastically again and again. The Birmingham, Derbyshire, and 2nd Manchester corps were almost as good; they were certainly equal to any corps present, if the Nottingham men be deducted. Bearing in mind that most of these Volunteers had made a journey longer than that which metropolitan undertake when they go to Brighton, and that, in the aggregate, they composed a Brigade of nearly 3000 men—exclusive of the Somersetshire and Berkshire regiments, not less efficient, which were classed in other Brigades—it will be manifest with what spirit drill must be pursued in the provinces.

"The march-past began shortly after a quarter past six, and terminated at two minutes past eight o'clock. It was estimated that an hour and forty minutes would be occupied in the proceedings, from the time the troops were set in motion, and it will be seen from this how accurately the Volunteers must have carried out their instructions. The programme was adhered to with such literal fidelity, that the occasion was almost devoid of incidents. The directions as to equalizing the strength of companies had, on the whole, been very fairly attended to, but there were still some instances in which blank files—say a regiment of grey uniform, had been filled up with 'casuals' dressed in green, inconsistencies which detract very much from the appearance of a regiment on parade, and ought not to be allowed by officers in command. Moreover, there is a manifest want of head somewhere, when a mounted officer sits his horse as if it was an easy chair, and lounges past the flag-staff without giving himself the trouble to draw his sword; and when the tallest member of a cadet corps struts by in plain clothes and a 'billycock' hat. Matters like these, the Volunteers, for their own credit, will do well to keep their eyes upon, as they would never be tolerated in the military service to which it is their desire to approximate as closely as possible.

"When the last corps had passed the flag-staff, and it became evident that the Prince and Princess of Wales were about to leave the ground, there was one general impulsive rush to see and cheer them. The carriage in which the Princess sat was surrounded in a moment, swallowed up, almost climbed into, by eager thousands, who bestowed upon her Royal Highness such a greeting as has not been heard since she passed through London on the day of her public entry. It was with the utmost difficulty that a way was at last cleared for the carriage to take its departure, but, once it was in motion, a troop of Lancers, forming in rear, was enabled to check the pressure."

The next, and last occasion, up to date, of a Review in Hyde Park was on July 1st, 1876, when the Prince of Wales reviewed about 30,000 Volunteers, and *The Times* of July 3rd thus criticizes it.

"The review of Volunteers on Saturday, in Hyde Park, was a complete success. There were some trifling errors, due to inexperience, and in the interest of the Volunteers themselves, we shall not hesitate to point out such as fell under our observation; but there can be no question that the force has entered on a new stage in its history. All competent critics seem to agree that the whole tone has altered for the better. It is difficult to define the exact meaning of the word 'soldier-like,' but no other word nor phrase would express so well what the Volunteers failed to be a few years ago, and what they are now. Formerly, at any great assembly, like that on Saturday, there was noise and fuss on parade, unsteadiness in the ranks, want of due obedience and discipline, bad marching, carried off by a sort of defiant recklessness, which said, 'We could do better if we would, but we don't choose;' and, speaking generally, the absence of all the qualities which, from time immemorial, have been held to characterize the true soldier.

"On Saturday, there was a radical change. The battalions which paraded in different parts of London were quiet, orderly, and obedient. They waited patiently for their commanding Generals, and obeyed orders with complete docility. They were composed of good-looking, well drilled men, whose anxiety to deserve commendation was as conspicuous as formerly was their determination to have praise whether they deserved it or not. There was little talking in the ranks, and less confusion. The result was a general steadiness and dignity of demeanour which carried them well through a day full of difficulties, and gained the respect of all the officers of the Regular forces who had to deal with them.

"There were, of course, some exceptions to the rule, and we must confess to a feeling of positive annoyance against those men who absented themselves from their regiments during the march-past, or joined them only when they were drawn up in the Park. We saw numerous instances of men pushing their way through the lines of spectators a very short time before the arrival of the Prince, and others never joined at all. It may be ungracious to point out this fault on the part of men who came to Hyde Park at their own expense, and, naturally enough, found many an Armida to tempt them from the weary parade; but the Volunteers may be assured that the fact attracted much attention, and elicited many an unfavourable remark. The absence of men from the ranks till the last moment, and sometimes altogether, had a direct tendency to spoil the look of those ranks on parade, and was probably the cause of the irregular 'sizing,' which was so conspicuous in some of the battalions. Tall men and short men were mingled together, standing anyhow side by side, and the bad effect for parade purposes was very evident.

" Yet in common fairness we must consider what many of the Volunteers had been about. Some of them, and by no means the worst regiments, had come from the Midland counties by train, and moved to their places of rendezvous, where they had long to wait before the order to march-off came. It is said that many men who appeared before the Prince at half-past 5, had been at work that morning, up to 1 o'clock, at Nottingham. This much, at least, is certain, that they had walked or marched from their homes to the station, performed a long railway journey, and then marched again through the streets of London. Doubtless, such as these needed refreshment, and nothing was more satisfactory than the fact that they did not refresh themselves so much as to appear other than steady on parade. Indeed, we are under the impression that the offenders were not chiefly from the country."

From this time there has been no great military display in Hyde Park: it is unsuitable for it, and the grass is quite enough spoilt by the mobs of fanatic, idle, mischievous, or seditious persons who there assemble at oft-recurring intervals, and destroy the peace and comfort of those, who are the vast majority, who wish to enjoy the verdant pleasures of the Park. Besides, railways have multiplied, and the facilities of holding real reviews and military manœuvres in places where there is far more room, have so increased, that it is probable that we have seen the last great military gathering in the Park. The Foot Guards still assemble here occasionally for exercise, and in the autumn it is a favourite spot for the annual inspection of Volunteer regiments, but then these are inspected singly, and without fuss.

It now becomes my very disagreeable task to chronicle the scenes of disorder which have taken place in the Park, and which, owing to the growth of democratic feeling, have only occurred this century, our ancestors being wisely content to use the Park as a place of sensible recreation, or at the very worst, as one for settling private differences quietly, and without observation. The change begun in 1821 at the removal of the corpse of Queen Caroline, wife of George IV., but this was unpremeditated, and need not have occurred. This took place on August 14.

It is not my place to comment on the marital relations of the King and Queen, or of the behaviour of the latter, who stood her trial and was acquitted of the charges brought against her. Suffice it to say that the popular voice was in her favour, and, on the occasion of the removal of her body to Brunswick (her final resting-place), the natural and most direct route lay through the City. Those in authority knew what an ovation the corpse would receive if it went that way, and sought to take a different route. From Brandenburgh House, where the Queen died, through Hammersmith, to turn round by Kensington Gravel Pits, near the church, into the Uxbridge Road, to Bayswater : thence to Tyburn turnpike, down the Edgware Road, along the New Road to Islington, down the City Road, Old Street, Mile End, to Romford, etc.

But this the mob would not allow : the corpse *should go through the City*, and *The Morning Chronicle* of Aug. 15 gives the following account of how the procession fared.

" It was at eight o'clock in the morning, when the procession reached Kensington Church, that public opinion made its first indication ; the whole procession was suspended. The multitude, proceeding from the eastward, here assumed a determined attitude. The first object was the seizure of an ammunition-waggon, with an escort of the Foot Guards. The soldiers endeavoured to maintain their charge, but the pressure of the crowd rendered their efforts impotent; the ammunition-waggon was turned into an engine of defensive war. The people were determined not to let the Royal remains be smuggled through a bye-lane. Waggons, carts, hackney-coaches, with the lynch-pins taken out, were, almost by a talismanic agency, converted into a barrier of obstruction, calculated to prevent the progress to the New Road. After two hours delay, an express having been, it was understood, sent to the Earl of Liverpool, a detachment of the Life Guards, with Sir Robert Baker at their head, at full gallop, with sabres drawn, reached the High Street, Kensington, at twenty-two minutes past 10. He, with the military officers, reconnoitred the position taken by the people, and they at once perceived that the passage by Kensington Gravel-pits was impossible. When it was announced that the Royal *cortège* was to proceed along the Hyde Park Road, the interest of the public feeling was then strenuously directed to prevent its being directed into Hyde Park. The cry was for 'The City, the City, the City,' etc. At the request of Mr. Hume, the ammunition-waggon, which was the first seizure, was released by the people.

"The Park now presented the spectacle of an immense multitude. As far as the eye could reach, the space was covered with umbrellas. Some of the Life Guards rode to and fro, which seemed to excite much displeasure among the crowd, which was testified by hissings and hootings. When the head of the procession reached Cumberland Gate, about half-past 12, a stoppage took place; the people crowded and wedged together at the end of Oxford Street and the gates were not very willing nor very able to make way. We saw an officer ride down Park Lane, for the purpose, as it appeared, of bringing up another body of soldiers. A troop of Horse Guards then appeared, and galloped at full speed towards the gate.

"As the Horse Guards advanced towards Cumberland Gate the people crowded forward, and manifested an intention of preventing the hearse from passing through. The Guards, who were not only hissed, but pelted with mud and stones, attempted to proceed, but the crowd rushed forward and closed one side of the gate. The soldiers then charged upon the people, and the gate was forced open, but was again closed for a few moments. The soldiers having at length got through, were again pelted with mud and stones. Some persons attempted to block up the entrance to the Edgware Road, and posts, stones, etc., were torn up for that purpose. The Guards now charged a second time, and many severe wounds were inflicted. The Riot Act having (as we understand) been read by Sir R. Baker, the Horse Guards fired upon the people, and did serious injury. One of the sufferers is a man named Honey, a cabinet-maker, Compton St., Soho; he lies at the General Wetherell, Oxford Street, and has just been recognized by his brother. Another lies dead at Mr. Lightfoot's, surgeon, Oxford Street. An unfortunate man who had been carried to the hospital, shortly afterwards died of his wounds. The firing, single shots, lasted four or five minutes, during which period it is impossible to describe the distress and confusion which prevailed; men and women were seen running in all directions, endeavouring to avoid the attacks of the soldiers, who brandished their swords, and pushed forward with the most determined boldness and intrepidity.

"We must here observe, that the Oxford Blues took no part whatever in this attack upon the people—their conduct throughout was highly praiseworthy. The obstructions to the entrance of the Edgware Road having been at length removed, the procession moved forward, but not quietly. The people continued throwing mud, and calling out 'Piccadilly Butchers,' and 'The Blues for ever.'"

The people had their way. When the procession came to Tottenham Court Road, it was found that the New Road, Hampstead Road, and all the streets near, were so barricaded, that it was utterly impossible to proceed. It, therefore, turned down Tottenham Court Road, Bloomsbury High Street, High Holborn, Drury Lane, to the Strand. The Lord Mayor and one of the Sheriffs met it at the foot of Ludgate Hill, and accompanied it to the City boundary, in Aldgate. After turning down Tottenham Court Road, and it was certain that the popular will would be carried out, all went with the utmost decorum, and the passage of the body through the City was quiet and reverential.

CHAPTER XVI.

Commencement of the reign of King Mob—Sunday Trading Bill, 1855—Riots—Withdrawal of the Bill—Meetings about high price of food, 1855—Rough play and window smashing.

THIS riot was accidental and unpremeditated. We now come to the reign of King δῆμος in the Park, and it began on Sunday, July 1, 1855, in a demonstration against Lord Robert Grosvenor's "Sunday Trading Bill"—the following account of which is abridged from *The Times* of July 2, 1855.

"Three o'clock was the advertised time for the proceedings to begin, and, notwithstanding that Sir Richard Mayne[1] had had placards posted in the metropolis, announcing that the meeting would not be allowed to take place, long before that hour Constitution Hill, and the walks in St. James's Park, were literally crowded by thousands, who were all wending their way towards Hyde Park. By half-past two o'clock there must have been nearly 150,000 men, women and children present. Many, judging from their dress, were of the respectable class. The proceedings began by the usual stump oratory, which continued for some time, until a cry of 'the Police' being raised put an abrupt termination to it.

"About 30 or 40 policemen made their way

[1] The then Chief Commissioner of Police.

towards the man, but he had decamped, and a great number of men, finding that he was not allowed to address them, commenced hissing and hooting at the police, and some cried out, 'Down with the Crushers!' This gave rise to an extraordinary scene of confusion. Some of the men commenced knocking the constables' hats off, and, to protect themselves, the men were obliged to use their truncheons with considerable force. Several carriages containing company came in sight, when every one present commenced crying out, 'Go to church,' and 'Take your horses out.' The police, finding that this frightened the horses, commenced seizing those who uttered the expressions. In return, the crowd laid hold of the officers, and endeavoured to rescue their prisoners. Of course, this could not be allowed, and the police were compelled to use their staves vigorously, and with marked effect on the mob—but they kept their prisoners, and sent them off to the police-station in cabs. One man, to escape capture, plunged into the Serpentine, but had not got more than half across, when he seemed likely to sink. He was rescued by an officer of the Royal Humane Society, and duly was enrolled in the ranks of the captured. The police were heavily reinforced, and the riot was put down—but not before 104 rioters were lodged in the police cells, who were in time dealt with by the magistrate.

"On the next day, Lord Robert Grosvenor withdrew the objectionable Bill; but this did not satisfy the mob, who met again in Hyde Park on the following Sunday, 8th July, but, finding no excitement there, they went into Belgravia, and took to the pleasant pastime of window smashing, the houses which suffered most being those of the Earl of Sefton, Duke of Marlborough, Lady Somers, Count Kielmansegge, and the Archbishop of York. Lord Palmerston, who was then Prime Minister, and Lord Brougham, both had a narrow escape from stoning."

This making Hyde Park a Cave of Adullam, was too great a novelty to be let rest; so we find, that it being war time, and provisions somewhat high, a meeting must needs be held to talk about the high price of food—and one took place on Sunday, 14th October, 1855. *The Times* of next day says :—

" For many days past large placards have been posted on the hoardings about London, deploring the present high price of bread, setting forth possible causes and certain remedies for the evil, and calling on the working men of the metropolis to meet in ' Our Park ' on Sunday next (yesterday) for the purpose of giving expression to their feelings on the subject, and taking measures for bringing about a change in so sad a state of affairs. Accordingly, yesterday, about 2 o'clock, great numbers of persons were found wending their way towards the Park, where already had assembled many, not of the best orders of society, and of those itinerant gentry who ply their various callings on such occasions.

" Until 3 o'clock nothing of an unusual character occurred; but, shortly after the hour named, a movement towards the centre of the Park gave indication of something exciting, and a rush from all parts to the point of attraction brought together, of a sudden, a crowd that continually increased, until, at last, as many as 5000 persons must have assembled together, the majority of them being of respectable appearance. All the available men of the police force, and those who would have been, otherwise, off duty for the day, were disposed about the Park, in case their services should be required, but not the slightest interference in the subsequent proceedings took place.

"Presently, two immense rings were formed, and a man of serious aspect, with a profusion of hair about his face, made his way to one of the spaces thus made, and addressed the people. He said he was a hard-working man; that it was no vain desire for popularity that had induced him to leave his large family on the Sabbath for the purpose of meeting his fellows in Hyde Park; it was because he believed he had it in his power to help his fellow-countrymen to a right understanding of the purpose for which they had assembled together. After two of the most plenteous harvests that ever blessed the earth, bread was at famine prices. The war was set forth as the cause of this. There was plenty of corn in Turkey, which could be imported at 20s. a quarter, and yet Russian corn at 73s. a quarter was permitted to be brought over. The speaker, who was said to be an eloquent carpenter, had proceeded in this strain for upwards of an hour, when a counter-agitation seemed to be rising within twenty yards of the crowd which had gathered around him.

"A baker by trade was endeavouring to defend the corn-factors and landed proprietors, against whom his opponent had been inveighing; but the mob was in no humour to listen to the 'other side,' and a cry of 'Out with him' having been raised, the baker was pushed and dragged, and carried off in the direction of the Marble Arch. Two or three gentlemen interfered to defend the unfortunate man from the usage to which his boldness had subjected him; but he did not escape even then, and he would, undoubtedly, have received some rough treatment, had not a body of police appeared to the rescue. The inspector on duty at that spot evidently saw an admirable chance of giving a favourable turn to the events of the day. Eight officers, surrounding the baker, trotted off with him at a smart pace, followed by an immense number of persons, among whom were those who appeared to be most bent on mischief; they ran on, following the baker and his guard towards Apsley House and outside the Park. Returning to the carpenter, whose audience had been considerably thinned, he was found to be still holding forth; he continued to speak and to declaim against 'the powers that be,' until dusk, when he brought his harangue to a close."

On the next Sunday, Oct. 21st, another meeting took place in the Park, upon the same subject, when the same speaker congratulated his audience on again exercising their now recognized privilege of meeting in "their own Park." Of course he wandered from his subject, and became violently political. "He also propounded a plan of attaching the police to the cause of the working classes, by appealing to them, as men and brothers, through the intervention of tracts, adding that every citizen should be a soldier, and every man a voter. He was winding up in a magniloquent peroration, when a diversion in his immediate neighbourhood attracted the attention of the greater portion of his audience towards a new object. This was an unfortunate young man dressed in livery, apparently an officer's servant, whom a great crowd was chasing, hooting, and pelting with turf. What umbrage he had given them—whether it was his connection with a wealthy or an aristocratic master, as indicated by his dress, or what else, it was difficult to ascertain. Some said he had been circulating a tract among the crowd which was obnoxious to them; others, that he was the servant of a nobleman equally obnoxious; but be that as it may, he was followed and pelted without mercy for a considerable distance. Being hotly pressed, he took refuge behind a tree, but this availed him little, and he started afresh, but only to be subjected to renewed ill-treatment. At last he took to his heels, contrived to elude or outstrip his tormentors, and to get beyond their reach.

"This incident over, the idler and more wanton part of the crowd amused themselves by throwing tufts of grass and other missiles at a number of police who had returned in front of the magazine guard-house, from protecting the unfortunate footman. This continued for some little time, and, at one time, looked threatening; but the policemen, who showed the greatest forbearance under the annoyance, contrived to separate, and the delinquents gradually became tired of the fun. Proceeding, after this, in the direction of the Marble Arch, to a spot where a crowd had collected, we found another orator holding forth in a style of rude eloquence, which, both in its matter and manner, was not without its attractions to many. He was relating the history of the appropriation of land in this country, and, at the point when we came within reach of his voice, he was telling how William the Conqueror parcelled out the English territory among his followers. Another philanthropist, with a brown-paper parcel under his arm, and somewhat advanced in life, was advocating, in another part of the Park, the system of Communism as a panacea for the high price of food and almost every other evil."

Of the next meeting *The Times* of October 29, 1855, says, " Yesterday (Sunday) another unseemly assemblage of persons congregated in Hyde Park, partly under the auspices, and at the bidding of a small knot of individuals who, under the pretext of agitating for cheap bread, really seek to disseminate political doctrines, which the people of this country, including almost every class of them, have long since, and over and over again, refused to endorse, and who, for the last few weeks, have converted a place to which thousands of the inhabitants of this metropolis, of all ranks, were accustomed to resort for agreeable and healthy recreation, into the rendezvous of a mob. It is however, satisfactory to be able to add, on the assurance of those persons themselves, given yesterday, and in the course of the week, that this is to be the last of the gatherings, as far as they are concerned." The mob wound up their day's amusement by smashing windows at the West End, the value of the glass broken in Curzon Street alone being over £150.

Of course, the promise that the meeting of 28th

October was to be the last was not kept, and another, and, if possible, more disgraceful riot took place on Sunday, November 4. Commenting upon it, *The Times* of next day observes:—

"Yesterday, from about 3 o'clock in the afternoon, till about nightfall, Hyde Park was the scene of one continual riot, of a disgraceful and intolerable description; and not the less so, perhaps, because it was not accompanied by any serious injury to property, nor any loss of life—results with which the mind is apt to connect great popular tumults—though in many instances it was attended with the commission of personal violence on a number of unoffending persons. It is a naked, incontrovertible fact, let it bear what interpretation it may, and with whomsoever the blame may rest, that a place set apart for the recreation of the people of all ranks and classes, without distinction, was, yesterday (a Sunday), almost wholly surrendered to a lawless, ruffianly mob, without anything like an organized attempt to suppress the tumult to which they gave themselves up, or to prevent the violence they were ever ready to inflict, although some creditable, but isolated, and not always successful efforts were certainly made by individual members of the police force, at the inevitable risk of great violence to themselves, to secure the most conspicuous of the ringleaders.

"And who were the persons, and what was their character, by whom this reckless and unprovoked attack was made to disturb the public peace? No section of the middle—still less of the upper class of inhabitants; none of the community of artisans; nobody having a just, or well-defined grievance

High Price of Food Riots, 1855.

to complain of—none even, perhaps, of the parties by whom these Sunday gatherings were originally convened; but a pack of contemptible boys and lads, including a large proportion of vagabonds and ruffians of all kinds and degrees, with which this metropolis abounds, some thousands strong in the aggregate, who had collected there for no other purpose than that of the most wanton mischief, and from no other but the most insensate motives."

There was the same rioting next Sunday (11th November), only this time some arrests were made. One man got a month's imprisonment for obstructing the police, another two months for assaulting two policemen, a boy had fourteen days for disorderly conduct, and a man was fined £3 1s. for distributing handbills.

Sunday, 18th November, was the last of these series of riots, and on this occasion there were plenty of police—some 700 or 800, and they seem to have been better handled than usual. "Towards 4 o'clock a rush was made in the direction of the bridge at the east end of the Serpentine, and the crowd followed in considerable numbers, as did also a portion of the police. Crossing the bridge at a run, the crowd—chiefly boys—made for the Albert Gate, for a purpose, probably, which had better be imagined than stated in terms; but there they were received by two mounted inspectors and a company of policemen on foot, who guarded the outlet, and effectually prevented their escaping into the adjacent streets. The youngsters, thus foiled, stood for some time in a body in front of the residence of the French ambassador, and eventually dispersed, some returning into the Park. This incident had the effect of thinning the crowd considerably in the middle of the enclosure, but night had set in before those who lingered there could be persuaded to depart. Captain Labalmondière kept moving his patrols through and through the crowd in every direction, without any very perceptible effect in lessening their number. At length the police completely tired them down, and the people slowly retreated into the streets, without, so far as we could ascertain, doing any damage."

CHAPTER XVII.

Sympathy with Italy, 1859—Garibaldi riots, 1862—Reform League Meeting, 23rd July, 1866—Police proclamation against it—Attempt to hold it—Hyde Park railings destroyed.

THERE were no more meetings in the Park for a long time, but there was one on Sunday, 8th May, 1859, to propose an address to the Emperor Napoleon, sympathizing with the Emperor in the course he had taken with respect to the war in Italy.

This meeting passed off quietly, which was a great deal more than another did, which took place on Sunday, 28th September, 1862. This was, presumably, to express sympathy with General Garibaldi, and to protest against the French occupation of Rome. It was numerously attended, and especially by large numbers of Irish labourers, whose hatred of Garibaldi excited their fighting blood to such an extent that a serious riot ensued, which a violent downpour of rain helped to stop. Several arrests were made, and the prisoners duly fined.

But this was mild to what occurred the next Sunday, 5th October. The Irish had had time to brood over it, and although " The Working Men's Garibaldian Fund" had not convened any meeting, it was generally understood that something would take place. By half-past four there must have been some 80 or 90,000 people present, and to hold them in order there were but about 400 police, who were ordered not to interrupt any speaker, nor, if possible to avoid it, to ascend the mound of earth, or rubbish, which had been chosen by the speakers as the platform from which to address the meeting. The following is *The Times* (Oct. 6) account of what occurred:—

"It appears that the possession of this mound of rubbish was the great object of contention between the rival supporters of Garibaldi and the Pope on Sunday week, and so it was yesterday. It appears to have been first occupied by a mixed body of people, but, owing to an aggressive movement of Irish labourers, it was soon held exclusively by the champions of the Papacy. The Garibaldians submitted reluctantly to this state of things for a short time, and, when two or three soldiers appeared, belonging to the Foot Guards, a cry was raised for 'Garibaldi,' and some dozen or so men attempted to regain a footing upon the mound.

"This was the signal for a fearful conflict. It became apparent, in a moment, that almost every Irishman had a stick or bludgeon in his possession, and with these they struck about them right and left, crushing hats and breaking heads with relentless brutality. The Garibaldians struck back in return, some with sticks, and some without, and, for some ten minutes, the struggle was sufficiently fierce to awaken fears among the spectators that loss of life would ensue. One stalwart Irishman laid about him with a heavy-looking stick four feet long and two inches in diameter, and another with a roughly squared piece of wood, equally long and equally strong, and with sharp edges, until both were disarmed by the Garibaldians, without the intervention of the police.

"At the end of this struggle the Irish remained masters of the 'Redan,' as it was termed ; but suddenly there came up about a dozen soldiers—Coldstreams and Grenadiers—who shouted for Garibaldi, and charged up the mound with desperate gallantry. Twice they charged in vain, but the third charge was successful. Up they went, amid loud cheers, and cries of 'Go it, brave Guards,' and followed by some 200 people. The front ranks of the Irish gave way; then there was another fierce struggle with sticks and fists on the summit of the mound, and then the Irish were kept off to a man, leaving the position in the hands of the Guards and the Garibaldians. Suddenly some sticks and stones were thrown at them from below, and the Guards plunged down to punish the aggressors. Away went the Irish, away went the Guards in pursuit, and, in a minute, a dense disorderly mass of 5000 or 6000 people was flying across the Park, spreading fear and confusion around them.

"Like a herd of infuriated oxen, they rushed onward, carrying all before them, till it seemed to occur to them that they were running for nothing, and then they returned to the mound. This occurred again and again, women being sometimes thrown down and trampled upon, and men compelled to turn and fly, till the wonder was that serious injuries were not inflicted upon many. Then, at short intervals, whenever the police fixed their eyes on some prominent aggressor, they made a plunge into the heaving mass, and resolutely brought out their man, generally, but not always, succeeded in conveying him away in safe custody. It is impossible to overrate the cool manner in which they set to work. Three or four officers would thrust themselves fearlessly into a mob of 200 or 300 infuriated men, collar one, cling to him, and hold him, despite the attempts made to favour his escape, never drawing a staff, nor striking a blow but holding their man by the bare assertion of the authority of the law, and this not for a brief period, but during the course of several hours.

" The Guards and the Garibaldians having firmly established their supremacy, quiet reigned, at one time for about a quarter of an hour; and, taking advantage of this interval of rest, a working man, came forward, who, in a brief speech, denounced the Emperor of the French as the would-be Dictator of Europe, and the enemy of Italy, the opponent of liberty everywhere, and, above all, the hater of liberty in England. In conclusion he called for three cheers for Garibaldi, which were lustily given, and, when he asked all those who sympathized with Garibaldi to hold up their hands, a forest of dirty hands were extended.

" Then another speaker followed, who, with great common sense, said, ' Enough has been done. It had been made plain to the world that the feeling of the people of London was in favour of the great patriot, Garibaldi; and with that assurance, they might settle down without any more speeches.' This speaker had hardly concluded when the tumult was renewed, the mound being lost and won several times, and the rushes through the Park followed close upon each other; while conflicts with sticks and stones were both frequent and severe. Knives were drawn several times, and one formidable weapon, apparently a shoemaker's knife, with a wooden handle, and a blade nine inches long, was taken from a man, who said he found it lying on the grass after one of the tumultuous rushes. This was delivered up to Sergeant Savage, who forthwith shivered the blade to fragments.

"During one of the assaults upon the mound, a corporal in the Coldstreams had his bayonet snatched from its sheath, and later in the afternoon when it was recovered, the Irishman who had taken it was soundly thrashed, and threatened with a ducking in the Serpentine, towards which he was carried by several soldiers, who, however, yielded to the persuasion of others, and permitted him to go at large.

"At half-past five, two strong pickets, one of Grenadiers, and one of the Fusileers, marched into the Park, for the purpose of carrying off the men belonging to their respective battalions. They marched straight to the mound, and, just as they ascended it, a soldier received a terrific blow on the head from a thick club, wielded by an Irishman. The blood ran down the face of the soldier, who was led away in a fainting condition, his dastardly assailant escaping by plunging into a mass of his sympathizing countrymen. After this, the pickets cleared the mound, of which they held possession till a body of police approached, half an hour later, when the military power yielded to the civil. From that time the police held the mound, and, although there was a great deal of disorderly and tumultuous rushing to and fro, with an occasional scuffle, and wholesale destruction of hats, the fear of any very serious outbreak was passed. The people had begun to disperse at five o'clock, when a few drops of rain fell, and gradually thinned afterwards. But a fine moonlight night was the means of prolonging the demonstration; at seven o'clock, there were still some thousands of people remaining on the ground, and it was late before the Park was restored to its usual peaceful aspect."

During the next week a strong body of men were engaged in levelling the objectionable mounds, the Guards were forbidden to enter the Park on the following Sunday, and a notice was issued by the Commissioner of Police :—

"WHEREAS numbers of persons have been in the habit of assembling and holding meetings on Sundays in Hyde Park, and the other parks in the metropolis, for the purpose of delivering and hearing speeches, and for the public discussion of popular and exciting topics; and, whereas such meetings are inconsistent with the purposes for which the parks are thrown open to, and used by the public; and the excitement occasioned by such discussions at such meetings has frequently led to tumults and disorder, so as to endanger the public peace; and on last Sunday and the Sunday before, large numbers assembled in Hyde Park, for the purposes aforesaid, and, when so assembled, conducted themselves in a disorderly and riotous manner, so as to endanger the public peace; and, by the use of sticks, and throwing stones and other missiles, committed many violent assaults upon persons quietly passing along the Park, and interrupted the thoroughfares; and, whereas it is necessary to prevent such illegal proceedings in future:

"Notice is hereby given, that no such meeting, or assemblage of persons, for any of the purposes aforesaid, will be allowed, hereafter, to take place in any of the parks in the metropolis; and all well-disposed persons are hereby cautioned and requested to abstain from joining, or attending any such meeting or assemblage.

"And notice is further given, that all necessary measures will be adopted to prevent any such meeting, or assemblage, and effectually to preserve the public peace, and to suppress any attempt at the disturbance thereof.

"RICHARD MAYNE,
"The Commissioner of Police of the Metropolis.
"October 9."

The appearance of about 800 policemen in the Park, and a pitiless rain in the afternoon of the 12th October, probably prevented a repetition of the scene of the 5th, as a sufficient number of suspicious characters were there, but did not stop long. There was an attempt, in Ireland, to get up a subscription for the injured Irish, but I cannot find that it met with any success.

For three or four years the Park was not troubled with noisy demagogues, until there arose an association called "The Reform League," of whom a Mr. Edmond Beales, a barrister, was a prime mover. This association gave out publicly that they would hold a meeting in Hyde Park on

Monday, July 23rd, 1866, and Sir Richard Mayne, in consequence, issued the following notice on July 17th :—

" WHEREAS information has been received, and it has been publicly announced in various printed notices, that it is the intention of certain persons to assemble in the open air at several places in various parts of the metropolis on the evening of Monday, July 23rd, and to walk from thence through the streets in procession, with banners, and preceded by bands of music, to Hyde Park, to hold a meeting there for the purposes of political demonstration and discussion :

" And, whereas such a meeting, being inconsistent with the purposes for which the Park is thrown open to, and used by the public, is illegal, and cannot be permitted, and such an assemblage there of large numbers of persons is calculated to lead to riotous and disorderly conduct, and to endanger the public peace :

" And, whereas it is necessary to prevent such proceedings, and to preserve the public peace : notice is hereby given that NO such MEETING, or ASSEMBLAGE of persons in large numbers will be allowed to TAKE PLACE in Hyde Park, and all well-disposed persons are hereby cautioned and requested to abstain from joining, or attending any such meeting, or assemblage ; and notice is further given, that all necessary measures will be adopted to prevent any such meeting, or assemblage, and effectually to preserve the public peace, and to suppress any attempt at the disturbance thereof."

A copy of this notice was sent by the Commissioner to Mr. Beales, with a request that he would exert his influence to prevent any attempt to hold the meeting. This, in his reply to Sir Richard Mayne, Mr. Beales declined to do, unless he could be shown by what statute, or law, or principle of law, the Commissioner was acting in declaring the meeting illegal: and he went on to say, "The Park is either the property of the nation, as there are strong reasons for contending it is, under the transactions which have taken place between the Crown and the people, through Parliament, respecting it; or it is still Crown property, though kept up and maintained out of the public purse. If the former be the fact, where is your authority for excluding the public from their own property? If the latter be the case, then show me that you are acting under the express authority of the Crown, as claiming to be the exclusive owner of the Park."

An attempt was made to carry out the meeting, and the following is a portion of *The Times* account of it. "Meanwhile vast crowds had collected in the neighbourhood of Hyde Park. A force of foot and mounted police, numbering 1600, or 1800, were assembled under the direction of Sir Richard Mayne and Captain Harris, and at 5 o'clock the gates were closed. Before that hour a considerable number of people had collected inside, in order to witness what was about to take place, and these were permitted to remain there. Outside, the throng was, as might be supposed, much greater. Masses of people had assembled at all the approaches. The Marble Arch was the centre of attraction, and for an hour or two previous to the proposed commencement of the demonstration, traffic was seriously impeded. The windows and balconies of the neighbouring houses were also crowded with spectators.

"Shortly after 7 o'clock Mr. Edmond Beales, Lieut. Col. Dickson, and other leading members of the Reform League, in a line of cabs which headed the Clerkenwell, Islington and other processions, advanced to the Arch; and, the sub-committee having succeeded in making a clear passage, Mr. Beales and his friends went up to the police, who were drawn up in line, staves in hand, some of them being mounted. The crowd immediately closed in, and endeavoured, by an 'ugly rush,' to effect admission. The police used their staves freely to defeat this attempt; and, it is stated that both Mr. Beales and Col. Dickson were struck in the scuffle. At any rate, after having been refused admission, and having raised the question in the form they desired, they went back to their vehicles, and, with some difficulty, managed to make their way through the crowd, in order to proceed to Trafalgar Square, there to hold the meeting, according to the programme which had been laid down.

"Printed bills were distributed among the various detachments as they came up from Clerkenwell, Southwark, Finsbury, etc., directing them not to attempt to force an entrance into the Park, but to proceed to Trafalgar Square. It is much easier, however, to collect throngs of people, than to keep them in leading-strings when collected; and a large portion of the 'masses' were not disposed to follow implicitly the instructions of their leaders. The gates, it is true, were strongly fortified, but to throw down the railings seemed a feasible undertaking, and this was promptly attempted. The police, indeed, hastened to every point that was attacked, and, for a short time, kept the multitude at bay; but their numbers were utterly insufficient to guard so long a line of frontier, and breach after breach was made, the stonework, together with the railings, yielding easily to the pressure of the crowd. The first opening was made in the Bayswater Road, where the police, rushing to the spot, prevented, for a time, any considerable influx of people; but they could not be ubiquitous, and along Park Lane especially a great extent of railing was speedily overturned, till in the end the crowd entered *ad libitum.*

"A good deal of scuffling attended these incursions. The police brought their truncheons into active use, and a number of the roughs were somewhat severely handled. One man, who was stated to be a mechanic, named Field, received serious injury on the head, and was carried off insensible to St. George's Hospital. It is said that he had just thrown a brickbat at a policeman. A man named Tyler, living at New Road, Chelsea, also received blows on the head, and was taken to the hospital, as were, likewise, others, whose injuries were of a less serious character. The police, on the other hand, did not come off unscathed. One of them, named Penny, received a thrust in the side from an iron bar; another was knocked off his horse by sticks and stones, and several others sustained slight injuries. Stones were thrown at Sir Richard Mayne, who, as well as his men, was much hooted. Between forty and fifty persons were taken into custody in the vicinity of the Marble Arch, and about as many more at the other approaches. Many of the leaders of the crowd exerted themselves to prevent a breach of the peace, and Mr. Bradlaugh got considerably hustled for so doing, falling under the suspicion of being a Government spy.

"About eight o'clock, a company of the Grenadier Guards, and a troop of the Life Guards, entered the Park, but it was then too late to prevent the influx of people; for though the gates were still jealously guarded, breaches had been effected in every direction in the palings, and the military, who were loudly cheered by the crowd, confined themselves to manœuvres, the only effect of which was to oblige the mob occasionally to shift their position. The numbers in the park were, by this time, very large; and although, of course, there were a considerable number of 'roughs,' who look on the police as their natural enemies, many of the persons present appeared to be quiet and respectably-dressed people who had simply been attracted by curiosity, and showed no uproarious, nor even any political proclivities. Speeches were made at various spots, one of the orators being a Miss Harriet Laws, who delivered a very fervid address on the political and social rights of the people."

The Times of next day (July 25th) says:—

"Yesterday morning Hyde Park presented, along its eastern extremity, a pitiable spectacle. Between the Marble Arch and Grosvenor Gate the railings were entirely demolished, and the flower-beds were ruined. Between the Grosvenor and Stanhope Gates, moreover, not a railing remained erect, those not actually levelled being forced considerably out of the perpendicular. This had been done out of mere wantoness, after ingress had been effected at other points, as was evident from the fact of the flowers and shrubs having escaped damage. On the north and south sides of the Park much damage had also been done, the railings having been overturned in numerous places. In many cases the masonry had given way, and was still attached to the ironwork, while in others the rails had been forced from their sockets; and one could not but reflect what appalling results might have ensued had the mob used them as weapons. The trees and shrubs were greatly injured, and, in fact, the appearance of the north-western portion of the Park was as if it had been overrun by an invading army. Waggons were engaged, yesterday, in removing the broken railings and shattered masonry, and a considerable sum will, certainly, be required to restore the Park to its original condition."

CHAPTER XVIII.

Reform League Meeting of 25th July, 1866—Burning a tree—Stone-throwing—Temporizing policy of the Government—Special constables sworn in—Meeting abandoned—Return of police injured—Meeting of "Working Men's Rights Association," 1867—Reform League Meeting of 6th May, 1867—Police warning—Legal opinions—Meeting held—Meeting on 5th August, 1867.

But the London rough had tasted blood, and as a Reform Meeting was to be held in the Park on 25th, they gathered there in force. How the Park looked may be judged from the following, in *The Times* of July 26th :—

"The gathering in Hyde Park yesterday was, on the whole, probably of a more respectable and orderly character than on the previous day. It was generally believed that the rioting would diminish, if not entirely cease, and that the Government would adopt such precautions as would be likely to conduce to that result. The Park was, consequently, visited by large numbers of persons desirous of viewing the havoc which had been committed by the mob. During the morning, however, and the earlier portion of the afternoon, the roughs congregated largely, and spread themselves over the Park in search of amusement. For some time, this amusement appeared to be derivable only from an increase of the general destruction. The plantations especially have suffered severely from the hands of a ruthless mob, who appear, for the most part, to comprise the lowest scum of the London population. Shrubs and saplings have been broken near the ground, or forcibly torn out by the roots; and, in several instances, where the young trees were able to defy the strength of the attacks, the bark has been pealed off in every direction. This state of things is especially perceivable on the side of the Park facing the Bayswater Road; and from the Marble Arch for some little way down the Park Lane side, damage of a similar nature, but much less extensive, has been committed. Below Grosvenor Gate, however, the flower-beds remain untouched, the people, in entering the Park on Monday night, having seemingly avoided them. The railings lie in all directions, mingled with broken stones; for, as a rule, the wall itself seems to have given way, the railings, in many instances, though overthrown, still being connected for yards.

"In the Park itself, however, the damage, though not so great, is even more apparent. Many of the young trees have been broken off close to the ground, while branches have been wrenched off in all directions. Some little distance from the Marble Arch stands, or rather stood till yesterday morning, one of those venerable trunks, covered with foliage, which always invest the spots where they are to be found with an air of picturesqueness and wild beauty. But this tree has now shared in the general fate. After the mob had run riot over the plantations, the dryness and age of the trunk presented a temptation which it was evidently impossible for them to resist. They gathered together as much dry wood as they could find, and placed it at the foot of the tree, setting light to the pile. Dry as tinder, it was soon on fire, and throughout the day and night the smouldering tree afforded continual amusement. The police would not—at all events, did not—interfere, but two or three of the park-keepers were attracted to the spot by the crowd and the smoke. The roughs, however, were masters of the situation, and the keepers were consequently informed that if they remained long in the neighbourhood they would stand a good chance of being roasted. The fellows looked as if they would not require much provocation to induce them to fulfil their threat; and the keepers, fully believing discretion to be the better part of valour, at once beat a retreat.

"Even a burning tree, however rare as the sight is, will fail after a time to satisfy a London mob's craving for mischief, and the fellows soon began to exert themselves in other ways. They attempted to fire some more trees, but without success, and then returned to the old trunk, where they occasionally diversified the proceedings by an exhilarating *mêlée* with brickbats, stones, and pieces of burning wood. It was soon found that on being struck by a stick, the burning trunk would send forth showers of sparks, and the young trees in the neighbourhood were denuded of their branches, and in some instances broken off bodily for service in this way. But something still more exciting was needed, and it was soon determined in what quarter this might be obtained. The roughs then seized possession of the gates at the Marble Arch, and closed them, after which they commenced stoning the riders and the carriages passing along the drive in the Park, extending their favours in some instances to the more respectably dressed pedestrians and lookers on. These excesses rendered the interference of the police indispensable, and, accordingly, a strong reinforcement soon arrived. A fight, of course, ensued, in which stones formed the favourite weapons of the one side, and truncheons of the other. Several men were captured and confined in the Arch, until about five o'clock, when they were removed in cabs to the police-station.

"From five o'clock, the crowd increased considerably, but the fresh arrivals comprised a large proportion of respectable working men, who appeared, for the most part, to be actuated only by curiosity. Some short time afterwards, Mr. Beales and some of his friends came into the park. Mr. Beales was, of course, immediately surrounded by an admiring multitude, and for the rest of the evening was the centre of attraction. Wherever he went, he moved, so to speak, in crowds. A rumour had for some time prevailed to the effect that the police were to be withdrawn, and this rumour was now developed into a certainty. Mr. Beales informed the people that his visit to Mr. Walpole had resulted in that gentleman's promising that the right of public meeting in the Park should be legally tested at as early a moment as possible. Mr. Walpole had agreed to permit the holding of a meeting in the Park on Monday next,[1] and, in the meanwhile, it was expected that the Reformers should abstain from any proceedings, the Govern-

[1] This Mr. Walpole denied in a letter to *The Times*, July 26th.

ment having undertaken not to make any demonstration of police or military force. One of the leading reformers now arrived with a paste-pot and bills; and soon the various gates of the Park were covered with the following official announcement:—

"THE REFORM LEAGUE AND THE GOVERNMENT.

"The Government, by the Right Hon. Spencer Walpole, the Home Secretary, have this day agreed with the Council of the Reform League, to facilitate in every way their obtaining a speedy decision, either in Parliament or a court of law, as to the right of the people to hold public meetings in the parks, and it is earnestly requested that in the meantime, and until the question is decided, no further attempt be made to hold a meeting in Hyde Park, except, only, on next Monday afternoon, July 30th, at 6 o'clock, by arrangement with the Government. And it is further earnestly requested that all will abstain from disorderly acts, and do everything in their power to preserve the peace, and protect property, the Government undertaking, on their part, not to make any further demonstration of the military or police.

"EDMOND BEALES, President."

This had the desired effect. Several speeches were made, the mob was congratulated on its "great and glorious victory," and, in spite of the bitter feeling against the police, there was no further rioting; but the truth of the placard just given was denied by the Government, vide *Times*, July 26th, 1866.

"A placard having been extensively circulated on behalf of the Reform League to the effect that, in consequence of an agreement with the Government, every facility would be given to try the legal question of the right of the public to free admission to the parks for any purpose, no further attempt would be made to hold a meeting in Hyde Park, except only on next Monday afternoon ; and such placard leading to the inference that the consent of the Government had been given to such meeting, we are authorized to state that no such consent has been given: and that on an application from the leaders of the League to be allowed to hold such meeting, by permission of the Crown, they were asked by the Secretary of State for the Home Department to prefer their request in writing, that they might receive a written reply."

The Home Secretary in Parliament (26th July) said that, "In the meantime it is impossible for her Majesty's Government to sanction that which they believe to be a violation of the law. It is added that if they desire to hold an open-air meeting, no objection will be raised to their meeting, as on former occasions, on Primrose Hill, but a meeting in any of the Royal Parks will not be sanctioned. . . . If, after the warning which has been given, after the voluntary offer to permit a meeting upon Primrose Hill, they persist in what we believe to be a violation of the law, they must be held responsible for all the consequences which must follow from such a reckless course of procedure."

Special constables were sworn in, the railings were removed and carted away, and a strong hoarding about ten or eleven feet high erected in their place. The projected meeting for 30th July was abandoned, and the Park was once more given up to the recreation and amusement of the people.

Many arrests had been made, especially for throwing stones at the police, and punishment was duly meted out. Many people were taken to the hospitals, and there treated for injuries inflicted on them by the mob and the police, the latter of whom, however, had suffered severely, vide the following return (*Times*, Aug. 2nd, 1866) :—

" Return of the number of each rank of Police injured during the meetings in Hyde Park, on Monday, Tuesday and Wednesday, the 23rd, 24th and 25th July :—

"*Rendered unfit for duty.*—Superintendent, 1; inspectors, 2; police sergeants, 9; police constables, 33; total, 45.

" *Slightly injured.*—Superintendents, 10 ; inspectors, 18; police sergeants, 23 ; police constables, 170; total, 221.

" The Commissioner was struck several times by stones thrown at him ; he received a severe contusion on the side of the head, and a cut on the temple, which blackened his eye. Each of the assistant Commissioners was struck several times by stones thrown at them."

Mr. Beales was, not long after, made a County Court Judge.

On 19th April, 1867, there was a meeting, convened by the "Working Men's Rights Association," held in Hyde Park, for the purpose of denouncing the Government Reform Bill, and to express their opinion "That the Parks are the People's, and we hereby claim the right to the use of them for the purpose of discussing our political wrongs." They had a red flag, surmounted by a Cap of Liberty, but, as they were quiet, the police did not interfere with their proceedings, although there was a reserve of mounted and foot police at the Magazine, to act in case their services were required.

On 17th April, 1867, it was resolved, at a meeting of the Council and delegates of the various branches of the Reform League, "That a demonstration of the Reformers of London be held in Hyde Park at 6 o'clock in the evening of Monday, the 6th of May." This provoked much comment from the inhabitants of the neighbourhood, and from those who looked upon the Park as a place of recreation and innocent enjoyment ; and on 1st May Mr. Walpole issued the following proclamation :—

" WHEREAS it has been publicly announced that a meeting will be held in Hyde Park on Monday, the 6th of May, for the purpose of political discussion ; AND WHEREAS the use of the park for the purpose of holding such meeting is not permitted, and interferes with the object for which her Majesty has been pleased to open the Park for the general enjoyment of her people : Now all persons are hereby warned and admonished to abstain from attending, aiding, or taking part in any such meeting, or from entering the park with a view to attend, aid, or take part in such meeting."

This was received with ridicule by some of the meeting, and Col. Dickson elegantly pointed out that it was a very milk-and-watery affair, and showed that there was some " funking" in official quarters ; and Mr. Bradlaugh moved a resolution which, somewhat altered in words, was carried unanimously : "That this meeting, denying the right of S. H. Walpole, or any other person in this realm, to issue such a proclamation, and, regarding the parks as places open for the purpose of holding public meetings, which are the right of all Englishmen, reply to the proclamation, that they intend holding the meeting of Monday, and that the consequences of endeavouring to prevent it must rest with those who are wicked enough to take this course."

Men's minds were much exercised as to this meeting. Petitions, signed by upwards of 16,000 persons in the metropolis against the proposed demonstration in the Park, were presented to Mr. Walpole; and the question of the law on the subject was authoritatively laid down; which was, that in November, 1856, the law advisers of the Crown—Sir Alexander Cockburn, Sir Richard Bethell, and Mr. (afterwards Justice) Willes—signed an opinion to the effect that there is a right to close the gates and exclude the public : or, the gates being open, to exclude persons; but that persons who have once entered, cannot be turned out without notice that the license is withdrawn.

In July, 1866, this opinion was submitted to Sir William Bovill and Sir Hugh (afterwards Earl) Cairns, who were particularly requested to say whether there was any legal authority to disperse by force any meeting for political purposes in the Park.

Their answer was, that there is no such authority for any practical purpose.

They stated that when persons had once entered the Park, they could only be ejected after notice being served on, or brought home to each individually. Publication, they said, is not enough, for many cannot, and many would not read, and an express warning must be shown. They particularly impressed that the right of removal is a separate right against each individual who has had notice. No force, therefore, can be brought to bear against bodies, or masses, which may contain many who have not had notice. They also said that it would not be practicable to remove any number, individually, and prevent them from returning, and remarked on the probability of disorder, if even an individual were turned out. The effect, consequently, was that the Government had nothing but the common law of trespass to rely upon.

The Government, however, relied upon the strong arm; and on May 6th special constables were sworn in in different parts of London, whilst the several police magistrates were in attendance at their Courts for a like purpose. The public were officially warned that a force of over 5000 mounted and foot police would be in the Park, as well as Sir Thomas Henry, the Chief Magistrate, upon whose word would rest the employment of troops, who were, for that day, confined to barracks, in order to be in readiness at a moment's notice. But the futility of guarding the railings and hoardings of the whole Park was so forcible that it was determined not to attempt to keep anybody out; and, at the last moment, it was decided to permit the demonstration, and not to interfere with it, so long as the peace was preserved.

Well, the day came, and so did the people, in their thousands, until it was reckoned that there were about 30,000 present; and soon after six the speechifying began. And when that was over, the people dispersed without the slightest disturbance worth mentioning, or without more than a dozen policemen being, at any one time, seen upon the ground. *The Times* of May 7th thus winds up its account of the meeting :

" At a little before 8 o'clock most of the meetings began to disperse, and the crowd to quit the Park, in a quiet and orderly manner. In some cases, where the stations were quitted early, speakers not named in the programme took the places of the official orators, and held forth for a time; but the interest had died away, and none could retain their audiences long, even where, in one case, the speaker was a lady, and declaimed, with singular vehemence, about the rights of women. As the crowd from one of the stations was leaving, one of the reformers seized a pickpocket, who had taken a gentleman's watch, and who succeeded in passing it away to a confederate, in an instant. Others of the same gang made an effort to rescue the prisoner; but, with the aid of some detectives, who instantly came up, he was forced along in the direction of the police barracks. Thither an immense crowd followed, which, passing in through the narrow, funnel-shaped entrance, between walls, made, for a time, a crowd so dense, that it seemed as if some lamentable result would ensue. Yet the reformer and the detectives stuck to their prisoner, and the great mass of the concourse around them most earnestly cheered them in their endeavour to secure him. When at length he was forced through the pressure of the mass into the station, great cheers and clapping of hands arose on all sides at the success of the capture, and those who at first had attempted to rescue the prisoner at once slunk away. After this nothing worth notice occurred. Only five prisoners were apprehended, three for picking pockets, and two for gambling.

" At ten o'clock the police and military were withdrawn; at eleven the Park was quite clear, and all the streets adjoining even emptier than usual. No accident of any kind took place, as far as the police were able to ascertain."

The Reform League had not done with Hyde Park yet awhile. On July 31, 1867, it issued the following poster and handbill:—" REFORM LEAGUE. 'To your tents, Oh! Israel.'—A monster meeting of the working men and other inhabitants of the metropolis will be held in Hyde Park, on Monday evening next, August 5th, at 7 o'clock, under the presidency of the Reform League, to express the public indignation at the Parks Prohibition Bill, attempted to be passed through an expiring and self-condemned Parliament, by the enemies of all popular rights; and also to protest against the attempt of the House of Lords to rob the lodger of his franchise."

The meeting duly took place, and passed away without event. The League was on its last legs. As *The Times* observed,—" Yesterday, however, the League put forth its strength for a final effort, but sad to say, it failed egregiously. It made a grand effort of despair, but it lacked the strengthening impulse which that feeling ordinarily instils. A dull, lethargic passiveness pervaded every movement of the demonstration."

CHAPTER XIX.

Demonstrations against the Irish Church, 1868—In favour of Fenians, 1869—Regulations made by Commissioners of Works—Fenian Demonstration, 1872—A speaker sentenced —Meeting about the Eastern Question, 1878—Fight— Preaching in the Park—Modern instances—May-Day and May 6, 1894—Against the House of Lords, Aug. 26, 1894.

On Sunday, July 19, 1868, there was a demonstration in the Park against the Irish Church: then there was one in favour of the Fenians in Oct., 1869. But it is not worth chronicling all the meetings that have taken place since the time when the Commissioners of Works settled upon the place of public meetings, and the routine necessary before they were held.

Times, Oct. 15, 1872: "The Commissioners of Works have caused to be erected in Hyde Park, at exactly 150 yards distance from the so-called 'Reformers' Tree,'[1] a granite pedestal and iron standard, surmounted by a board, to mark the spot where it shall be lawful (and there only) to hold public meetings, and inscribed with the following announcement: 'The Notice Board respecting Public Addresses.— No public address may be delivered except within 40 yards of the notice board on which this rule is inscribed.' The rule is to the following effect, and in addition, posted at all the entrances to the Park:

[1] So called because it was there that the Reform League used to hold their meetings.

'No public address may be delivered unless a written notice of the intention to deliver the same, signed with the names and addresses of two householders residing in the metropolis, be left at the offices of Her Majesty's Works and Public Buildings, at least two clear days before: such notice must state the day and hour of intended delivery. After such notice has been received, no other notice for the delivery of an address on the same day will be valid.'"

Because the concession had been made, of course it was forthwith to be set at nought—by a Fenian Demonstration. The following is the commencement of an account of the meeting in *The Standard* of Nov. 4, 1872.

"The late Mr. O'Connell was in the habit of boasting that he could drive a coach-and-four through an Act of Parliament. The sympathizers with political discontent, or disturbance rather, in London, transcended the rhetorical flourish of *the agitator, par excellence,* yesterday. They had been bragging at Convention for some time past that they would hold a meeting in Hyde Park, 'the people's Park,' in the teeth of Mr. Ayrton and the Parks Regulation Bill,[1] and yesterday they carried out their threat. The day was the day consecrated to God's worship, but these disciples of 'the revolution' held their demonstration all the same, evidently acting on the principle of the proverb 'the better the day, the better the deed.' The object of the gathering was to seek for the amnesty

[1] 35 and 36 Vic. C. 15 (June 27, 1872); by which it is set forth in the first Schedule, "That no person shall deliver, or invite any person to deliver any public address in a park, except in accordance with the rules of the park."

of the political prisoners (by political prisoners being understood sundry soldiers who had forsworn their allegiance to join a conspiracy against the Queen's Government, and the lives of their own comrades), and various other culprits who, under the pretence of patriotism, had transgressed the laws that regulate the order of the community by acts of violence."

This led to twelve of the speakers being summoned to Marlborough Street Police Court, and one of them, a man named Bailey, was tried before the magistrate as a test of the whole, on Nov. 19, and fined 5*l*. or a month's imprisonment, but it was agreed that a case should be stated, and taken to a higher Court, the other summonses being adjourned *sine die*. The Appeal came on at the Queen's Bench, on Jan. 23, 1873, before three judges, who all concurred in affirming the conviction. The Treasury, to the very great disgust of the Fenian sympathizers, presented them with a bill of costs for 100*l*., but I do not know whether it was ever paid.

The effect of licensing public meetings in Hyde Park has been to turn that place into a bear-garden on most Sundays during fine weather, and one-sided meetings, more or less orderly, have been held on almost every subject, social and political. Is there a strike, the strikers must needs go and bellow their grievances—be they cabmen, laundresses, bakers, or unemployed. What good they think can accrue from it, they themselves cannot answer. As to the Trades' Unions who go there periodically, I fancy very few would go were it not to show their regalia, air their banners, and march to the sound of a brass band; while of late years it has become to very many a Sunday picnic, to which they and their wives go in brakes. Nay, sometimes they meddle with things wholly out of their sphere; as, for instance, the demonstration on the Eastern Question on Feb. 24, 1878, at which the following handbill was distributed:—

"RUSSIAN MEETING IN HYDE PARK:—Englishmen! A last attempt is to be made by the baffled agents of Russia, on Sunday, Feb. 24 (to-day), to corrupt and undermine the patriotism of our countrymen. Do you wish Count Schouvaloff to telegraph to the Czar that any meeting of Englishmen have passed resolutions in favour of the policy of the most despotic and cruel Power in Europe, a Power that deliberately crushes all 'national freedom' with the iron heel of military force, and shuts out British industry from all her territories? Any resolution passed at their meeting will be a direct encouragement to Russia. Nothing but a vigorous and determined policy will prevent war, which the Russian party, if successful, will inevitably bring about, as they brought about the Crimean War, in 1853."

While Mr. Auberon Herbert was speaking, *The Times* says that "A rush was made by a number of well-dressed young men on the south-east, at the same time that a huge column, with banners spread, was advancing from the north-east. It was easy to see that the 'specials' in the ring had had no military training, for some left the part which needed the most strength to repel the attack made by the young men. The chairman and the clergyman disappeared, and the Peace party then stood ready to greet the on-coming column. Mr. Bradlaugh had a special constable's staff in his hand;

and, parleying with the head of the column, demanded that their flags should be put down. Each of the men who had composed the circle brought out a constable's staff. The platform was, meanwhile, left in the possession of one person. The Peace party tore down the Turkish and Polish banners from the poles, and thereupon the anti-Russian party made a rush to, and broke up the platform.

"The *mêlée* now became almost general, for all classes of persons had got mixed up together, and in the struggle of those who wanted to pass out of harm's way, an extraordinary scene was presented. There must have been 60,000 or 70,000 people, but only a very small number was inclined to take active part in the proceedings. The fight, which was more noisy than hurtful, did not occupy much time. One or two men climbed small trees, where they took up the remains of the Turkish flag, and displayed it upon the leafless branches. It was draped too low, however, and was seized and lost. One of the events of the day was a regular fight in a tree, between two well-matched antagonists. The fight was witnessed by the whole crowd, some of whom took it upon themselves to dislodge the fellows from the trees, by pelting them with heavy sticks and stones."

But public meetings were not the only nuisance occasioned by throwing open the Park. It at once became a place for every shade of religious and secular doctrine to be preached; and the first notice I can find of these practices is in a letter in *The Times* of Nov. 27, 1872.

"The public are not aware of what occurs on

Sundays in Hyde Park. Here is what I have seen.

"A man dressed as a clergyman was standing on a seat near the Serpentine, and preaching to a few listeners, a very sensible sermon. A policeman advanced and told him, 'This is not allowed.' The preacher at once discontinued. Scene the second. A considerable crowd near what is called the Reformers' Tree : three men, dressed in cassocks and caps, preaching such terrible blasphemy that I quite shuddered to hear it, our Saviour's name and His words being travestied in the most awful and obscene manner. The policeman there stood outside the crowd, but made no attempt to interfere."

Are things better now? Let anyone go and see for himself; or, if that is inconvenient or impossible, let him read these two recent newspaper cuttings (*Globe*, April 16, 1894) :—

"DISORDERLY SCENE IN HYDE PARK.

"Yesterday afternoon a disorderly scene took place in Hyde Park. Two persons who were endeavouring to hold a religious meeting near the Serpentine, were surrounded by a crowd of men and boys, and, owing to some peculiarity, were frequently interrupted and prevented from proceeding with the service they were attempting to conduct. Finally, the opposition became so demonstrative that the two men were compelled to beat a retreat, a small banner they had with them being torn. Their hats were knocked off, and they were otherwise subjected to considerable hustling and ill-usage. Some disorder also occurred at a meeting which was being held close by. Scenes of this character have recently become very common in the Park."

"THE BISHOP OF HYDE PARK.

"At the Marlborough Street Police Court, John Mullane, thirty-seven, labourer, Circus Street, Marylebone; John Hayes, twenty-three, painter, John Street, Marylebone; and John Henlay, thirty, labourer, Carlisle Street, Marylebone; were charged with fighting together in Hyde Park. A police sergeant said that on Sunday evening, a man named Scully was addressing a meeting in Hyde Park, close to the Marble Arch. Presently, the three prisoners began to fight with each other, apparently over some argument with Scully. To prevent further disturbance, he obtained assistance, and took the men into custody.

"In defence, Mullane said he was listening to Scully, and noticed that he had a bottle in his pocket. Scully said it was water, but Hayes smelt it, and said it was gin. Then Scully knocked him (Hayes) down. He (Mullane) then struck Scully, when Henlay came up and struck him (Mullane) and knocked him down. Henlay said that he was standing behind Scully, when Hayes took the bottle out of his (Scully's) pocket, struck Scully, and threw him on the top of him (Henlay). Peter Scully deposed that he lived in Stanhope Street, Deptford, and got a living by selling 'good' books. He had been in the habit of lecturing in Hyde Park, in favour of religion, for the last twelve years. While he was speaking on Sunday night, a bottle of water was pulled away from him, his hand was cut, and his chair was pulled from under him. People called him the 'Bishop' of Hyde Park, because he had such large audiences. He saw two young fellows struck.

"Mr. Newton: 'You see all these disturbances are caused by your preaching.'—Scully: 'I cannot help that.'—Mr. Newton: 'Yes, you can, because you need not preach there.'—Scully: 'Many other persons speak there as well as myself, and if I should stop speaking there, the other speakers should do the same.'—Mr. Newton: 'I think it would be a good thing if all of them were stopped. If there were no speakers in the Park, there would be no fights.'—Scully: 'I should not mind if speaking in the Park were stopped, for I can always get an audience, and could address meetings elsewhere.'— Mr. Newton (addressing the defendants) said, they 'should not misbehave themselves in the Park,' and ordered them to enter into their own recognizances to be of good behaviour in the future."—*Daily Graphic*, May 1st, 1894.

Here, also, in the Park, men's minds are poisoned by the doctrines of Socialist and Anarchist; but the latter, at present, is somewhat out of favour with King δῆμος—probably on account of the Anarchist predilection for bombs, against which even his majesty is not proof. Here is an account from the *Daily Graphic* of last

"MAY DAY IN HYDE PARK.

" The May Day celebration in London has been marked by one of the most extraordinary scenes ever witnessed in Hyde Park. The occasion was a demonstration organized by the Social Democratic Federation to unite with the demonstrations on the

Continent in making the first of May Labour Day. There was, of course, a procession, which formed up on the Embankment, and was about as imposing as that which follows a drunken man to the police-station.

"There was the difference that it had a few waggonettes and greengrocers' carts to lengthen it out. Some of the waggonettes and the greengrocers' carts were arched in with green branches, and the drivers wore red caps of the sort usually associated with burlesque. They were understood to represent 'caps of liberty.' A few bakers' carts displayed specimens of French loaves and horse-shoe rolls. In some of the carts were children who sang the 'Marseillaise,' as the carts trailed through Piccadilly. Girls of an older growth had donned white dresses trimmed with a virulent red, and marshalled the younger ones. Mr. Keir Hardie, with his tweed cap and his pipe, walked through the crowd like one who expected the homage due to a hero. Mr. William Morris was also there, but one could not help thinking that he was, and felt, out of place. There were speeches, of course. These were laudatory, for the most part, of the workers and the Social Democratic Federation.

"But the Anarchists had, somehow, recovered their spirits, and had ventured to join in the procession. Agnes Henry, in her inevitable yellow ulster and cloth shoes, plodded indefatigably on the outskirts of the crowd. Louise Michel hovered here and there. They had their flags—red with black fringes—with them. One was an imposing banner on two poles, with an appeal to put down all government and authority. The Anarchists took up their position as side shows to the main demonstration. The crowd had paid no attention to the Social Democrats, but the Anarchists drew them like a magnet. A man, named Leggatt, a well known anarchist, declaimed from one platform; a succession of speakers, including Louise Michel, Mowbray, Dr Macdonald, and others, from another, which was intended to be more important. Sullivan, of Tower Hill fame, had a little show of his own. There was an evident desire to listen to the Anarchists patiently at first. Then the listeners had their feelings jarred by some outrageous exposition of the doctrine of explosives. They groaned and hooted. Leggatt, with clumsy retort, said they should be at a Board School, or playing marbles. So far as he was concerned, the result was disastrous. There was a spring at him, and he swayed for a moment on his perch, and then came down full length, while his platform was soon in little bits. The police, who had been observing the ugly temper of the crowd, rushed in, just in time to save him from worse injury. The banner was promptly in ribbons, and its pole was broken up. On this the people at the other platform discreetly folded their banner, and took it away.

"They would have done as well to have taken themselves away also. One man, whose vanity shall not be gratified by having his name mentioned here, said the police were keeping down the workers. 'You will never be free while you have such men as Melville.'[1] He was answered with a cheer for

[1] A police inspector specially active in pursuit of Anarchists —knowing all their haunts, etc.

the police, and, in a second more, was in the hands of the crowd. There were cries of 'In the Serp. with him,' and again Chief-Inspector Peters and his men had to rush in to save the demonstrators from the consequences of their own folly. A red tie became a dangerous article of adornment—there were threats to lynch the wearers. It was now becoming more and more difficult to keep the crowd in hand. Big as the A.R. division men are, they could hardly force their way through the dense masses.

"Never has there been such a scene in the Park. Racing across it came the hunted Anarchists, surrounded by a yelling, fist-using crowd, with the police protecting, as well as they could, the objects of the public wrath. At the Marble Arch, the police formed a *cordon* across the gates and closed all passage, and it was then only that the Anarchists, bleeding and bruised, were able to get into cabs and be driven to safety."

Any one would have thought that this lesson would have lasted them some time, but it was not so. On the first Sunday in the month (6th May) the annual demonstration in favour of a "Legal Eight Hours Day" took place in Hyde Park; and, although the Anarchists had nothing whatever to do with the meeting, yet the irrepressibles were there, and succeeded in marching to their usual speaking-place near the Reformers' Tree; but their reception by the sympathizers with the demonstration was of so hostile a character, that before the head of the procession arrived, they were hunted out of the Park, and, but for the protection afforded by the police, several would have been severely handled.

Perhaps the greatest fiasco of any of these meetings was one held Aug. 26th, 1894, with a view of abolishing the House of Lords. There were comparatively few people, the procession being made up of banners and bands.

CHAPTER XX.

The Children's Fête in Hyde Park, 1887.

As a refreshing set-off to the mouthings of mobs in Hyde Park, let us turn to the prettiest and pleasantest sight that the Park ever beheld, namely, the Children's Fête in Hyde Park, on June 22, 1887, in commemoration of the Queen's Jubilee, the following account of which is taken from *The Times* of June 23 :—

" Hyde Park yesterday was the scene both of festivity and ceremonial, the children being the happy mortals who were especially privileged to take part in the former, and witness the latter. It was a kind thought that prompted the organization of a monster treat for the boys and girls of the poorer classes in this season of general jubilation, and equally kind was the interest at once taken in the matter by the heads of our Royal house. It would be hard to conceive any form of enjoyment more calculated to impress upon youthful minds the exceptional circumstances of the present week, than yesterday's *fête*. Even if it had not been graced with the presence of her Majesty, and of the members of her family, the occasion would, probably, never have slipped from the memory of any child who shared in the day's amusements ; but, as the little ones were not only entertained on a scale which must have surprised the most imaginative of them, but were actually honoured by a special visit from the Sovereign herself, it is, indeed, likely to remain for ever indelibly fixed on their minds. To Mr. E. Lawson,[1] who originated the idea which was realized yesterday, the children owe a debt of gratitude. Thanks are also due from them to the many donors who supplied the funds required to defray the costs of the *fête*. First among these were the proprietors of *The Daily Telegraph*, who headed the list of subscriptions with a very large sum,[2] and undertook the collection of subscriptions, and the general management of the festival. To the Committee of Organization also the gratitude of the children ought to extend. The task of arranging for their safety, and providing for their wants, involved no slight amount of forethought and care, and was fulfilled with a conscientiousness which deserved and commanded success.

"The portion of the Park which was the scene of the festivity was that which is seldom visited by any large concourse of civilians, except for the purpose of expressing dissatisfaction with the laws, or the system of government. On this occasion, however, the Reformers' Tree was forgotten, and nothing but expressions of satisfaction were heard. The playground of the children extended from the drive, on the north of the Serpentine, to the north of the Park: it was bounded on the east by the trees which shadow the roadway leading to the Marble Arch, and its breadth westward was about a

---

[1] Now Sir E. Lawson, Bart., editor of *The Daily Telegraph*.
[2] 1000*l*.

quarter of a mile. On this level expanse, about 26,000 children disported themselves from noon till dewy eve. All were in the highest spirits, and all behaved as well as the best friends could wish. The amusements provided were multifarious and varied, and supplemented by impromptu additions, such as racing and dancing, which gave scope for physical exercise. The day was lovely, and not oppressively hot. With such conditions, what wonder that the children enjoyed themselves!

"The duty of selecting them—for, of course, they were but representative of their class—had been performed under the supervision of Mr. J. Diggle, chairman of the London School Board. The selection had been made among the Board Schools and Voluntary Schools of the metropolis, and that it had been made with care was evident. The children were all spruce and clean, and in many cases attired with unostentatious taste. The dresses of many of the girls were simple white, the sashes which bound them being blue or yellow. The prognostications of ill fortune, which had come from some quarters, were wholly unfulfilled, no greater mishap occurring to any child than a temporary indisposition brought on by heat and excitement. More than one case of this kind occurred, but the possibility that medical aid might be required in the course of the day had been provided for, and the little patients were not left long unsoothed and unrelieved. That any child, however young, should be lost, with so many friends at hand ready to aid, was scarcely within the bounds of probability, but in case of emergency a special tent had been erected for the reception of stragglers who might be unable to give any lucid description of the direction in which they wished to go. The difficulties which straying children might otherwise have caused were also obviated by the simple expedient of requiring each boy and girl to wear a ticket bearing the name of the holder, and the number of the tent allotted to his or her school. The watchful interest extended to their charges by the teachers who accompanied the small folk, was almost in itself sufficient to reassure the most nervous of mothers.

"The playground was surrounded with Venetian masts, erected at short distances from one another. Near the Achilles statue there were clusters of these masts. A gilt crown shone at the top of each, and between them hung a banner of plush velvet, exhibiting, in gold letters, the following fervent wish for the Queen's welfare :—

'God bless our Queen—not Queen alone,
But Mother, Queen, and Friend in one.'

"Though the children were not expected till nearly 1 o'clock, several members of the Committee were on the ground long before this, completing the necessary arrangements. Little, however, remained to be done; and when the guests of the day did arrive, everything was in perfect readiness. About 9 o'clock the police, whom, to the number of over 3000, Sir Charles Warren [1] had detailed for different duties in connection with the fête, commenced operations by clearing the enclosed ground of all unauthorized persons. During the day admission was strictly confined to those armed with invitation tickets, the issue of which had been by no means lavish,

---

[1] Then Chief Commissioner of Police.

so that adults present bore but a very small proportion to the juveniles. The general public, numbering many thousands, took up positions upon the outskirts of the reserved space, which was, at points of the greatest pressure, fenced in with iron hurdles, to prevent the encroachments of the crowd. Among those who, in this somewhat disadvantageous position, patiently waited several hours were very many of the children's parents, and these can have obtained only a passing glimpse of the Queen, and but a distant view of the doings with the privileged circle.

"About 11 o'clock, a squadron of the 2nd Life Guards, and 200 men of the Foot Guards, arrived to assist in keeping the ground, and, later in the day, these were reinforced by two more troops of the 2nd Life Guards, to keep the roadway clear for the Queen. The presence of the military added greatly to the brightness of the scene. Soon after 1 o'clock all the children had safely passed into the Park, and reached their allotted playground. About 13,000, belonging to schools on the south side of London, assembled in St. James's Park at 12 o'clock; and, having been marshalled by some 30 sergeants from Wellington Barracks, marched off, four abreast, headed by Mr. Bennet Burleigh, and Mr. J. T. Helby, of the London School Board. Proceeding past Buckingham Palace and up Constitution Hill, they entered Hyde Park by the Grosvenor Gate, and reached their destination, without mishap, and in capital order. A column almost as large, consisting of children from the northern districts of London, assembled in Regent's Park soon after 11 o'clock, and were put in position by Mr.

Howard Vincent, M.P., Mr. H. Lawson, M.P., Capt. E. Brodie, and Mr. W. Sheffield (drill instructor to the London School Board). This column also reached the Park in good time, and in good order. Smaller contingents that had assembled, the one in Battersea Park and the other in Kensington Gardens, also arrived.

"Twenty-six thousand children had now to be fed, and to be amused for several hours. The first thing was to feed them, and they were accordingly marched off to the different tents, which were ranged at intervals of fifty yards, five on either side, about fifty yards distant from the central roadway, up which the Queen was later to proceed. Each tent was 140 feet long, by 40 feet wide, but its accommodation was severely tried, in ministering to the wants of 2500 children. There was, however, no confusion. Each school knew the tent to which it was to proceed; and, having marched thither, drew up outside. Then, in their turn, the children in batches of 250 proceeded into the tent, and received ia paper bag containing their rations—a meat pie, a piece of cake, a bun, and an orange— and were also presented with a silver-plated memorial medal, having on one side a portrait of the Queen in 1837, and, on the other, a portrait of her Majesty in 1887. During the afternoon, lemonade, ginger beer, and milk were to be had in each tent, and there were four large water-carts stationed in different parts of the ground, which dispensed a plentiful supply of water to the thirsty. Each tent was in charge of one lady, who was assisted by eleven other ladies and twelve gentlemen. With such a staff, the work of dissemination rapidly proceeded, and the children were soon supplied with their much appreciated paper parcels.

"The children having picnicked on the grass, proceeded to roam at large in search of amusement. They could not go far without finding it. It was, indeed, a case of *l'embarras des richesses*, for the counter attractions were many and various. There were a score of Punch and Judy shows, eight Marionette theatres, eighty-six Cosmoramic Views and Peep-shows, nine troups of performing dogs, monkeys and ponies; and, for the special benefit of the boys, several hundred 'Aunt Sallies' and 'Knock 'em downs.' There were 100 large lucky-dip barrels, and a great distribution of presents, to the number of 42,000, consisting of skipping-ropes, money-boxes, dolls, pencil-cases, tin whistles, walking sticks, pop-guns, and *hoc genus omne*. Ten thousand small balloons, inflated with gas, also afforded the children considerable amusement. Meanwhile, the proceedings were enlivened with much good music. The bands of the 2nd Life Guards, the Royal Horse Guards, Royal Artillery, Royal Engineers and Grenadier Guards, with two or three civilian bands, were stationed at different points, at such distances apart as to allow of their playing simultaneously without conflicting, and the children had the good taste to listen, and apparently to appreciate. Flitting to and fro, from one point of attraction to the other, the young folks seemed to be enjoying themselves greatly, and the time went quickly by.

"The Prince and Princess of Wales, with the three Princesses, arrived soon after 4 o'clock, and appeared much pleased by the manifest gratification which their presence afforded to the children. Their Royal Highnesses, after having been received by Mr. Lawson, and conducted to the Committee tent, proceeded to one of the ordinary tents, where the distribution of memorial cups was going on. Having made their way through the juvenile and excited throng which pressed around them, the Prince and Princess handed a cup each to several of the children. The visit was quite unpremeditated, and no arrangements had been made. It was, therefore, a case of first come first served, and the children struggled hard, with outstretched hands, in their efforts to secure a cup from the hands of their Royal Highnesses. The Prince smiled good-humouredly at their eagerness; and as he left the tent 'God bless the Prince of Wales' was sung with much heartiness. Their Royal Highnesses then returned to the Committee tent, where the gentlemen and ladies who, earlier in the day, had assisted in the tents, and other invited guests, were assembled. At half-past 4 o'clock the bugle sound announced that the amusements must end, and the music cease. The children betook themselves to their respective tents, and, having been duly collected together, under the charge of their masters and mistresses, proceeded to take up positions along the road to be traversed by the Queen. The bands were massed under the direction of Mr. Dan Godfrey, and drawn up opposite the flag-staff where the Queen's carriage was expected to stop.

"The Queen was expected on the ground at half-past 5, but it was considerably later before her

Majesty's procession arrived. In the interval, several of the Royal guests joined the Prince and Princess of Wales in the reserved enclosure, the children cheering lustily as they drove past. When the time approached for her Majesty's appearance, even Mr. Dale's huge balloon, which was unloosed from its fastenings, and soared at once high into the air, failed to rouse anything approaching to the excitement which so interesting an event was calculated to arouse. The thoughts of the children were intent upon the Queen, and for the moment they were engrossed with the prospect of seeing her. It may be doubted even whether they paid much attention to the pealing of the sweet-toned bells which Mr. Irving had allowed the Committee to remove from the Lyceum Theatre, where until recently they were nightly heard in the cathedral scene in *Faust*, and which now began to send across the playground their soft and modulated sounds.

"At last, the appearance of a dozen mounted constables, trotting up the roadway, betokened that the chief event of the day might shortly be expected. Nor were the children disappointed this time, as they had been once or twice previously, when carriages had driven up which they thought might have contained the Queen, but which held occupants who were unknown to them. The hoisting of the Royal Standard to the top of the flag-staff, and the strains of the National Anthem, played by the massed bands, removed the last doubt as to the nature of the *cortége* which now slowly entered the Park by the Achilles statue. First came a party of Life Guards, with their flashing breast-plates and plume-crested helmets, and then the Indian escort, who had played so conspicuous a part in the pageant of the preceding day. Their swarthy faces and stolid demeanour, and the strange beauty of their uniforms, will long linger in the recollection of the youthful spectators. The Royal carriages, which were immediately preceded by outriders in scarlet, were all open, and some were drawn by four horses.

"The Queen's carriage was stopped opposite the flag-staff, and the chief ceremony of the day was at once begun. Miss Lawson, on behalf of the children of the London Board and Voluntary schools, presented a bouquet, and the Prince of Wales then led up to the carriage a little girl named Florence Dunn, to whom her Majesty gave one of the memorial cups. The Prince having explained that the child had never missed a single attendance during the seven years she had passed at school, the Queen expressed the pleasure which she felt in rewarding so industrious a scholar. To Mr. Edward Lawson, who was also presented to her, she intimated that she was extremely gratified to see the charming scene which the Park presented. The Royal procession remained stationary a few moments longer, while a verse of the 'Old Hundredth' was sung by the children, and then resumed its progress northwards, leaving the Park by the Fountain Gate, for Paddington station.

"The Prince and Princess of Wales, and the Royal guests who had not left with the Queen, took their departure shortly afterwards, and the children then returned to the tents, where simple refreshments were again served out. Their red-letter day had come to an end, as even the best things must, and, marshalled by their officers, they prepared to return to their homes, where the story of their doings on the occasion of the Queen's Jubilee is pretty certain to be repeated many and many a time."

The memorial cups alluded to were of earthenware, specially manufactured by Messrs. Doulton and Sons, at their potteries, Lambeth, and they had on one side a portrait of the Queen as she was at her Accession in 1837, and on the other a portrait of her at her Jubilee in 1887.

CHAPTER XXI.

List of Rangers—A horse jumping the wall—Highwaymen—Horace Walpole robbed—Other robberies—Assaults, offences, etc., in the present reign—A very recent case.

THE nominal head or Keeper of the Park is called the *Ranger*, and the first Keeper was made in the reign of Henry VIII. His name was George Roper, and besides lodging, fire, etc., venison, cattle grazing, etc., his salary was sixpence a day; and he kept this position until his death in 1553, when he was succeeded by Francis Nevell, whose salary was reduced to fourpence a day.

In 1574 a coadjutor was appointed to relieve him of some of his arduous duties, and he was a first cousin to Queen Elizabeth, being a son of Anne Boleyn's younger sister Mary. He was Henry Carey, first Lord Hunsdon. This shows that the office of Keeper was one of honour, for Hunsdon certainly could not have cared for the 4*d.* a day attached to the office, as he was not only well-to-do, and lord of several manors, but a Knight of the Garter, Privy Councillor, Captain of the Gentlemen Pensioners, Governor of Berwick, Chamberlain of the Queen's Household, etc., etc. At Nevell's death Lord Hunsdon became sole Keeper, and his fee was then 8*d.* per day. At his death, in 1596, his fourth son, Sir Edward Carey, knight, succeeded him in sole occupancy of the post. In 1607 he was followed by Robert Cecil, Earl of Salisbury, the son of Queen Elizabeth's Lord Burghley; but, for some reason or other, a coadjutor was appointed in 1610, Sir Walter Cope, who built the greater part of Holland House, Kensington. But he only kept it for a couple of years, and on the Earl of Salisbury's death, in 1612, and his consequent accession to the undivided keepership, he surrendered it for life to his son-in-law, Sir Henry Rich, who was created Earl of Holland in 1624, and beheaded in 1649. In 1630, he had asked, as a favour, that the succession might be given to the Earl of Newport (afterwards the Earl of Warwick), and at his death he asked for its reversion to Sir John Smith.

At the Commonwealth, it was proposed that Lord Howard of Escricke should be the Keeper, but the Earl of Warwick pleaded the Earl of Holland's grant so effectually, that he obtained the appointment; not, however, to enjoy it long, for, when the Parliament sold Hyde Park, the office of Keeper was, necessarily, abolished. At the restoration, Charles II. made his younger brother Henry, Duke of Gloucester, Keeper of the Park, but he dying four months afterwards, the place was given (Sept., 1660), to James Hamilton, Esq. He got from it something more substantial than any of his predecessors, for he was granted the triangular piece of land where the fort had been built, at the south-eastern portion of the Park, by Hyde Park Corner, and now known as Hamilton Place. He also had a concession of 55 acres, whereon to grow apples in the Park. Of this he had a lease for 49 years, on condition that he surrounded it with a brick wall eight feet high, and gave the King half the produce of the orchard, in apples or in cider, at his Majesty's option. Hamilton was killed at sea, in an engagement with the Dutch, in 1673, and the office of Keeper was vacant till 1684, when it was filled up by the appointment of Wm. Harbord, Esq., M.P. for Launceston.

The title of "Keeper" now disappears, and in its stead the officer is styled, as now, Ranger of St. James's, Green and Hyde Parks, and in 1694 the Earl of Bath was made Ranger. In 1700, Edward Villiers, first Earl of Jersey, was appointed to the post, but he only held it three years, relinquishing it in 1703 to Henry Portman, Esq., who succeeded to the enormous property of his cousin Sir William Portman. This gentleman must have resigned the Rangership before his death, for, in 1714, it was given to Walter Chetwynd, Esq., who had been Queen Anne's Master of the Buckhounds. He kept it until the accession of George II., when this noble piece of patronage was bestowed upon the Earl of Essex, who having resigned it in 1739, his place was taken by Viscount Weymouth, afterwards Marquis of Bath, who held it until his death in 1751.

He was succeeded by Thomas, first Earl of Pomfret, who died in 1753, and the vacant Rangership was conferred on the Earl of Ashburnham, who resigned it in 1762. The position was then accepted by the Earl of Orford, who kept it till 1778, when he was succeeded by General Charles Fitzroy, afterwards Lord Southampton. He resigned it in 1783, and then it was taken by the Earl of Sandwich, better known by his nickname of

Jemmy Twitcher; but he only retained it one year, and it was then resumed by the Earl of Orford, until his death in 1791. Next to him came Lord William Wyndham Grenville, who resigned in 1793, and was followed by the Earl of Euston, afterwards Duke of Grafton. He kept in office till 1807, and after him came Viscount Sydney, who kept it till his death in 1831. Then the office came into the hands of royalty, in the person of the Duke of Sussex, who was Ranger till his death in 1843, when it was taken by his brother, the Duke of Cambridge. At his death in 1850, the Rangership was conferred on the Duke of Wellington, and on his death on the Duke of Cambridge, the present Duke, who still holds the office, which is entirely honorary: but he has under him a Superintendent Ranger, with a salary of 191*l*., and a Superintendent of Works, at 260*l*. per annum.

It was during Col. Hamilton's keepership that Hyde Park was enclosed with a brick wall, high enough to keep in the deer with which the Park had been restocked; and this wall lasted till 1726, when a new wall was built six feet six inches high on the inside, and eight feet on the outside, a wall which one might well think could not be negotiated by any horse. Yet a horse belonging to a Mr. Bingham did twice clear it, in 1792; once in a standing leap, and once in a flying leap. This wall continued till 1828, when it was replaced by the iron railings which were demolished by the mob in 1866, they in their turn giving place to those which now surround the Park.

What are the duties of a Ranger I have no idea, except that we see his name attached at the bottom of the rules and regulations of the Park; but seeing that the position is honorary, and that he has a deputy, they cannot be very onerous. One thing is certain, he seems to have no power to put down acts of violence, which have occurred, and still are occurring in Hyde Park, nor does the personal safety of those who use the Park for purposes of recreation seem to be one of his functions.

Larwood says that robberies in Hyde Park were so common in the reign of William III. that the King ordered the Guards to patrol the Park till eleven o'clock at night, and " In addition to this a guard house was built in the Park in 1699, ' for securing the road against footpads, who,' according to the *London Post,* Dec. 16, 1699, ' continue to be very troublesome.' " This assertion may be correct, but there is no mention of it in the newspaper named, nor in any other contemporaneous journal; nor can I find any account of a highway robbery in the Park in Feb., 1749. *The Penny London Post,* 12-15 May, 1749, says, " On Wednesday Night (May 10) Mr. Hoskins, a Pale Ale Brewer in Tyburn Road, was robbed by three footpads near the Serpentine River, in Hyde Park, of a purse of silver, to the amount of eighteen pounds, which he had a little before received at a Publick house at Kensington."

But a famous person, no less than Horace Walpole, was robbed in the Park, on Nov. 8, 1749, of which he gives the following account, in his *Short Notes.* " One night, in the beginning of November, 1749, as I was returning from Holland House by moonlight, about ten at night, I was attacked by two highwaymen (McLean and Plunket) in Hyde

Park, and the pistol of one of them (the accomplished McLean) going off accidentally, grazed the skin under my eye, left some marks of shot on my face, and stunned me. The ball went through the top of the chariot, and, if I had sat an inch nearer to the left side, must have gone through my head." *The General Advertiser* of Nov. 15, 1749, says : " We hear that the Hon. Horace Walpole Esqre, who was lately robb'd in Hyde Park, has received a letter, intimating that if he would send his Footman, to a House in Tyburn Road, with 30 Guineas he should have his Watch restor'd, and also that of his Coachman, provided the Footman behaved as directed in the said letter."

In No. 103 of *The World* (Dec. 19, 1754) this robbery is commented on. "An acquaintance of mine was robbed a few years ago, and very near shot through the head by the going off of the pistol of the accomplished Mr. McLEAN; yet the whole affair was conducted with the greatest good breeding on both sides. The robber, who had only taken a purse *this way* because he had that morning been disappointed of marrying a great fortune, no sooner returned to his lodgings than he sent the gentleman two letters of excuses, which, with less wit than the epistles of Voiture, had ten times more natural and easy politeness in the turn of their expression. In the postscript he appointed a meeting at Tyburn, at twelve at night, where the gentleman might *purchase again* any trifles he had lost; and my friend has been blamed for not accepting the rendezvous, as it seemed liable to be construed by ill-natured people into a doubt of the *honour* of a man who had given him all the satisfaction in his power, for having, *unluckily*, been near shooting him through the head."

It was not only in Hyde Park, but all over London, that these highway robberies took place, but, naturally, they were more prevalent at the West End, because the inhabitants were richer. People were convoyed home from the suburbs, such as Hampstead and Kensington, and *The Penny London Post* (Jan. 26-29, 1750) says : " So many Robberies have been committed lately in the New Buildings at the Court end of the Town, that the Servants go armed with Blunderbusses and Pistols, with both Coaches and Chairs on Nights."

Generally, people seem to have taken their robbery very calmly, and made no attempt to capture the thief, but one met with his deserts at Hyde Park Corner, as we see in *Read's Weekly Journal* of June 29, 1751 : " Last Friday 7-night, as Mr. Hornsby and his Lady, and Mr. Harding, were returning from Ranelagh Gardens, in a Coach, they were stopped between the Lock and St. George's Hospitals, Hyde Park Corner, by a single Highwayman, well mounted, who presented a Pistol, and demanded their Money : and while Mr. Harding was amusing him with a few Shillings, Mr. Hornsby clapt a Pistol to his breast and fired, which frighten'd the Highwayman's Horse, and gave the Coachman an Opportunity of driving off. 'Tis apprehended the Highwayman is either killed or dangerously wounded, the Pistol touching his Breast when Mr. Hornsby fired. The next Morning, the Highwayman's Pistol was found by the Watch, loaded with a Brace of Slugs."

Singularly ungallant, too, were some of the footpads, as we may read in *The London Chronicle,* July 28-30, 1774: " Sunday evening, two Ladies walking in Kensington Gardens were met by two Gentlemen, who entered into Conversation with them; and, after walking together for some time in the Gardens, the Gentlemen begged permission to accompany them home, to which the Ladies consented. When they came near Grosvenor Gate, the pretended Gentlemen pulled out their pistols and demanded their money, which amounted to near two guineas, and their gold watches, with which they made off."

But this is sufficient of old outrages : let us see whether we have amended our ways, taking only a few instances in the present reign. The following is the statement of a young woman, aged 26, as recorded in *The Times* of Dec. 11, 1840 :—

"She had been that afternoon to Hammersmith to see a lady respecting a situation; and on returning, at Kensington, was induced by the bright moonlight to proceed through the Park, as the nearest way to town. She, however, by mistake took the footpath to Kensington Gardens—instead of that at the side of the carriage road, which closely abuts on the high road ; and had not proceeded far when she passed a tall, stout man, of respectable appearance, who followed her ; and, on approaching the one-arched bridge, accosted her, and wanted to enter into conversation, which she avoided by walking fast. About the centre of the bridge, he suddenly caught hold of her, pushed her against the balustrades of the bridge, which at that spot consists of ornamental iron railings about 3 feet high, and forcibly attempted to take liberties with her, which she strongly resisted; and, being a powerful woman, struggled desperately with him, calling out 'Murder' at the utmost pitch of her voice; when the villain suddenly stooped down, and catching hold of her legs, threw her, with great violence, over the bridge into the water, and instantly effected his escape. From her appearance, when brought to the Receiving House, it was evident that she had fallen head first into the water, as her head and shoulders were thickly incrusted with the mud at the bottom of the stream." I fail to trace that this ruffian was ever caught.

The Times, Oct. 13, 1842:—

"HYDE PARK AFTER DARK.

" Saturday evening, about half past 8, as a person named Newport was walking along Rotten Row, he was accosted by a man who asked him the time, and said, 'Let me see your watch.' Mr. Newport refused to tell him, or pull out his watch, upon which the ruffian instantly seized him by the collar, and said, 'You are my prisoner, you have been acting improperly'; but on Mr. Newport immediately calling out 'Murder! Police!' his assailant let go his hold, and running away, effected his escape." —"On Sunday night, about five minutes before 10, a young man named Pummell was returning from town along the carriage road leading from Hyde Park Corner to the Kensington Gate, which is close to the high road, when he was stopped by a man, who said to him, 'Are you going to stand half a pint of beer, old fellow?' Pummell told him 'he should not, indeed'; when the fellow said, 'You had better stand it before you go any further.' Pummell, however, repeated he would not, and was walking away, when another man, whom he had not before observed, jumped from the ditch under the rails at the side of the path, and said, 'We are hard up, and on the tramp, so you must give us half a pint of beer, or something, before you go on.' Pummell, becoming alarmed, raised a walking stick he had in his hand, and called loudly for assistance, upon which, one of the fellows snatched at his stick, but only caught hold of the tassel, which was torn away in the attempt. Pummell then ran off, at his utmost speed, towards the Kensington Gate, from which he was not far distant, and the two fellows ran across the Park, and effected their escape."

A few years later, things were not much better, as we find in a letter in *The Times* of Aug. 7th, 1847. "It is now proved beyond a doubt that any blackguard may insult, attack and rob you with perfect impunity, unless you can induce him to wait patiently whilst you scour the park in search of a policeman to take possession of him. Here is a case in point. I was in the park last evening. Some children were amusing themselves with a kite. Two blackguards crossed their path, and at once took possession of their ball of string. I desired them to return it, otherwise I should give them in charge. They very complacently glanced around them, and then began to pour forth, within the hearing of several women and children, a torrent of the most filthy language. A gentleman who came up at the time interfered, and the abuse was at once turned upon him; the intention of the men being, evidently, to create a disturbance, and then profit by it. I at once went in search of a policeman: after walking about a quarter of a mile, I met a park-keeper. His answer to my request was, 'Oh! I can't interfere, you'll find a policeman somewhere.' I proceeded in my search, and at last found one on the other side of the Serpentine, amongst the bathers: he very readily accompanied me, although leaving his especial duty, and the matter was soon settled."

Complaints were also made of the inadequacy of the police during the building of the Great Exhibition of 1851. Crowds used to go every Sunday to see how it had progressed, and a dweller in Park Place thus writes to *The Times* (*vide* Feb. 18, 1851): "I will content myself by merely stating that scarcely a Sunday now passes that the disturbance does not terminate in a fight. On one occasion, a soldier and a civilian, each striving to go contrary ways through the gate, at length came to blows. On a subsequent Sunday a similar conflict took place between a soldier and a policeman; and yesterday two men were fighting under my sitting-room windows for some considerable time. This latter encounter, especially, was not a mere skirmish; on the contrary, a ring was made, the men were each backed by a second: in fact, there was all the formula of a regular pitched battle."

Take, again, a short letter in *The Times* of March 15th, 1855 : "Allow me, through your columns, to caution the frequenters of Hyde Park against a gang of ruffians, who are in the habit of accosting ladies and female servants, and, under the pretence of asking the time of day, endeavouring to pick their pockets. Several ladies of my acquaintance, when walking in the Park with their children, have had narrow escapes of being robbed in this manner."

In *The Times* of July 1st, 1858, a Resident near Hyde Park writes that "it is perfectly notorious that in all of our parks, but most especially in Hyde Park, it is impolitic, in the highest degree, for young girls to take exercise unattended. I, for one, have been obliged to prohibit my daughter, aged 13 years, from taking her hitherto pleasant morning walks, in company with her little brother, for precisely the same reason as a thousand other parents could assign—namely, because of the hoary-headed ruffians, dressed in the garb of gentlemen, who systematically lay in wait for young girls, with an intent too horrible for mention."

Here is a sketch of the Park, in the *Pall Mall Gazette* of May 21, 1866, endorsed by being copied into *The Times*, May 22nd :—

"The Police of Hyde Park.

"Urgent remonstrances have recently been made to the Chief Commissioner of Works, from various quarters, and, more especially, by the parochial authorities of St. George's, Hanover Square, against the misrule and vice which is allowed by the Ranger of Hyde Park to prevail unchecked within its precincts after the Park is closed at night. The gates are then locked, the park-keepers go to their homes, the lodge-keepers go to bed, and the Park is utterly given up to hoards of tramps and roughs of both sexes, who, during the summer months, pass their nights there. Any decent persons caught in crossing the Park at the hour for locking up, have no choice but to remain prisoners until the morning, if they are not sufficiently active to climb the iron railings; for it is a point of professional honour with the lodge-keepers, to resist all attempts at rousing them after they have once turned in. A number of prostitutes, too, of the very lowest grade, ply, unmolested, in the Park, their dismal calling, spreading around them disease, until they are themselves stricken down by it, and perish in the neighbouring workhouses.

"And it is this wretched fact that has, at last, set the authorities of St. George's Parish in action. It is now required that the incompetent and useless park-keepers, to whose care the Park has hitherto been intrusted, shall be superseded, and that they shall be replaced by the Metropolitan Police, who shall supervise and patrol its area by night, as well as by day; that policemen shall be on duty all night, at all its gates, to let out persons who may have been accidentally shut in; and that two or three of the mounted police shall be stationed in Rotten Row, between the hours of 12 and 2 p.m. and of 5 and 8 p.m., to keep in check the galloping snobs, grooms and horsebreakers of both sexes, by whose reckless brutality the lives and limbs of her Majesty's lieges are daily endangered. To effect this reform, mere management, not money, is wanted.

"The discreditable condition in which the police of Hyde Park now is, distinctly indicates want of ability or attention on the part of its Ranger; and the costly landscape and flower gardening, so extensively and successfully carried out by Mr. Cowper, as clearly shows that that condition is owing to no lack of funds. It is of far more importance to the inhabitants of the West End of London, that the Park to which they and their families resort should be orderly, cleanly and well watched, than that it should be picturesque and gay with flowers: and, in the case of Hyde Park, there seems to be no reason why its police should not be as effective as its horticulture."

It would almost seem as if everyone was doing their utmost to spoil the Park, and divert it from its assumed purpose of reasonable recreation; for, at one time, the betting men got hold of it, and made it the scene of their unhealthy calling, *vide* a letter in *The Times* of June 1, 1866:—"I have frequently occasion to cross Hyde Park between the hours of 12 and 1, and I have watched with surprise the operations of a numerous betting ring, the members of which hold daily undisturbed possession of a large group of trees in the centre of the Park. It is becoming so popular a resort of servants, that I was not astonished, last week, to hear of a footman, when applying for a situation, stipulating for a mid-day walk in the Park. Yesterday, I saw one of the park-keepers apparently busily engaged in the ring." And this letter was fully endorsed in another which appeared in next day's *Times*.

If betting were allowed, why not other forms of gambling? So we find that on June 25, 1866, at Marlborough Street, Thomas Davids, who is described as being "well-dressed," was charged with setting up a roulette table in Hyde Park. Inspector Green, of the A Division, said he was in Hyde Park on June 23rd about six o'clock, when he saw the prisoner with a roulette table, and a large number of persons round him. The prisoner was playing, and on seeing him take up some money from the board, he seized him, and charged him with gambling. The prisoner admitted that he was playing at roulette, but he was not aware it was illegal. He found £1 10s. in gold and £1 12s. in silver in his possession. The prisoner's father was a respectable person. The prisoner, in defence, said that he was in such a novel position that he hardly knew what to say. Mr. Tyrwhitt said everybody must know that gambling in the parks was not permitted. He considered the prisoner's conduct most mischievous in robbing persons of their money, for it was well known that the chances in favour of the keeper of the gaming-table were 100 per cent. Davids was fined 40s. and costs.

It is impossible to chronicle all the scandals of the Park, we may think they belong to a past age, and that Board Schools and their enlightening influences, and with the "sweetness and light" they should have brought with them, have for ever banished evil from it, but I will only give two modern instances, and I have done with this portion of its history. First take a letter in *The Times* of Dec. 26, 1891, in which the writer says : " It is impossible for any respectable woman, after dark, to pass through even from the Marble Arch to Hyde Park Corner, without being insulted by men, or groups of low women. For young people who have to come from the other side to work, there is no alternative for them, on their return home at night, but to walk right round ; as after dark no respectable girl could pass through, unaccompanied, without molestation."

And, last of all, because I have not chronicled one out of the hundreds of atrocities committed by soldiers in the Park—assaults, robberies, vile accusations, etc.—I will give a very mild and recent case reported in the *Daily Graphic*, May 22nd, 1894 :—

"Violent Guardsmen.

"At the Marlborough Street Police Court, Augustus Fitzgerald, 24, and Frank Burton, 24, privates in the 1st Battalion Grenadier Guards, were charged with being drunk and disorderly, and using obscene language in Hyde Park, and Fitzgerald was also charged with assaulting Police-Sergeant Cooke, and Burton with assaulting two constables in the execution of their duty. Sergeant Cooke stated that about 12 o'clock on Saturday night, he was on duty near the Marble Arch. A gentleman complained to him that the prisoners had pushed him and his wife, and also used very bad language. Both prisoners then attempted to get at the gentleman, and used very bad language. The sergeant advised them to go quietly to barracks. Fitzgerald tried to get Burton to go, but he would not, and the officers had to take him into custody. Fitzgerald then struck the sergeant on the face, cutting his cheek. A constable then took Burton, and the sergeant, Fitzgerald. The latter then kicked his captor on the knee. The officers blew their whistles, and assistance arrived. While the sergeant was struggling with Fitzgerald, Burton came up and kicked him, making his leg black and blue. Fitzgerald went quietly to the station, but Burton continued to struggle so violently that the ambulance was sent for, and then it took seven constables to get him on it. The prisoners used most disgusting language to the officer who took the charge, and when in the cells, kicked the doors till they loosened the frames. The constable who was on duty with Sergeant Cooke corroborated his statement, and said that Fitzgerald kicked him in the lower part of the abdomen. Both officers are now on the sick list. Fitzgerald said, if he struck the sergeant, it was a pure accident. Burton asserted that the constables shoved them about, and prevented them leaving the park by the nearest gate. An officer present gave Fitzgerald a bad character, and Burton a fairly good one. Mr. Hannay sentenced them to one month's hard labour each."

"EXCITING SCENE IN HYDE PARK.

"Last night[1] an extraordinary and violent scene (a correspondent writes) took place in Hyde Park. In the evening the park is now frequented by large crowds of people, who listen to speeches, recitations, &c., delivered near the Marble Arch, and considerable hostility has, it appears, been aroused by the action of some soldiers in persistently creating a disturbance among the crowd, with the object of breaking up any meeting that may be held. Last night, while a small knot of people were listening to a reciter, four soldiers, whose movements had hitherto been unobserved, suddenly ran in, and without giving any warning flung themselves with great force on those on the outside of the crowd. A struggle at once ensued, and before many moments had elapsed the soldiers found themselves surrounded by an infuriated crowd of some 300 persons, who pelted them with hands full of pebbles picked up from the ground, and, at the same time, indulged freely in hooting. The soldiers struck out vigorously to right

[1] Probably meaning Sunday, 24th March.

and left with their canes, retiring close together, and for some time managed to keep the crowd at a respectful distance. One of them, however, being struck suddenly in the face with a missile, drew his bayonet, and breaking away from his comrades, furiously charged the crowd. Immediately a general stampede took place, but though the enraged soldier speedily gave up the pursuit, it was some minutes before he sheathed his weapon. No sooner had he done so than the crowd again returned, and forming round the troopers, recommenced booing and hooting, though at a longer distance than before. By this time, however, notification of the occurrence had been conveyed to the police, and they coming up, were able, though not without difficulty, to get the soldiers out of the park without further violence from the mob. No one, fortunately, was seriously injured, but both the soldiers and some civilians had their faces cut."—*Globe*, March 26, 1895.

CHAPTER XXII.

The Gates—That into Kensington Gardens—Improvements in the Park—Encroachments—The case of Ann Hicks and the other fruit-sellers—Seats in the Park—New house in ditto.

THERE are several entrances into Hyde Park—those called Gates being passable for carriages. These lead into the Bayswater Road, Park Lane, and Knightsbridge, but there is also one connecting it with Kensington Gardens, concerning which there are several paragraphs in *The Times* of 1794-1795 :—

"The access to KENSINGTON GARDENS is so inconvenient to the visitors, that it is to be hoped the politeness of those who have the direction of it will induce them to give orders for another door to be made for the convenience of the public—one door for admission, and another for departure, would prove a great convenience to the visitors. For want of this regulation the Ladies frequently have their cloaths torn to pieces: and are much hurt by the crowd passing different ways." (*March* 28, 1794.)

"Two ladies were lucky enough to escape thro' the gate of Kensington Gardens, on Sunday last, with only a broken arm each. When a few lives have been lost, perchance then a door or two more may be made for the convenience of the families of the survivors." (*May* 8, 1794.)

"We noticed last year the nuisance at the door of

Kensington Gardens, leading from Hyde Park, and was (*sic*) in hopes those who have the care would attend to it. As the season is approaching when company frequent it, we again recommend that an additional door should be made, and an inscription put over it—' The company to go in at this gate, and return at the other '—by which means the press will be avoided, and directions given, that all servants do keep away from the doors, who behave with great impertinence to their superiors, as the company go in. If the gardens are to be a public accommodation, surely so trifling an expense can be no object. A greater number of seats in the gardens is very desirable." (*April* 24, 1795.)

"The public in general, and the ladies in particular, are much obliged to the Ranger of Hyde Park, for having taken the hint given in the paper towards their accommodation, by ordering a new gate to be made, as an entrance into Kensington Gardens. This convenience was, yesterday, much noticed, as there is now one gate for the entrance, and another for leaving the gardens, which were extremely crowded. But so little regularity was observed in the procession of carriages, on the Park Road, that there was a general stoppage about four o'clock, for nearly an hour; in the throng several carriages were overset, and many much injured. We never witnessed so much confusion on any similar occasion." (*May* 4, 1795.)

The first gate in the Bayswater Road, starting from Kensington Gardens, is called the Victoria Gate, and it is opposite Sussex Place—there is an entrance by the drinking fountain—but there is no other *gate* till Cumberland Gate, or the Marble

Arch, as it is more generally called. Turning down Park Lane we have first Grosvenor Gate, and then Stanhope Gate; whilst on the Knightsbridge side is the principal entrance, or Hyde Park Corner. Next comes Albert Gate, the roadway of which was finished and opened to the public on April 6th, 1842. The present gates were not then erected, nor the noble mansions which stand on either side of the entrance. Then comes the Prince of Wales' Gate, and the Alexandra Gate—both modern entrances in the Park—and are among the many improvements effected in Queen Victoria's reign.

At its commencement, the Park was not altogether a place of beauty, or of " sweetness and light "—gravel used to be dug there, as we see by the following letter to *The Times*, Oct. 18th, 1838 :—" I beg through your columns to remonstrate with the Commissioners of Woods and Forests, on the extreme negligence of leaving the gravel pit in Hyde Park in its present dangerous state. Two sides of it are very deep and precipitous, without any fence whatever to protect the unwary traveller, when darkness conceals the danger from him. I wonder, Sir, that fatal accidents do not nightly happen; if neck or limbs escape fracture in the fall, there is now water enough in the pit to drown anyone stunned by the accident."

There is a letter in *The Times* of April 11, 1839, from Mr. I. C. Loudon, the eminent authority on gardening—speaking of the improvements which had taken place in the Park during the past five or six years; how the pasture had been renovated by manuring, and other means, the carriage roads had been altered, the footpaths gravelled, and greatest of all, in his estimation, the number of *single* trees which had been planted in different situations; but he anathematises the planting them in *clumps,* as the Commissioners of Woods and Forests were then doing. Probably this generation, who have benefited by the Commissioners' planting, will not endorse Mr. Loudon's opinion, but then letters to *The Times* are not always temperate, *vide* the following—in that paper of Feb. 13, 1844 :—

" Sir, permit me, through your columns, to call the attention of the Commissioners of Woods and Forests to a serious nuisance in Hyde Park, which, if continued and increased, will be a permanent injury to the Park and its neighbourhood. A large excavation has been made in the south-western side of the Park, for the purpose of procuring gravel; and this excavation, extending over more than an acre of ground, and 15 or 20 feet deep, is being filled up with the refuse from a nightman's or dustman's yard. The stench which proceeds from the spot, whilst the work is in progress, is of a most pestiferous description; but this is not the worst of the mischief. The real damage is in altering the character of the superficial strata; so that, hereafter, the moisture which heretofore drained off through the gravel, will be retained near the surface, and generate miasma."

Then came the grievance of so called " encroachment "—and a gentleman asks in *The Times* of March 21, 1845 : " Why have several hundred yards of Hyde Park been enclosed during the last weeks— not by a low wooden rail, but a high iron fence? This encroachment is making in the space between Albert Gate and the Piccadilly Gate; and, by it, the public must be for ever excluded. Is it to be planted, or converted into a garden for the benefit of the twin giants,[1] untenanted as yet, after the precedent set some years ago of taking a considerable plot of ground between Stanhope Street Gate and the Piccadilly one, for the exclusive advantage of a very few houses in Hamilton Place and Park Lane?"

And the same gentleman in another letter (March 27, 1845) says: "The expense, also, of maintaining these enclosures is very heavy, for not less than £500 a year is spent on the small plot between Stanhope Gate and Piccadilly. This outlay seems enormous, but the authority on which it rests is unquestionable, and it furnishes, on the score of economy, a strong argument for its restoration to the Park, from which it was taken about twenty years ago. This concession would be a gracious act on the part of the Crown, save much charge, and be highly estimated by the people. So little was the public health and pleasure considered formerly, that a plan was proposed by the Woods and Forests, when presided over by Mr. Huskisson, for building a line of houses from the reservoir, near Grosvenor Gate, towards Piccadilly, and the aggression was only quelled by Lord Sudeley, and another member of the House of Commons."

From the grumbles, it is refreshing to turn to the improvements—and in April, 1845, upwards of 150 labourers were employed for some time in levelling the grass, new gravelling the paths, and generally making very considerable improvements

---

[1] Now the French Embassy, and the London and County Banking Company.

throughout the whole of Hyde Park. On the 8th August, same year, the erection of the new iron gates at the Albert Gate entrance was completed, and the stags appeared to public gaze.

In 1851, the Park had to be set in order—for the Great Exhibition, and some old established privileges had to give way—one of which was the famous case of Ann Hicks, which came before the House of Commons on July 29, 1851. The following is the report in *Hansard* :—

"Mr. BERNAL OSBORNE wished to ask the noble lord, the First Commissioner of Woods and Forests, whether Ann Hicks held a house in Hyde Park by the gift of George II., or by what tenure she occupied the house from which she had been evicted? and, also, whether the noble lord had permitted any other house to be erected in the Park?

"Lord SEYMOUR said, that in answer to the first question of the hon. gentleman, he had to state that Ann Hicks did not hold any house by the gift of George II. or of any other Royal personage at all. The first time he (Lord Seymour) ever heard of her claim to a house as the gift of any Royal personage, was a few weeks ago. In 1843, Ann Hicks, like several other persons, had a little stall, where she sold apples and ginger-bread in the Park. Previous to that, she had occupied one of the old conduits there. She subsequently wrote to the Commissioners of Woods and Forests, and requested leave to build a place to lock up her ginger-beer bottles in; and after some correspondence with the Commissioners, they told her she might have a wooden stand, the same as some persons had near where the cows are kept in St.

James's Park. Shortly afterwards, she wrote to the Commissioners again, saying she was very much obliged by their reply, but that she should like to build her stall of brick, instead of wood, as a wooden one was insecure, and liable to be broken open; but in all those applications she never made any allusion to any Royal gift, but always rested her claim on her having fifteen children to support.

"After some time, the Commissioners allowed her to have her stand of brick instead of wood. Having got that leave, she wrote to the Commissioners, and said that her stand was not quite large enough, and she wished to make it larger, as she had so many ginger-beer bottles, she did not know where to put them. The Commissioners gave way to her, and said she might make her stand five feet high, but no higher. She then wrote again in the following year, and said she was very much obliged for the little hut she had got, and that it was a great accommodation to her, and that she had not the least wish to make a residence of it; but, that if the Commissioners would allow her to have a little fireplace in it, it would be of great use to her to make a cup of tea. The Commissioners resisted that, and told her they could not allow her to have a fireplace; that her hut was merely a place allowed her to put her bottles in, and that she must not use it as a residence.

"She again wrote to the Commissioners, saying that the roof of her shed wanted repair, that the rain came in, and might she be allowed to repair it, and keep the rain out? The Board told her she might repair it so as to keep the rain out, but that she must make no alteration in it. However, shortly afterwards, the Commissioners found that the hut had a roof and chimney. When he (Lord Seymour) came into office, in 1850, the hut had not only got a roof and a chimney, but there was a little garden to it, with hurdles round. Ann Hicks said the hurdles were put up because it was so disagreeable to have people looking in at her window. His attention had been called to the matter from the frequent disputes between the authorities of the Park and Ann Hicks. The hurdles were continually advancing and encroaching on the Park. She was told to put them back; but she made so much noise and abuse about it, that none of the Park authorities cared to meddle with her. They all gave him very bad accounts of her. He also asked a gentleman who was connected with the management of the Park, though not with his (Lord Seymour's) department, and he gave him an account, equally unfavourable, of Ann Hicks. Upon that, he thought it time that some proceedings should be taken against her, because it was quite unusual to allow any residence in the Park. The law was decidedly against it; and he was told that, if they sanction this for a few years, there would be great difficulty in removing her.

"Before he took any step, however, he wrote to the Duke of Wellington, as Ranger of the Park; and his Grace, with that consideration which he gave to the minutest details, wrote him word that he was coming to town, and would inquire into the whole case. Accordingly, when his Grace came to town, he wrote to him (Lord Seymour) and said that he ought to apply for legal advice, and remove Ann Hicks from the Park at once. He then referred all the correspondence to the solicitors of the office, and Ann Hicks was served with a notice to remove; but he told her, that if she would go from the Park and not give them any trouble, he would take care that some allowance should be made to her. But she would not go; she said it was her ground, and that nothing could remove her. He then gave directions that proceedings should be taken to remove her, and she would not move until those proceedings were actually taken.

"She then wrote again to the Commissioners, and said that she owed a small debt of £6 or £7 for the repairs of her cottage, but she said nothing of a Royal gift. He thereupon told her that if she went, she should have five shillings a week for the next year, and that would secure her a house in lieu of the one to which she had no legal right. He also gave her some money at once to pay for the repairs; but a builder afterwards called upon him, and said that she owed him his debt for the repairs of the cottage still. In fact, instead of paying the debt with the money he (Lord Seymour) had given her, she spent it in getting some placards printed and placing them about the Park, charging the Commissioners of Woods and Forests with hardship and oppression towards her.

"As to any other cottage being erected in the Park, the only one he was aware of was the cottage proposed to be built by Prince Albert, as a model cottage. When it was built, he (Lord Seymour) said it could not be allowed to remain, and his Royal Highness promised that it should be taken down next November."

Besides this extremely grateful old lady, there

were four other fruit-sellers evicted, and one of them afterwards memorialized a new Chief Commissioner as to compensation, or renewal, and some of the grounds on which the claim is based are somewhat curious : " That your petitioner, Charles Lacey, has several times assisted the park-keepers and other officials in the apprehension of various offenders, and also that he has himself, without the aid of either park-keepers, or other officials, apprehended and caused to be convicted other offenders, which must show to the public that he was not there for his interest alone, but that he protected the visitors from injury and insult; we therefore placed a firm reliance in the hope that a renewal would be granted for our 'stand,' which was neither unsightly, nor an obstruction; however, to our great disappointment, our appeal was non-suited.

"The removal of our 'stand' has not only deprived us of the means of obtaining an honest livelihood, but, in fact, has compelled us to pledge and sell our very clothes to provide a subsistence. Nor is this the worst; the deprivation of the 'stand' occasioned such a shock to the female petitioner (Lacey's wife) as to bring upon her a nervous excitement, under which she suffered intensely for upwards of eight months, and great doubts were entertained that she would have been deprived of her reason altogether. In addition to their other distresses, your petitioners regret, most painfully, to add that their daughter, eighteen years of age, at the present time lies dangerously ill of scarlet fever."

At the end of June, 1852, the drive and promenade on the north side of the Serpentine were widened and improved; whilst the old wooden railing was replaced by the iron rail now existing, in August of the same year. In March, 1854, the principal promenades were relaid with gravel, and the site of the exhibition of 1851, being entirely covered with grass, and no trace of the huge building left, was thrown open once more to the public. In September, 1855, at the close of the season, the Serpentine underwent a thorough revision, the holes in which many persons had lost their lives were filled up, and the bed of the pond levelled, whilst the various sewers which had so long run into it from Notting Hill to Bayswater were diverted into a different channel in the main road.

We have no evidence when free seats began in Hyde Park; they were probably in existence when the Park was first thrown open to the public; but we do know when the movable chairs, for which a charge was and is made, were introduced—in 1820, when some twenty or thirty were placed near Stanhope Gate. Sir Benjamin Hall, when Chief Commissioner of Works, provided free seats in plenty along the north side of Rotten Row; but when he was succeeded by Lord John Manners, the latter had them all removed early in 1859, and an abundance of chairs for hire was substituted in their place. This doubtless tended to make that lounging place more select, but a popular outcry was raised about it, and a few of the free seats were grudgingly reinstated. In 1859 the band stand was erected, since when most excellent music has been discoursed there, for the delectation of her Majesty's lieges.

In *The Times* of July 30, 1864, is a letter complaining of the disgraceful state of Hyde Park—

"where may be seen, every day, hordes of half dressed, filthy men and women, lying about in parties, and no doubt concocting midnight robberies. There appear to be police and park-keepers enough to prevent this, but they state they have no orders to remove them. The evil is increasing, and it is hardly safe to allow ladies and children, who are anxious to have their daily walks in Hyde Park without being disgusted at the proceedings practised there daily."

That the state of the Park has not improved, especially on Sundays, or at night, see the correspondence on the subject in *The Times*, Sept. and Oct., 1895.

From this time to the present, there is little to chronicle of the Park, except that in 1877 a three-storied villa containing some thirteen rooms was erected in the Park, as a residence for the head gardener, at the expense of Mr. Albert Grant, in lieu of a lodge in Kensington Gardens, which was demolished, by permission, because it interfered with an uninterrupted view of the Gardens from Kensington House, which Mr. Grant was then building at a fabulous cost, for his residence, but which was pulled down before it was ever inhabited. Of course there have been, and are still, grumbles, but they are about trifles—and, as a rule, the Park is very well kept, there being a shade of partiality towards the south side, in preference to the north, as anyone can see who draws an imaginary line from the middle of Park Lane to the centre of Kensington Gardens.

CHAPTER XXIII.

Works of art in the Park—Drinking fountain—Marble Arch—Hyde Park Corner—Achilles statue—Walk round the Park—Cemetery of St. George's, Hanover Square—Sterne's tomb and burial—Tyburn tree—The Tybourne—People executed—Henrietta Maria's penance—Locality of the gallows—Princess Charlotte—Gloucester House—Dorchester House—Londonderry House—Apsley House—Allen's apple stall—The Wellington Arch—Statues of the Duke—St. George's Hospital, Knightsbridge—A fight on the bridge—Albert Gate and George Hudson—Knightsbridge Barracks.

WORKS of Art in the Park are conspicuous by their general absence. There is a drinking fountain near the Bayswater Road, a fountain on the site of the Chelsea Waterworks reservoir—the statue of Achilles, the Marble Arch, and the Gate at Hyde Park Corner.

The drinking fountain was dedicated on Feb. 29, 1868, with a great function in which figured the Archbishop of Canterbury, the Duke of Cambridge, Lord Harris, and many other noblemen. This fountain was the gift of the Maharajah of Vizianagram, K.C.S.I., and cost about £1200. The material employed is box-ground stone, the columns being blue pennant, and the bowls polished granite. The form of the fountain is quadrangular, and the style early Gothic. On two sides are the portrait and arms of the Maharajah; and on the remaining two sides the portrait and arms of her Majesty

Queen Victoria. On one of the recesses is the following inscription, in old English character:—
"This fountain, the gift of the Maharajah Murza Vizeram Gujaputty Raj Munca Sooltan, Bahadoor of Vizianagram, K.C.S.I., was erected by the Metropolitan Drinking Fountain Association, 1868."

The old Cumberland Gate, which was built about 1744, was, as may be seen by a water-colour drawing in the Crace Collection (Port. ix. 75), a very ugly brick construction with wooden gates—but it was removed in 1822, and handsome iron gates substituted for it. But 1851—which turned Hyde Park topsy-turvy—did away with them, and in their place was erected the present Marble Arch, which was originally the chief entrance to Buckingham Palace. The original estimate for it was £31,000, but that included £6000 for an equestrian statue of George IV., which was to surmount it, but was placed instead in Trafalgar Square. One authority says it cost £80,000, whilst its metal gates cost £3000. It was designed by Nash, the favourite architect of the Regency and reign of George IV., and is an adaptation from the Arch of Constantine at Rome. Flaxman, Westmeath, and Rossi did the ornamentation, and, being of Carrara marble, and kept scrupulously clean, it forms a very effective entrance to the north of the Park.

Its removal was effected with great rapidity—for the foundations were not begun to be dug till the middle of January, 1851. We hear of it in *The Times* of Feb. 25, that "the Arch is in a very advanced state, and is, in fact, fast approaching towards completion. The works are so far advanced that the massive gates have been fixed in their places, and the whole of the superstructure is in a very forward condition." And in *The Times* of April 1, 1851, we read : " On Saturday (March 29) the re-erection of the Marble Arch at Cumberland Gate was completed ; and, in the course of the week, the carriage drive will be opened to the public. The blocks of marble of which the Arch is composed have all been fresh polished, and the structure has altogether a very chaste appearance. The upper part of the Arch has been constructed as a police-station, and will contain a reserve of men."

In 1756, as we may see by a water-colour drawing by *Jones* (Crace Collection, Port. x. 39), the Piccadilly entrance to Hyde Park consisted only of wooden gates, and so it remained until the present entrance was made from designs by Decimus Burton in 1827. This is a screen of fluted Ionic columns, supporting an entablature. This is divided into three arched entrances for carriages, and two for foot passengers. The frieze, which represents a naval and military triumph, was designed by Henning—and if it were finished as he wanted it, with groups of statuary on the top, it would be very fine. By the way, talking of statuary at this spot, in " A New Guide to London," 1726, p. 83, we find : "If you please, you may see a great many Statues at the Statuaries at Hyde-Park Corner."

Visible from this entrance is the Achilles Statue —the first public nude statue in England. A great deal of rubbish has been talked about this statue, especially in attributing its original to Pheidias. Whoever was its sculptor, it was a marble statue which formed part of a group on the Quirinal Hill at Rome—which has been christened Achilles for no particular reason, but that it seemed applicable to a monument from the ladies of England to the hero of the day, the great Duke of Wellington. The Pope gave the casts, the Ordnance Office found the metal from captured French cannon, the Government gave the site, and yet it cost £10,000 before it was erected. True, Westmacott furnished it with a sword and shield which were not in the original, and part of the Park wall had to be taken down in order to get it into the Park, an event which took place on June 18, 1822 (the anniversary of the Battle of Waterloo). But its beauties were not to be shown on that occasion, as weighing about 33 tons, it required a lot of fixing—but it was unveiled on July 14th. The height of this statue is more than 18 feet—and with the mound, base, plinth, pedestal and statue, it is 36 feet high from the road level. It was soon found necessary to surround it with an iron balustrade, as it became a favourite play place of the little *gamins* of the Park. On the pedestal is the following inscription :—

> TO ARTHUR, DUKE OF WELLINGTON,
> AND HIS BRAVE COMPANIONS IN ARMS,
> THIS STATUE OF ACHILLES,
> CAST FROM CANNON TAKEN ON THE VICTORIES OF
> SALAMANCA, VITTORIA, TOULOUSE,
> AND WATERLOO,
> IS INSCRIBED
> BY THEIR COUNTRYWOMEN.
> PLACED ON THIS SPOT
> ON THE XVIIITH OF JUNE MDCCCXXII
> BY COMMAND OF
> HIS MAJESTY GEORGE IV.

This statue was lampooned and caricatured very considerably, but both are somewhat too broad for reproduction nowadays.

Let us now take a walk round the Park—outside—beginning on the North side. All along the Park, till we come to Tyburn, was open fields and market gardens, except the mortuary chapel and cemetery of St. George's, Hanover Square, and its concomitant, St. George's Terrace, which we see in Sandby's camp picture of "The Toilet." This burial ground was enclosed and consecrated in 1764, and comprises an area of about four acres. It is popularly supposed that Laurence Sterne is buried here—and if you do not believe it, there is a tombstone to testify to the fact. It is near the centre of the west wall of the cemetery, and it bears the following inscription:—

> Alas, poor Yorick.
> Near to this Place
> Lies the body of
> The Reverend LAURENCE STERNE.
> Dyed September 13, 1768,
> Aged 53 years.
> Ah! Molliter, ossa quiescant.
>
> If a sound head, warm heart and breast humane,
> Unsully'd worth, and soul without a stain,
> If mental powers could ever justly claim
> The well-won tribute of immortal fame,
> Sterne was the Man who, with gigantic stride,
> Mow'd down luxuriant follies far and wide.
> Yet, what though keenest knowledge of mankind,
> Unseal'd to him the springs that move the mind,
> What did it boot him? Ridicul'd, abus'd,
> By foes insulted, and by prudes accus'd.
> In his, mild reader, view thy future fate,
> Like him despise what 'twere a sin to hate.

This monumental stone was erected to the memory of the deceased by two *Brother Masons*, for, although he did not live to be a member of their *Society*, yet all his incomparable performances evidently prove him to have acted by *Rule* and *Square*; they rejoice in this opportunity of perpetuating his high and unapproachable character to after ages. W & S.

If we analyze the above, and search out the truth

of it, we find that Sterne died on March 18th, and was buried in the cemetery on March 22nd, being followed to the grave by only two persons, his publisher, Becket, and Mr. Salt, of the India House. It is, and was, currently believed that two nights after his burial his body was exhumed by the body-snatchers, or "Resurrection Men," as they were called, and by them sold to M. Collignon, Professor of Anatomy at Cambridge: and the story goes on to show, how among the scientific people the Professor invited to witness his demonstration, there was one who had been personally acquainted with Sterne, and who fainted with horror at the sight of his corpse being thus anatomized. That this story is true is more than probable—exhumation being rife—so much so, that in the *St. James's Chronicle*, Nov. 24-26, 1767, it is thus recorded of this very Cemetery: "The Burying-Ground in Oxford Road, belonging to the Parish of St. George's, Hanover Square, having been lately robbed of several dead Bodies, a Watch was placed there, attended by a large Mastiff Dog, notwithstanding which, on Sunday last, some Villains found Means to steal out another dead Body, and carried off the very Dog."

Ann Radcliffe, the novelist, who died in 1823, was also buried here.

The old chapel is now pulled down, and a new and much handsomer one erected in its place; whilst the cemetery has been levelled, planted, pathed, and seated, in accordance with modern taste.

Continuing our walk, we come to dread Tyburn, with its fatal tree of which it was written :—

"Since Laws were made for ev'ry degree
To curb vice in others as well as me,
I wonder we ha'n't better Company
Upon Tyburn Tree.

. . . . .

In short, were Mankind their merits to have,
Could Justice mark out each particular knave,
Two-thirds the Creation would sing the last stave
Upon Tyburn Tree."

It derives its etymology either from Twy bourne— Two brooks, or the united brooks; or else from Aye-bourne[1]—t'Aye bourne—which rises in Hampstead, and receiving nine other rills, crossed Oxford Street about Stratford Place, by the Lord Mayor's Hunting Lodge, now Sedley Place, where conduits were built to receive water from it for the use of the City: which conduits were found in pretty fair repair in Aug., 1875. It ran by Lower Brook Street, which owes its name to it, as does also Hay (Aye) hill—Lansdowne Gardens, Half Moon Street, crossed Piccadilly, where it was spanned by a bridge, and thence into the Green Park, where it formed a pond. Running past Buckingham Palace, it divided and formed Thorney Island—or Westminster—one outfall turning the Abbey Mill.

Tyburn has been a place of execution for centuries, the earliest I can find being in "Roger de Wendover," who mentions that, A.D. 1196, William Fitz-osbert, or Longbeard, was drawn through the City of London, by horses, to the gallows at Tyburn. We hear occasionally of executions there in the 14th and 15th centuries, and Perkin Warbeck was hanged there in 1499—as was also Elizabeth Barton, the Holy Maid of Kent, in 1534—but I have no

---

[1] In a plan of "Part of Conduit Mead"—about 1720—the little stream is called "Aye brook."

wish to chronicle the people who were here done to death for crime, and religious and political offences, except to mention that the bodies of Oliver Cromwell, Ireton and Bradshaw, were exhumed, and on Jan. 30, 1661, dragged on sledges to Tyburn, where they were suspended till sunset on the "triple tree."

That the shape of the Tyburn Gallows was triangular is proved by many quotations, one of which, from Shakespeare's *Love's Labour's Lost* (Act iv. Sc. 3), will suffice :—

Biron.—Thou mak'st the triumviry, the corner cap of society,
 The shape of love's Tyburn, that hangs up simplicity.

There is a story that Queen Henrietta Maria did penance under the gallows at Tyburn in expiation of the blood of the martyrs who had suffered thereon. That it was a matter of public report there can be no doubt, as we may read in the "*Reply of the Commissioners of his Majesty the King of Great Britain, to the proposition presented by Mons. le Maréschal de Bassompierre, Ambassador Extraordinary from his most Christian Majesty.*"[1] "They (*the Bishop of Mande and his priests*) abused the influence which they had acquired over the tender and religious mind of her majesty, so far as to lead her a long way on foot, through a park, the gates of which had been expressly ordered by Count de Tilliers to be kept open, to go in devotion to a place (*Tyburn*) where it had been the custom to execute the most infamous malefactors and criminals of all sorts, exposed on the entrance of a high road; an act, not only of shame and mockery towards the queen, but of reproach and calumny of

---

[1] "Memoirs of the Embassy of the Marshal de Bassompierre to the Court of England in 1626," p. 138. Translated. Lond. 1819.

the king's predecessors, of glorious memory, as accusing them of tyranny in having put to death innocent persons, whom these people look upon as martyrs, although, on the contrary, not one of them had been executed on account of religion, but for high treason. And it was this last act, above all, which provoked the royal resentment and anger of his Majesty beyond the bounds of his patience, which, until then, had enabled him to support all the rest; but he could now no longer endure to see in his house, and in his kingdom, people who, even in the person of his dearly beloved consort, had brought such a scandal upon his religion; and violated, in such a manner, the respect due to the sacred memory of so many great monarchs, his illustrious predecessors, upon whom the Pope had never attempted, nor had ever been able, to impose such a mark of indignity, under pretext of penitence, or submission due to his see."

That Charles I. believed this story, there can be but little doubt, for, on July 12, 1626, he writes to his Ambassador in France : " I can no longer suffer those that I know to be the cause and fomenters of these humours, to be about my wife any longer, which I must do if it were but for one action they made my wife do; which is to make her go to Tyburn in devotion to pray, which action can have no greater invective made against it than the relation."

Replying to the Commissioners, Bassompierre takes up the cudgels for the Queen, and denies the accusation thus : " The Queen of Great Britain, with the permission of the King, her husband, gained the jubilee at the Chapel of the Fathers of the Oratory at St. James's (*Saint Gemmes*) with the devotion suitable to a great Princess, so well born, and so zealous for her religion—which devotions terminated with Vespers; and some time after the heat of the day having passed, she went for a walk in the Park of St. James', and also in Hyde Park (*Hipparc*), which adjoins it, as she had, at other times, been accustomed to do, and frequently in the company of the King, her husband; but that she has done so in procession, that there have there been made any prayers, public or private, high or low—that she has approached the gallows within 50 paces—that she has been on her knees, holding a book of Hours or a Chaplet in her hands, is what those that impose these matters do not believe themselves."

In the Print Room of the British Museum, in that fine collection of pictures relating to London— Crowle's interleaved edition of Pennant's London— is a very fine engraving of the Queen, praying under the gallows by moonlight, assisted by a torchbearer—a coach and six awaiting her return; but as this picture is manifestly of the last century, it is not worth reproducing in any way.

Where the gallows stood is still a moot point— but evidence points that No. 49, Connaught Square was built on its site, and in the lease of the house from the Bishop of London it is so expressed. Against this a correspondent in "Notes and Queries" (2 S. x. 198) says, "that the late Mr. Lawford, the bookseller of Saville Passage, told me that he had been informed by a very old gentleman who frequented his shop, that the Tyburn Tree stood as nearly as possible to the public house in the Edgware Road, now known by the sign of the 'Hoppoles,' which is at the corner of Upper Seymour Street; he having several times witnessed executions there. Amongst them, Dr. Dodd's, which had made a strong impression on his memory, on account of the celebrity of the culprit, and because, when the hangman was going to put the halter round the doctor's neck, the latter removed his wig, showing his bald shaved head; and a shower of rain coming on at the same time, someone on the platform hastily put up an umbrella, and held it over the head of the man who had but a minute to live, as if in fear that he might catch cold."

Another correspondent (4 S. xi. 98) practically endorses this site. He says : " The *potence* itself was in Upper Bryanston Street, a few doors from Edgware Road, on the northern side. The whole of this side of the street is occupied by squalid tenements and sheds, now (Feb. 1, 1873) in the course of demolition, and on the site of one of these, under the level of the present street, is to be seen a massive brickwork pillar, in the centre of which is a large socket, evidently for one of the pillars of the old gallows. An ancient house at the corner of Upper Bryanston Street and Edgware Road, which has been pulled down within the last few weeks was described to me as the only one existing in the neighbourhood when executions took place at Tyburn, and from the balcony in front of which the Sheriffs of London used to take their official view of the proceedings."

The date of the last hanging at Tyburn was Nov. 7, 1783.

A curious thing connected with Tyburn was the

"Tyburn Ticket." In the *Morning Herald*, March 17, 1802, is this advertisement: "Wanted, one or two Tyburn Tickets, for the Parish of St. George's, Hanover Square. Any person or persons having the same to dispose of may hear of a purchaser," etc. These tickets were granted to a prosecutor who succeeded in getting a felon convicted, and they carried with them the privilege of immunity from serving all parochial offices. They were transferable by sale (but only once), and the purchaser enjoyed its privileges. They were abolished in 1818. They had a considerable pecuniary value, and, in the year of their abolition, one was sold for £280.

Tyburnia is that part of London bounded south by the Bayswater Road, east by the Edgware Road, and the west includes Lancaster Gate.

There was a Turnpike called Tyburn Gate which commanded the Edgware and Uxbridge Roads; and close by, on the north side of the Bayswater Road—from the corner of the Edgware Road—is Connaught Terrace; No. 7 of which was, in 1814, the residence of Queen Caroline—wife of George IV. It was here, and to her mother, that the Princess Charlotte ran, rather than live at Carlton House, or marry the Prince of Orange. Then there was great consternation, and the Lord Chancellor, the Chancellor of the Duchy of Lancaster, and others, came to reason with her, but she would none of them, and not even her kind uncle, the Duke of Sussex, could prevail with her to go back.

Lord Brougham was more successful, and this is a portion of his account of how he managed the wayward girl: "We then conversed upon the subject with the others, and after a long discussion on that and her lesser grievances, she took me aside, and asked me what, upon the whole, I advised her to do. I said at once, 'Return to Warwick House, or Carlton House, and on no account to pass a night out of her own house.' She was extremely affected and cried, asking if I, too, refused to stand by her. I said, quite the contrary, and that as to the marriage, I gave no opinion, except that she must follow her own inclination entirely, but that her returning home was absolutely necessary; and in this all the rest fully agreed—her mother, the Duke of Sussex, Miss Mercer and Lady Charlotte Lindsay, for whom she had a great respect and regard. I said, that however painful it was to me, the necessity was so clear, and so strong, that I had not the least hesitation in advising it. She again and again begged me to consider her situation, and to think whether, looking to that, it was absolutely necessary she should return.

" The day now began to dawn, and I took her to the window. The election of Cochrane (after his expulsion, owing to the sentence of the Court, which both insured his re-election and abolished the pillory) was to take place that day. I said, 'Look there, Madam; in a few hours all the streets and the park, now empty, will be crowded with tens of thousands. I have only to take you to the window, show you to the crowd, and tell them your grievances, and they will rise in your behalf.' 'And why should they not?' I think she said, or some such words. 'The commotion,' I answered, 'will be excessive; Carlton House will be attacked, —perhaps pulled down; the soldiers will be ordered out; blood will be shed; and if your

Royal Highness were to live a hundred years, it never would be forgotten that your running away from your father's house was the cause of the mischief; and you may depend upon it, such is the English people's horror of bloodshed, you would never get over it.' She at once felt the truth of my assertion, and consented to see her uncle Frederic (the Duke of York) below stairs, and return with him. But she required one of the Royal carriages should be sent for, which came with her governess, and they, with the Duke of York, went home about five o'clock."

Turning down Park Lane, we find Gloucester House, the residence of H.R.H. the Duke of Cambridge, and it is so called because it was bought by the late Duke of Gloucester on his marriage. Formerly the Earl of Elgin lived here, and here he exhibited the "Elgin Marbles" which are now the pride of the classical section of the British Museum. Byron, in his *Curse of Minerva*, thus writes of them :—

"While brawny brutes, in stupid wonder stare,
And marvel at his lordship's 'stone shop' there."

Lower down is Dorchester House, the residence of Capt. Holford, erected in 1852-4. It is so named because it stands on the site of a house belonging to the Damers, Earls of Dorchester. It is celebrated for its libraries, engravings, and paintings by the old masters. Yet nearer Hyde Park Corner is Londonderry House, the town house of the Marquess of Londonderry, K.G.

Hyde Park Corner, as shown in a water-colour drawing of 1756 in the Crace Collection, gives us a good idea of what it was like—its wooden gates, its apple stall, the row of squalid cottages, and the public-house called the " Hercules' Pillars "—where now stand Apsley House and the houses of the Rothschilds. Anent the apple stall, the story is told that the wife of a discharged soldier named Allen kept it during the reign of George II. Allen somehow attracted the notice of the King, who, upon learning that he had fought at Dettingen, asked what he could do for him. Allen asked for the grant of the bit of land on which his hut and apple stall stood, and the boon was granted. In 1784, Allen's representative sold the ground to Henry, Lord Apsley, who was then Lord Chancellor, who thereon built a red brick house, which he is said to have designed, and, having built the first floor, found that he had forgotten any staircases to go up higher.

In 1820 it was purchased by the nation and settled on the great Arthur, Duke of Wellington, and his heirs for ever, but it had to undergo many alterations before it took its present shape. Many of my readers will remember the bullet-proof iron shutters which were put up at every window facing Piccadilly, after all the windows had been smashed by a mob during the popular ferment caused by the Reform Bill. They were never opened during the old Duke's life, and were only taken down by his son in 1856. The story of these iron shutters is thus told by the Rev. R. Gleig, in his *Life of Arthur, Duke of Wellington* (ed. 1864, p. 360):—

"The Duke was not in his place in the House of Lords on that memorable day when the King went down to dissolve (prorogue) Parliament (April 22nd, 1831). He had been in attendance for some time previously at the sick bed of the Duchess, and she expired just as the Park guns began to fire. He was therefore ignorant of the state into which London had fallen, till a surging crowd swept up from Westminster to Piccadilly, shouting and yelling, and offering violence to all whom they suspected of being anti-reformers. By-and-by, volleys of stones came crashing through the windows at Apsley House, breaking them to pieces, and doing injury to more than one valuable picture in the gallery. The Duke bore the outrage as well as he could, but determined never to run a similar risk again. He guarded his windows, as soon as quiet was restored, with iron shutters, and left them there to the day of his death—a standing memento of a nation's ingratitude."

The illustration representing the Duke looking out of his smashed windows is taken from *Political Sketches by H.B.* (John Doyle), No. 267, June 10th, 1833, and is entitled "Taking an Airing in Hyde Park; a portrait, Framed but not YET *Glazed*."

Nearly opposite Apsley House, and at the top of Constitution Hill, stands an Arch which was originally intended as a private entrance to Buckingham Palace; but it was erected on its present site about 1828, when Burton put up his screen at the entrance to Hyde Park. It is now more generally known as the Wellington Arch, from its having been surmounted by a colossal bronze equestrian statue of the great Duke, by Matthew Cotes Wyatt, in 1846. This was the outcome of a public subscription for the purpose, which is said to have amounted to £36,000. So much ridicule, however, was heaped upon it, that it was taken

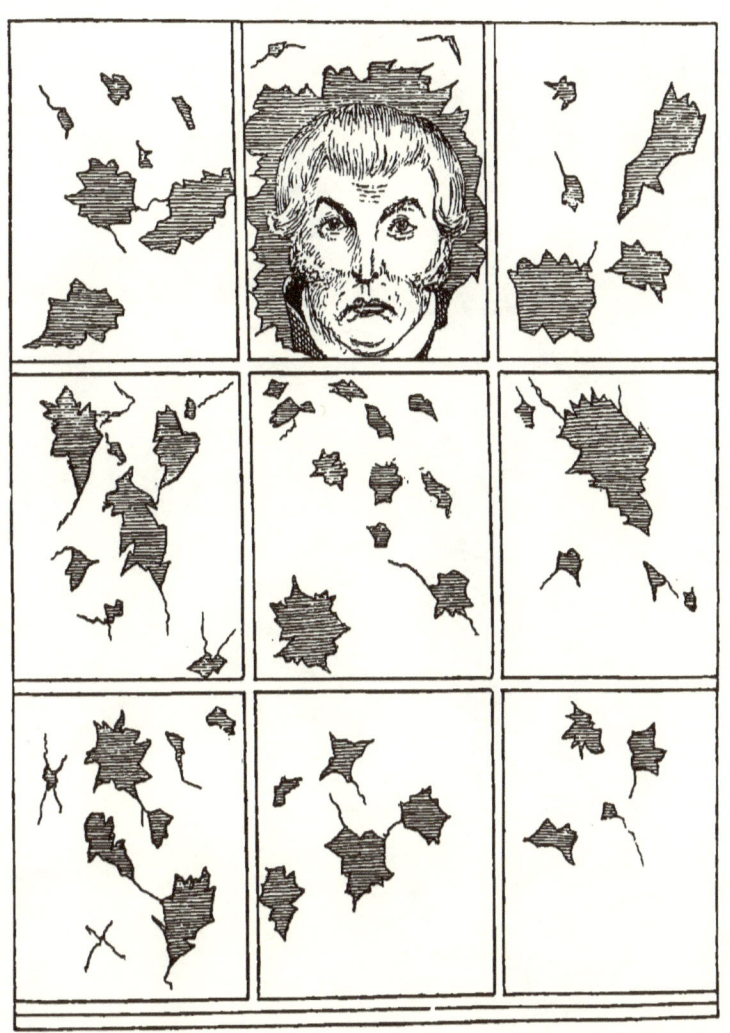

THE BROKEN WINDOWS AT APSLEY HOUSE, 1831.
Page 280.

www.ingramcontent.com/pod-product-compliance
Lightning Source LLC
Chambersburg PA
CBHW030012240426
43672CB00007B/916